INNOVATIONS IN INTERDISCIPLINARY TEACHING

Edited by
Carolyn Haynes

With the support of the
Association for Integrative Studies

AMERICAN COUNCIL ON EDUCATION
ORYX PRESS
Series on Higher Education
2002

The rare Arabian Oryx is believed to have inspired the myth of the unicorn. This desert antelope became virtually extinct in the early 1960s. At that time, several groups of international conservationists arranged to have nine animals sent to the Phoenix Zoo to be the nucleus of a captive breeding herd. Today, the Oryx population is over 1,000, and over 500 have been returned to the Middle East.

Library of Congress Cataloging-in-Publication Data

Innovations in interdisciplinary teaching / edited by Carolyn Haynes with the support of the Association for Integrative Studies.
    p.   cm.—(American Council on Education/Oryx Press series on higher education)
    Includes bibliographical references and index.
    ISBN 1-57356-393-5 (alk. paper)
    1. Education, Higher—Curricula.   2. Interdisciplinary approach in education.   3. College teaching.   I. Haynes, Carolyn.   II. Association for Integrative Studies.   III. Series.
LB2361.I44   2002
378.1'25—dc21   2001055183

British Library Cataloguing in Publication Data is available.

Library of Congress Catalog Card Number: 2001055183
ISBN: 1-57356-393-5

First published in 2002

Oryx Press, 88 Post Road West, Westport, CT 06881
An imprint of Greenwood Publishing Group, Inc.
www.oryxpress.com

Printed in the United States of America

The paper used in this book complies with the Permanent Paper Standard issued by the National Information Standards Organization (Z39.48–1984).

10 9 8 7 6 5 4 3 2 1

CONTENTS

ACKNOWLEDGMENTS

This book would not have been possible without the sponsorship and support of the Association for Integrative Studies (AIS) Board of Directors. This Board first initiated the idea for this book and contacted me about editing it. A special thanks goes to all of you for working with me over the past two years to bring this volume into its present form.

A special debt of gratitude goes to Julie Thompson Klein whose kind assistance, advice, and superb scholarship proved invaluable.

In addition, I wish to thank all the contributing authors for their creativity, thoughtfulness, and diligence in producing each chapter in a timely fashion and Susan Slesinger of Greenwood Press for her helpfulness in editing and publishing this book. Finally, I wish to express my gratitude to Sheila Croucher for her continuing support while I completed this project.

Carolyn Haynes
Miami University

ABOUT THE EDITOR
AND CONTRIBUTORS

Jeff Abell, Faculty, Interdisciplinary Arts Department, Columbia College, Chicago

Stanley Bailis, Professor, Center for Interdisciplinary Programs, Social Science Programs, San Francisco State University

Robert M. Bender, Professor of English and Women's Studies, Faculty Liaison, Information and Access Technology Services, University of Missouri, Columbia

Valerie Bystrom, Professor of English and Coordinated Studies, Seattle Community College

James R. Davis, Professor of Higher Education and Adult Studies, College of Education, University of Denver

Michael Field, Provost and Vice President for Academic Affairs, Shawnee State University

Faith Gabelnick, President, Pacific University

Virginia N. Gordon, Assistant Dean Emeritus, University College, The Ohio State University

Nancy M. Grace, Associate Professor, Department of English, College of Wooster

Carolyn Haynes, Associate Professor, School of Interdisciplinary Studies, Miami University

Debra Humphreys, Vice President for Communications and Public Affairs, Association of American Colleges and Universities

George Klein, Director, Office of Academic Programs Abroad, Eastern Michigan University

Christopher Myers, Professor, School of Interdisciplinary Studies, Miami University

Roslyn Abt Schindler, Associate Professor, Interdisciplinary Studies Program, College of Lifelong Learning, Wayne State University

Marcia Bundy Seabury, Professor of English, Hillyer College, and All-University Curriculum Faculty, University of Hartford

Don Stowe, Director of the Bachelor of Arts in Interdisciplinary Studies Program, University of South Carolina–Columbia

Jay Wentworth, Professor, Interdisciplinary Studies, Appalachian State University

INTRODUCTION

Laying a Foundation for Interdisciplinary Teaching

Carolyn Haynes

LAYING A FOUNDATION FOR INTERDISCIPLINARY TEACHING

The impetus for creating this book came from my own realization of the challenging nature of teaching interdisciplinary studies to undergraduate students. I vividly remember the terror I felt as a new faculty member when faced with the prospect of teaching an interdisciplinary undergraduate course. Teaching in itself—without even addressing the content area to be taught—was difficult enough for me. I had no idea what students' expectations of such a college course would be, nor was I clear about my own course expectations. A host of questions haunted me: How do students learn best? What skills must I cultivate in them, and what pedagogical approach should I use? To compound my confusion, I was unsure how even to define interdisciplinarity for myself, much less for a group of wide-eyed, curious, first-year students.

My ignorance was somewhat understandable given that my own graduate education had focused on a concentration in a disciplinary subject field and research applicable to that concentration, rather than on interdisciplinary or even disciplinary teaching; and, according to recent studies, my graduate experience was not atypical then or now (Boice; Menges). Moreover, I took little time to prepare for this initial experience, since I was warned by numerous mentors and advisors not to spend too much time on teaching. They rightly noted that it is rarely rewarded or supported as much as research (Cannon; Halpern). As a result of my lack of education in and preparation for teaching, I naturally depended during my first year on the instructional methodology that I had encountered during my own experience as a student (see Lucas). This reliance on my own personal experience led to unfortunate assumptions about learning and teaching:

> that passive verbal transfer is an effective mode of instruction; that college students have long attention spans; that if teachers prepare well and keep talking nothing bad can happen; and that authority and truth reside in the figure behind the lectern. (Eble 206)

Little did I know at the time that although the lecture method of teaching is "not *ineffective* . . . , the evidence is equally clear that these conventional methods are *not* as effective as some other, far less frequently used methods" (Terenzini and Pascarella 29). In fact, some studies have gone further in criticizing the traditional, lecture-based pedagogy: "The primary learning environment for undergraduate students, the fairly passive lecture-discussion format where faculty talk and most students listen, is contrary to almost every principle of an optimal student learning setting" (Guskin 6).

Lack of teacher preparation and little experience in interdisciplinary settings were not my only stumbling blocks as a new undergraduate interdisciplinary educator. Figuring out how to assist students to learn also afforded me enormous challenges. David Bartholomae wisely notes that the students' learning process is especially difficult because they must "learn to speak our language, to speak as we do, to try on the peculiar ways of knowing, selecting, evaluating, reporting, concluding, and arguing that define the discourse of our community" (134). As students advance in their major, they must "appropriate a specialized discourse," as if they were members of the academy. In this way, they must invent the discipline "by assembling and mimicking its language while finding some compromise between idiosyncrasy, a personal history, on the one hand, and the requirements of convention, the history of a discipline, on the other hand" (Bartholomae 135).

Helping students to learn one new and specialized disciplinary way of thinking is strenuous enough, but learning and then synthesizing two or more disciplinary discourses—the latter of which is the goal of interdisciplinary studies—poses an even more daunting challenge. As Newell and Green point out, disciplines are "socio-political organizations that concentrate on a historically linked set of problems" (25). They are "distinguished from one another by the questions they ask about the world, by their perspective or world view, by the set of assumptions they employ, and by the methods which they use to build up a body of knowledge (facts, concepts, theories) around a certain subject matter" (25). Given the inherent complexity of the disciplines, integrating disciplinary insights, then, is a tall order for even the best of learners. Any new faculty member confronted with teaching an interdisciplinary undergraduate course might feel as dismayed as I did at how to assist students in realizing this goal.

This collection is designed to assist new and experienced faculty members who are teaching in interdisciplinary settings and who want to advance the integrative learning of their students as well as administrators who want to encourage integrative and interdisciplinary teaching in their institutions. By integration, I have in mind the combining and synthesizing of various viewpoints, worldviews, or systems of thought. Some of these entities may be disciplinary in nature (which would constitute interdisciplinarity), others may not (as when students are asked to consider nonacademic viewpoints when addressing a problem). This volume is especially timely given that recent studies suggest that faculty are increasingly teaching in interdisciplinary settings. Not only do many general education programs, honors programs, and liberal studies programs feature interdisciplinary courses, but the number and types of more specialized interdisciplinary majors and concentrations, such as women's studies, cultural studies, international studies, and environmental studies, have burgeoned in the past thirty years (Klein and Newell 4–6). Yet, as was true in my case, most faculty members have disciplinary terminal degrees, have little preparation for teaching, and have previous experience learning and teaching solely in disciplinary classroom settings.

A number of questions, then, emerges: How can faculty be better prepared for interdisciplinary teaching? How can we better ensure excellence in interdisciplinary undergraduate education, and what are the foundational tenets of interdisciplinary learning and teaching? In her pioneering work on interdisciplinary theory, Julie Thompson Klein offers some clues:

> [I]nterdisciplinary work gets done by moving across the vertical plane of depth and the horizontal plane of breadth. Breadth connotes a comprehensive approach based in multiple variables and perspectives. Depth connotes competence in pertinent disciplinary, professional, and interdisciplinary approaches. Synthesis connotes creation of an interdisciplinary outcome through a series of integrative actions. Synthesis does not derive from simply mastering a body of knowledge, applying a formula, or moving in linear fashion from point A to point B. . . . It requires active triangulation of depth, breadth, and synthesis. (212)

Whereas many of the skills (e.g., differentiating, contrasting, relating, clarifying, reconciling, and synthesizing) she cites as necessary for interdisciplinarians are similar to those needed for students in most disciplines, Klein articulates some more specialized forms of thinking that are crucial for interdisciplinarians to achieve this active triangular process of depth, breadth, and synthesis. For her, most significant are the abilities to define the task at hand, to determine how best to use available approaches, to devise a working vocabulary that can be understood by all disciplinary audiences, and to extract the worldview and assumptions embedded in each discipline (213–14).

What Klein is calling for is not simply a series of prescribed interdisciplinary skills; in a more fundamental way, she is articulating a form of cognition or epistemology. Synthesis of the sort that she highlights necessitates that students make meaning in a particular way. Rather than view knowledge as certain and held by authorities, interdisciplinary students—in order to reconcile and synthesize the differing disciplinary and nondisciplinary worldviews—must believe that knowledge is relative to a context and acquired through inquiry. As Klein puts it, for interdisciplinarians, the "definition of intellectuality shifts from absolute answers and solutions to tentativeness and reflexivity" (214). A host of educational and psychological theorists (including Perry, Piaget, Kohlberg, and Baxter Magolda) contends that individuals actively construct their own sense of reality and that the way that they make meaning changes in regular and systematic ways throughout the life span. Most undergraduates begin their college career exhibiting absolute thinking that is authoritarian and organized in dualistic (true–false, right–wrong) terms. Eventually, many come to see multiple truths and phenomenological variations. Some go further by perceiving knowledge as relative to and constructed within a context. This latter, more contextual form of thinking is akin to what Klein claims is essential for interdisciplinary thinking.

Yet, according to Robert Kegan, how one understands knowledge is directly related to how one understands others and the self. In other words, interpersonal and intrapersonal awareness mediate the epistemological dimension of development. An individual's meaning-making undergoes changes that affect and are affected by his or her view of the self, relations to others, and understanding of experience. Kegan proposes a series of holistic and qualitatively different forms of meaning-making that individuals may evolve during their lifetime. He contends that the majority of the adult population (from late adolescence through adulthood) makes meaning at or between order three and order four. Order three meaning-makers co-construct their sense of meaning with other persons and sources in their environment. That is, the individual's sense of self is based on a fusion of others' expectations, theories, and ideas, and those expectations form how one thinks about oneself. Although an order three meaning-maker is masterful at comprehending others' points of view, he or she does not possess a coherent sense of meaning-making or self apart from those other people and sources.

Order four meaning-makers, by contrast, construct their sense of meaning and the self such that self-authorship is the key feature. The order four individual has the ability to differentiate a self-standard apart from, but in relation to, other people and sources. That is, the self can internalize multiple points of view, reflect on them, and construct them into one's own theory about oneself and one's experience. Thus, the individual's meaning-making is influenced but not determined by external sources. The self becomes identified through these self-authored conceptualizations, giving the self an enduring identity that remains fairly stable across contexts and interpersonal relationships.

Although order three meaning-makers can engage in many of the skills Klein lays out for interdisciplinarians, to fully accomplish what Klein calls "the active triangulation of depth, breadth, and synthesis," the learner must be at Kegan's order four dimension of meaning-making. Students who are intensely concerned about what others will think of them and who believe that truth is absolute and universal will have difficulty critically evaluating others' sometimes conflicting disciplinary perspectives and identifying hidden commonalties and inconsistencies among disciplinary bodies of knowledge, much less authoring their own integrated view.

Rather than being simply a "a process of answering a question, solving a problem, or addressing a topic that is too broad or complex to be dealt with adequately by a single discipline or profession . . . [and that] draws on disciplinary perspectives and integrates their insights" (Klein and Newell 3), interdisciplinary studies fundamentally entail a movement away from an absolutist conception of truth to a conception of truth that is situated, perspectival, and discursive and that informs and is informed by the investigator's own sense of self-authorship. The interdisciplinary epistemology is not one that posits a pure relativism in which all knowledge claims are always equal. Instead, it rests on the assumption that disciplines and its practitioners, as well as their activities and concepts, are already socially constituted. The task of the interdisciplinary investigator, then, is to invent a new discourse that critically combines key elements of several disciplinary discourses and that is in keeping with his or her own sense of self. No disciplinary viewpoint is inherently or universally true or superior to others. Within the context of a given problem or question, however, some viewpoints are more relevant or logical than others. It is up to the interdisciplinary investigator to decide which viewpoints are appropriate for the given context and how to integrate them.

Interdisciplinary pedagogy, then, is not synonymous with a single process, set of skills, method, or technique. Instead, it is concerned primarily with fostering in students a sense of self-authorship and a situated, partial, and perspectival notion of knowledge that they can use to respond to complex questions, issues, or problems. While it necessarily entails the cultivation of the many cognitive skills such as differentiating, reconciling, and synthesizing that Klein has so aptly delineated, it also involves much more, including the promotion of students' interpersonal and intrapersonal learning. Because interdisciplinarity is a complicated psychological and cognitive process, it cannot be taught with one approach.

The authors in this volume offer many intriguing pedagogical approaches for achieving these goals. While some authors integrate the interpersonal, intrapersonal, and cognitive dimensions of interdisciplinarity, others bring a particular dimension to the forefront. In all cases, however, the question of how each particular pedagogical approach can best facilitate interdisciplinary learning—and, in particular, the ability to integrate and synthesize disciplinary perspectives—is foregrounded. Moreover, although not all of the authors directly call for or refer to the epistemological and affective framework that I have discussed in this introduction, all do offer pedagogical guidelines and strategies that promote this holistic process of development.

Some of the authors, however, do provide stunning insights into this process of development and epistemology. In Chapter 8, for example, Nancy M. Grace provides an apt metaphor for this form of thinking and feeling. She describes an art object created by Marcel Duchamp and popularly known as the "Small Glass" which invites its viewers to move around the work and gaze into its various pieces of glass. Not only can viewers peer from various vantage points at the world around them, but they can also peer at themselves. Because the object is in continual motion, the images of oneself and others perpetually shift and transform. For Grace, this metaphor represents the interdisciplinary teaching paradigm. She and the other authors in this book offer numerous ideas for how interdisciplinary teachers can encourage this fluid and self-reflexive way of perceiving the self and the world in their students. For example, the authors not only question the top-down method of the teacher imparting knowledge to a passive student, but they also underscore the necessity of empowering students to probe and investigate their own questions, to think critically, to make unusual connections between their own and others' ideas, to gain confidence in communicating in multiple literacies (writing, technology), to collaborate effectively with others, and to reflect on the ethical, cultural, and political dimensions of their findings. Most important, each stresses the need for faculty to assist students in thinking self-consciously about the disciplines—how they differ from and complement one another.

INTRODUCING THE CHAPTERS

The chapters in Part I focus on pedagogical concerns and approaches that in recent years have come to be seen as crucial to interdisciplinary teaching: innovative curricular design, team teaching, and writing-intensive teaching. Even though the authors in this section address topics that have historically been associated with interdisciplinary teaching, each offers new and significant ideas on how to implement their approach to advance integrative thinking. In Chapter 1, Stanley Bailis provides readers with a valuable overview of the challenges of creating interdisciplinary curricula. He argues for the necessity of continually facilitating fresh patterns of study that can be gained through close advising, new degree-granting programs, and a curriculum that fosters innovative linkages among disciplines. In addition, he offers strategies for responding to two major concerns with creating interdisciplinary curricula—access to a range of disciplines and the ability to cultivate integration and coherency.

Perhaps the most common approach to interdisciplinary teaching is team teaching, the topic of Chapter 2. In this chapter, Jay Wentworth and James Davis argue that despite the many demands on instructors' time, patience, and resources, team teaching can enhance integrative learning in students, particularly when the faculty members have a shared understanding of interdisciplinarity, are willing to take risks, share power, confront issues of personality, and learn to collaborate in the classroom.

Because most interdisciplinary investigations involve communicating findings in writing, writing instruction is often integrally incorporated into most interdisciplinary courses. Marcia Bundy Seabury, the author of Chapter 3, contends that interdisciplinary, writing-intensive courses need to go beyond the two most frequently used approaches in writing-intensive courses: writing informally as a mode of discovery ("writing to learn") and learning to use the accepted genres of a discipline ("writing in the disciplines"). Instead, interdisciplinary educators wanting to teach writing must use a more flexible, fluid, and recursive model for writing instruction that combines these two approaches and helps students move and draw the fruitful connections among levels of abstraction and generalization that are necessary for interdisciplinary study. Seabury also suggests a range of practical guidelines and assignment ideas for interdisciplinary faculty members who want to teach writing.

The late Forrest H. Armstrong once noted that interdisciplinary faculty members "must be prepared to venture into perhaps uncharted waters" (174). The authors in Part II embody this ideal in that they discuss some of the more novel approaches to interdisciplinary teaching: learning communities, computer-assisted instruction, and multicultural education. In Chapter 4, Valerie Bystrom describes and analyzes the major forms of learning communities (linked classes, customized links, fully integrated links, small coordinated studies, fully integrated programs of study), noting their potential for integrative learning and enumerating their benefits and challenges to interdisciplinary students and faculty.

One of the most popular emerging form of pedagogy—technology-based teaching—is the topic of Chapter 5. In this chapter, Robert M. Bender cautions that, as with any interdisciplinary pedagogical approach, technology-based teaching should be used to advance learning outcomes and to focus attention away from the professor as information-giver and performer to students as active and interactive learners. He provides a sequence of technologically based classroom experiences of increasing complexity and levels of integration. In his analysis of each of these experiences, Bender outlines ways technology can promote the integrative process that Julie Klein and other interdisciplinary theorists have articulated. Part II concludes with an exploration into interdisciplinary approaches to multicultural curriculum and teaching. In this chapter, Debra Humphreys combines the theories of William H. Newell and James A. Banks to argue for a developmental process of curriculum reform that advances courses that integrate diverse cultural and disciplinary elements in sophisticated, critical ways.

Ingenuity is also exhibited by the authors of Part III. The authors of these three chapters address pedagogical approaches that have traditionally been utilized in specific disciplinary course settings and explain how they can be used to deepen interdisciplinary learning. Performance, for example, is normally associated with teaching would-be actors in a theatre practicum, but as Jeff Abell demonstrates in Chapter 7, it can be used effectively to promote interdisciplinary learning. Rather than focus solely on cognitive forms of analysis, using language and numbers as the means of learning, interdisciplinary teaching, according to Abell, should encourage a more broadly experiential approach to learning and acknowledge the unity of mind and body in the learning process. He offers concrete suggestions for how to accomplish these goals.

Feminist pedagogy, the topic of Chapter 8, also is typically associated solely with women's studies courses. Yet, the learning objectives and strategies that Nancy M. Grace offers in this chapter—addressing and incorporating difference meaningfully, valuing difference, honoring and exploring the notion of identity through voice, questioning assumptions, teaching process as well as product, and fostering learning in multiple contexts and in multiple ways—are especially appropriate to interdisciplinary courses. Grace also emphasizes the need for feminist interdisciplinary faculty to take a relational, dynamic, and mutable approach to teaching.

In the past two decades, inquiry-based teaching has become popular among science educators. In Chapter 9, my colleague Christopher Myers and I discuss how science inquiry can be used to advance interdisciplinary aims. For us, interdisciplinary science inquiry is the process of investigating questions that retains the hallmarks of science but combines them with relevant ideas, methods, and practices from other disciplines in the social sciences, humanities, and fine arts. In this chapter, we consider ways of transforming a traditional, lecture-based pedagogy to an interdisciplinary, inquiry-based one by shifting the focus from teaching to learning, building a co-intentional and dialogical community of learners, offering students opportunities to ask and investigate their own questions, and incorporating critical and personal reflection.

Innovation in interdisciplinary teaching entails not only an ingenious application of discipline-based pedagogical approaches to interdisciplinary contexts, but it also involves working with unique groups of students in unique settings. Part IV includes two chapters that address interdisciplinary teaching in an unusual setting or to nontraditional students. In Chapter 10, George Klein examines the various interdisciplinary patterns of study abroad programs, including areas studies, cultural history tours, and interdisciplinary fields. He argues that none of these patterns ensures that students will move toward integrative forms of thinking. Thus, he offers practical administrative and pedagogical guidelines that will help to promote a more fully integrative learning experience for students and faculty in study abroad programs.

Chapter 11 concerns adult interdisciplinary education. Because of the diverse experiences and greater maturity of nontraditional adult learners, Roslyn Abt Schindler argues that special focus should be placed on confidence-building, attention to context, practical problem-solving and job-related skills, individualized approaches, and collaborative learning. She offers guidelines and tips for how to develop these five key objectives to advance integrative learning.

Part V, the final section of this volume, concerns two crucial forms of support for interdisciplinary teaching: advising and assessment. Effective interdisciplinary teaching is dependent on knowledgeable advisors helping students to understand and select appropriate learning experiences as well as on useful means of assessing instruction and learning so that improvements can continually be made. According to Virginia N. Gordon, the author of Chapter 12, interdisciplinary advisors are most effective when they are attentive to the cognitive and affective developmental needs of their students, have a critical understanding of the disciplines, are familiar with the interdisciplinary options available to students and their benefits, and cultivate a continuous and ongoing mentoring relationship that prompts students to reflect critically on the integrative nature of their education.

Chapter 13 features Michael Field and Don Stowe's discussion of interdisciplinary assessment. According to them, interdisciplinarity offers unique challenges to assessment—due to the magnitude, complexity, and serendipitous nature of its intended outcomes. Although more traditional indirect and direct assessment measures can be used in the interdisciplinary context, the authors argue that qualitative, direct, performance-based, and narrative/descriptive assessment methods are probably most appropriate. They hypothesize that interdisciplinary approaches to knowledge result in conventional outcomes of communication (technology and writing) competency, critical thinking, and a variety of affective, developmental, as well as serendipitous outcomes that have yet to be placed in the canon of desired outcomes.

Although faculty members are often the primary agents of innovative interdisciplinary pedagogy, no interdisciplinary innovation can last without substantial support. The book concludes with Faith Gabelnick's discussion of how interdisciplinary leaders (administrators, advisors, faculty members, and students) can best enable interdisciplinary innovations to thrive in the increasingly complex and global future. Rather than simply gain the skills needed for implementing a new pedagogical approach, interdisciplinary leaders must literally shift their ways of looking at the world, of understanding relationships, and of making commitments so that interdisciplinary learning communities can emerge and flourish. In other words, to enact a climate conducive for interdisciplinary innovation, the entire institution must engage in systemic transformational change.

Although this book does not exhaust every pedagogical approach that could be used in an interdisciplinary classroom, the thirteen different topics covered do highlight the diversity and creativity of interdisciplinary teaching in higher education. Moreover, the availability of a variety of possible teaching approaches is important given the fact that faculty themselves are diverse in their abilities and preferences and college students learn in different ways (Cavanaugh et al.; Cornwell and Manfredo; Enns; Holley and Jenkins). The more strategies, approaches, and tips that faculty have at their disposal, the more likely they will be able to meet the challenging nature of interdisciplinary teaching and to experience the joy of integrative learning.

WORKS CITED

Bartholomae, David. "Inventing the University." *When a Writer Can't Write: Studies in Writer's Block and Other Composing Process Problems.* Ed. Mike Rose. New York: Guilford, 1985. 134–65.

Baxter Magolda, Marcia B. *Knowing and Reasoning in College: Gender-Related Patterns in Students' Intellectual Development.* San Francisco: Jossey-Bass, 1992.

Boice, Robert. *The New Faculty Member: Supporting and Fostering Professional Development.* San Francisco: Jossey-Bass, 1992.

Cannon, John. "Teaching History at University." *History Teacher* 22 (1989): 245–75.

Cavanaugh, Stephen, et al. "The Assessment of Student Nurse Learning Styles Using the Kolb Learning Inventory." *Nurse Education Today* 15, no. 3 (1995): 177–83.

Cornwell, J. M., and P. A. Manfredo. "Kolb's Learning Style Theory Revisited." *Educational and Psychological Measurement* 54 (1994): 317–27.

Eble, Kenneth E. *The Craft of Teaching: A Guide to Mastering the Professor's Art.* 2nd ed. San Francisco: Jossey-Bass, 1988.

Enns, Carolyn Z. "Integrating Separate and Connected Knowing: The Experimental Learning Model." *Teaching of Psychology* 20 (1993): 7–13.

Guskin, A. "Learning More, Spending Less." *About Campus* (July/August 1997): 4–9.

Halpern, Diane F. "Rethinking College Instruction for a Changing World." *Changing College Classrooms: New Teaching and Learning Strategies for an Increasingly Complex World.* Ed. D. F. Halpern and Associates. San Francisco: Jossey-Bass, 1994.

Holley, Joyce H., and Elizabeth K. Jenkins. "The Relationship Between Student Learning Style and Performance on Various Test Question Formats." *Journal of Education for Business* 68 (May/June 1993): 301–8.

Kegan, Robert. *In Over Our Heads: The Mental Demands of Modern Life.* Cambridge, MA: Harvard University Press, 1994.

Klein, Julie Thompson. *Crossing Boundaries: Knowledge, Disciplinarities, and Interdisciplinarities.* Charlottesville and London: University Press of Virginia, 1996.

Klein, Julie, and William H. Newell. "Advancing Interdisciplinary Studies." Newell, *Interdisciplinarity* 3–22.

Kohlberg, L. *The Psychology of Moral Development*. San Francisco: Harper, 1984.

Lucas, Ann F., ed. *The Department Chairperson's Role in Enhancing College Teaching*. New Directions for Teaching and Learning No. 37. San Francisco: Jossey-Bass, 1989.

Menges, Robert J. "Preparing New Faculty for the Future." *Thought and Action* 10, no. 2 (1994): 81–95.

Newell, William H., ed. *Interdisciplinarity: Essays from the Literature*. New York: College Entrance Examination Board, 1998.

Newell, William H., and William J. Green. "Defining and Teaching Interdisciplinary Studies." Newell, *Interdisciplinarity* 23–34.

Perry, W. G., Jr. *Forms of Intellectual and Ethical Development in the College Years: A Scheme*. Austin, TX: Holt, Rinehart and Winston, 1970.

Piaget, J. *Six Psychological Studies*. New York: Vintage, 1967.

Terenzini, P. T. and E. T. Pascarella. "Living with Myths: Undergraduate Education in America." *Change* (January/February 1994): 28–30.

PART I

Standard Approaches to Interdisciplinary Teaching

CHAPTER 1

Interdisciplinary Curriculum Design and Instructional Innovation

Notes on the Social Science Program at San Francisco State University

Stanley Bailis

FIRST THOUGHTS

It was Shaw, I think, who challenged the golden rule by pointing out that neighbors can have very different tastes: Imagine the local masochist doing unto others as she might wish them to do unto her! It was perhaps on this account that Max Dimont touted Rabbi Hillel's very different version of the rule—do *not* do as you *would not* be done to (43–44).

Certainly I feel safer with the negative formulation, and I have tried very hard to apply it to my roles in the university. As an undergraduate obliged to choose a major, I looked for one that would not do to me what I didn't want done—a major that would not unduly restrict the "breadth" portion of my education by taking breadth and depth to be mutually exclusive. I thought of what I wanted as a nonmajor major, and I found it in something called American Civilization at the University of Pennsylvania, a field that saw me right through to the doctorate. For the past thirty-six years and some, I have been working in the Interdisciplinary Social Science Program at San Francisco State, which, like my own major, serves undergraduate and graduate students who do not want a major done *to* them.[1]

The program, which has been operating in more or less its present form since the early 1960s, affords students interested in the study of human affairs an opportunity to experience the university as broadly accessible and coherent with respect to problems, topics, or themes of their own choosing. It has been extraordinarily productive of instructional novelty in two ways: first, by continuously facilitating fresh patterns of study for students as individuals; and, second, by generating new degree-granting programs. These two are closely related and have among their important enabling conditions certain features of the design of our program's curriculum—features that have been for many years an effective, reasonably low-cost way of meeting fresh curricular demands. What follows is a sketch of these design features that delineates their interdisciplinarity and their consequences for instructional innovation. The discussion should be of interest to university students, faculty, and administrators who in their various ways engage this kind of learning and teaching.

CURRICULUM

One important kind of interdisciplinary instruction involves presenting a domain of knowledge in terms of its constituent disciplines and their relations, its connections to other domains, and its uses in the workaday world. Commonly offered as a complement to specialization, this kind of instruction is often justified—in the social sciences at least—as preparing people to consider factors of behavior together that are usually examined separately and differently in the specialized disciplines. The purpose is to promote understandings of human phenomena that are more inclusive, more comprehensive even, than the necessarily partial products of specialized study—understandings that may move us closer to reality and to reliable bases for action.

Our program is of this sort and does make such claims for itself. Accordingly, it has two basic problems to solve:

1. How to ensure access to the range of disciplines that constitute the instructional domain and that are needed to deal with some problem, topic, or theme; and

2. How to make coherently integrated use of the instruction thus received.

"Access" here means taking instruction in a range of relevant fields and being prepared to understand the content of such instruction as it is meant. In the social sciences, "access" pertains minimally to history, geography, psychology, sociology, anthropology, political science, and economics, but can and does reach outwards from there along lines determined by a student's particular interests. "Access" in these senses depends on solid advising—a kind of instruction, really, in what the disciplines are about and how they might relate to each student's interests. And the advising must be offered by a program faculty member who is well enough connected in the university to ensure admission of its students into courses that are usually reserved by departments for their own majors.

"Coherency" and "integration" here mean bringing ideas and information from several disciplines to bear on each other as matters that are related or alike and, in that form, applicable to a student's own particular subject. Since few if any specialized disciplines are taught with this kind of associative goal in mind, the goal is one that any interdisciplinary curriculum worth its salt must pursue. Commonalties of assumption, approach, and subject matter among the disciplines that constitute a domain of knowledge must be delineated. Connections between that domain and other broad categories and types of knowledge must be identified. And, regarding the social sciences at least, examples must be provided of both conceptual and empirical works that posit similarities and interactions among factors of behavior that are treated as different and separable in the disciplines. These materials must be part of an interdisciplinary student's preparation for making good use of courses in several disciplines.[2]

Our program's curriculum addresses the problems of access and coherency through continuously available advising and a set of four required core courses and nine satellite electives. The core courses deal with the social science disciplines in terms of their differences, their relations, and their use in interdisciplinary scholarship, including projects that our students design and do. The satellite electives, selected through intensive advising, present materials relevant to each student's interest through courses offered in departments and programs across the university. The curriculum has been described as one that offers instruction in a discipline called social science that has as its subject matter the other social science disciplines, their connections, and their applications.

What does this curriculum contain? The first pair of core courses, taken sequentially in the junior year, are best understood as a single course that deals with four basic questions: Is there a common subject matter of the social and behavioral sciences that justifies grouping them together as an area or domain of knowledge? Is this subject matter pursued in each of the seven basic disciplines? How can the bodies of knowledge produced through the practice of these and related disciplines be rendered coherent, integrated?

Taking evolution to have produced in humans a distinctive set of adaptive instruments (brain/mind, culture, social structure, polity, economy), we contend that each of the disciplines may be understood as specialized in the study of one or another of these instruments or, regarding history and geography, in the study of their uses at particular times and places. A natural science theory is used to establish that the basic social and behavioral sciences have human adaptive behavior as their common subject matter.

Given that human adaptive behavior presents diversity, complexity, subjectivity, and change in ways that seem to express the workings of creativity, imagination, and choice, we ask whether such a subject matter is amenable to scientific study and understanding. Arguments pro and con are considered. In epistemological terms, the discussion focuses on the root conflict between positivist and instrumentalist views of science and human nature. In ethical terms, emphasis is given to four basic questions: What kinds of knowledge about humans are needed? Is getting and having such knowledge more dangerous than it is useful? Should the knowledge we acquire about humans be regarded as at all scientific? Who should be empowered to answer these kinds of questions?

This discussion presses for specificity and leads into the third line of questioning: How are the subject matter and science issues addressed in each of the seven basic disciplines? To get at this, we consider a book in each of the disciplines in terms of how its author conceptualizes the phenomena under study, how he or she justifies methods used to gather and interpret data, and how these conceptual and methodological positions generate both the objects and events actually examined by practitioners of the discipline and their characteristic empirical claims.

Recognizing that the practice of different disciplines produces bodies of knowledge that are at least different and often incommensurable, we come finally to the fourth question: Can these bodies of knowledge be integrated? Here we examine some of the history of interdisciplinarity and present forms of integrative work, much of it philosophically associated with various brands of holism and reductionism,[3] and with applications such as are taken up in our university's problem- and perspective-oriented courses and programs.

This first pair of core courses, then, makes the access problem real and immediate by exposing students to the languages in which practitioners of each of the social sciences express their claims to knowledge. As well, they introduce the coherency/integration problem: The idea of human adaptive behavior as a subject matter common to all the disciplines ties them to each other and, through evolutionary theory, to the natural sciences. The identification of common epistemological and ethical issues ties the disciplines again to each other and also to philosophy and the humanities. The discussions of integration per se and of integrative strategies tie the disciplines to each other theoretically and, in applied form, to topical and/or problem-oriented fields.

At the risk of repetition and overkill, let me make these last two references to integration a bit more specific. Discussions of "integration per se" take up the forms and grounds for bringing together ideas and information arising in different specialized disciplines. Regarding forms, we might here encounter highly generalized treatments of the fields comprising a domain of knowledge—for example, formulations of how psychological, social, cultural, political, economic, and geographic determinants of human behavior interact to produce stability and change in human affairs over time (A. Kuhn). Or we might encounter very specific treatments of some particular problem, topic or theme—for example, formulations of how socialization and enculturation in professional communities may trigger deutero-learning processes that produce beliefs so firmly held that they can only be dislodged by removing believers from positions of authority (T. S. Kuhn). In either case, the purpose is to develop formulations—conceptual, methodological, empirical—that are complementary with respect to the necessarily partial knowledges that specialization generates.

Discussions of "integrative strategies" take up ways of pursuing this purpose. Here we may encounter strongly reductionist approaches in which apparently different phenomena are represented as manifestations of the same underlying processes. Once grasped, such representations constitute syntheses in the sense of allowing the same or similar understandings of very different classes of things (Homans, *Social*). Often the basis for using this approach is the recognition of similar patterns in different objects of study—for example, noticing the basic dynamics of exchange—giving and getting, if you will—in such different categories of human interaction as buying, worshipping, courting, marrying, loving, child-rearing, voting, teaching/learning, governing, healing, and so on.

Alternatively, discussion of integrative strategies may point to holistic approaches in which the focus is on relationship rather than similarity, on the emergent properties of phenomena that only become apparent when things are examined in concert rather than in the controlled or isolated conditions favored by specialized disciplines. A common basis for using this approach is the suspicion or recognition that a phenomenon viewed in naturalistic conditions has characteristics not seen when it is studied in isolation. So, for example, errors of visual perception associated with specific illusions were found to differ markedly in size depending on the gross visual properties of the subjects' physical environments—something that never appeared when, in the interests of experimental control, this basic aspect of perception was studied using subjects from just one kind of physical environment (Herkovits, Campbell, and Segall).

Through these discussions of integration per se and integrative strategies, students are apt to make the acquaintance, for example, of classical treatments like Auguste Comte's ideas about an ordered hierarchy of knowledge and Herbert Spencer's notions of synthetic philosophy; or early to middle twentieth-century efforts like Otto Neurath's contributions to *The International Encyclopedia of Unified Science*, Kenneth Boulding's *The Image*, George Homans' *Human Behavior, Its Elementary Forms*, Alfred Kuhn's *The Study of Society, A Unified Approach*, or more recent discussions like E. O. Wilson's *Concilience* and the emerging methodological integrations summarized in Charles Mann's "Can Meta-Analysis Make Policy?" And, through the same discussions, students are likely to become aware of our university's courses and programs in American studies, criminal justice, environmental studies, ethnic studies, gerontology, human sexuality studies, international relations, labor studies, public administration, women's studies, world development studies—offerings that address a particular topical area through the perspectives of several disciplines that are taken to shed light on the subject better together than they could separately.

In the same semesters when the first pair of core courses are taken, students are advised to take at least six of their nine satellite electives. These cannot be substantively described, of course, because they are selected for relevance to each student's individual interests from the large pool of courses offered throughout the social sciences and related fields. What can be said is that in these courses, the students cope with the access and coherency problems they are examining in the core courses—they get to see how things of interest to them look when they are examined by different sorts of specialists, and they begin to learn how to find, understand, and use the knowledge on which they will draw in their individual efforts to accomplish an integrative study of their respective subjects. Included among these electives are methods courses in the disciplines on which a student expects to rely and at least two courses that illustrate the integrative work of professional interdisciplinarians.

In the remaining pair of core courses, taken in the senior year along with the remaining three electives, students turn from learning about interdisciplinarity and their chosen interests to doing scholarly work on them. In the first course, a senior seminar, students delineate the focus of their individual programs as a subject warranting interdisciplinary treatment. As well, they find, read, and report on the relevance to that focus of fifteen research papers published in the journals of two or more fields. And they describe both a question with which their interdisciplinary reading leaves them, and an approach to answering it that, when executed, will constitute a senior project. The final core course operates both as a project-based tutorial arrangement between each student and a program faculty member and as a seminar in which students working on their projects share their on-going problems and progress. The projects completed in the course are each student's best effort at handling the access and integration problems that form the intellectual core of the curriculum from start to finish.

FIRST INNOVATION—FROM TOPIC TO PROCESS

Let me return now to the two sorts of innovation with which I began. The first, the continuous facilitating of fresh patterns of study for students as individuals, is literally a consequence of the core-satellite design. It produces a different educational experience from conventional majors that prepackage or sharply restrict the courses a student can use to earn a degree.

At the outset, during the junior year, our students are dealing head-on with the access problem—with the large effort of learning about the elements of several disciplines while most of their schoolmates are dealing with just one. At the same time, our students are dealing with core courses that stress the partial nature of specialized knowledge. Not surprisingly, they begin to wonder why they should be putting so much effort into absorbing what their own core courses challenge on such a fundamental level. Why bother with the disciplines at all? It takes awhile for the necessity of specialized work to make itself clear—for students to realize that we can't know everything before knowing something, and, therefore, that most of what is known in any scholarly domain is known through the practice of specialized disciplines.

In the same period, our students begin to experience another kind of doubt about their curriculum—this time as a consequence of their engagement with the integration/coherency problem: What guarantees that our integrative approaches won't turn out to be limiting in the same way that disciplines are? Are we not making constructions that could be, like disciplines, generators of partial knowledge? It takes a while to realize that their doubt is well founded and, consequently, that bringing ideas and information from several fields together is a continuous process that challenges interdisciplinary formulations as well as specialized ones.

Two kinds of information indicate that the learning processes we expect in this unusual educational experience do happen. First, historically, our students complete their programs through courses taken in five or more departments other than ours and earn grade point averages not different from those earned by students majoring in a single department. Second, faculty in the specialized disciplines routinely describe our students as especially interesting because they ask questions that are relevant to the disciplines' concerns but that are based on considerations in other disciplines—precisely the kind of questions that their own majors seldom ask. On both accounts, we believe that something fresh is happening by virtue of our students' grappling with the access and coherency problems that are central to their course of study.

But there is something else that goes on here—something deeper and more interesting that is rooted in each student's development of a novel body of knowledge about a topic, problem, or theme of his or her own choosing. This "something" happens in the second part of the curriculum when students with the same core courses and very different electives must participate in the senior seminars.

For most of our students, the start of the final seminar amounts to hitting a wall. This is because of two assignments that mark the turn from learning about interdisciplinarity and their own topics to doing their own work on these matters. They are asked, first of all, to describe in writing the focus of their satellite elective courses and the sense in which that focus warrants interdisciplinary treatment. And, second, they are asked to begin assembling from the research literatures of two or more disciplines some fifteen published articles relevant to their topics that they will be reading and describing in three more papers during the semester. Each of these three papers is to be about five of the fifteen research articles they've collected; each is to discuss how the set of five articles has affected their views of their topics, and each is to be presented to their fellow students in seminar. This reading and writing are understood to be in the nature of a literature review for their senior projects, a basis for identifying the questions they'll want to pursue therein.

These assignments prove very hard to do. The called-for descriptions of topics come out as little more than very general, commonsense namings of things and a few muttered remarks to the effect that the named things have to be treated in an interdisciplinary way because, after all, everything is related to everything else. And bibliographic searches for the fifteen topically relevant readings produce serious discomfort when it turns out that the names students have given to their topics either don't occur in the various reference sources/devices consulted, or are tied to so many different things that the resulting lists are too large to be useful. It almost feels as if a year of work has had no effects, until the shock of being asked to work on one's own wears off and students begin to make use of materials from the classes they've already taken—going back to texts and lecture notes to see what things that interested them were called, checking out footnotes to see what research was referenced in support of claims that struck them as important, trying to remember the questions they'd asked that their teachers thought were interesting because they brought something from one field to bear on something in another.

The process of organizing all of this material is daunting; and even after there's been some recovery from the initial collision with the wall, things do not go smoothly. Still, development proceeds through the series of assignments—seminar presentations reflect revisions of initial statements of topics as students work their way through each set of five of the fifteen research papers they've collected, each time reflecting on how their reading of research done in at least two different disciplines has affected their sense of their topics. At the heart of this development is the fact that few students share the same topical focus. Presentations are made to people who have the same core courses, but who have to be made familiar with the speaker's body of topical knowledge acquired in six or so courses. The feedback from fellow students in this situation is, I think, the necessary element that makes the whole process work. A closer look at the process is in order.

Usually, the initial presentations tell why the speaker is interested in a topic and how he or she thinks the ideas and events that constitute the topic come about—they are, in effect, somewhat personalized causal scenarios. Usually, too, this kind of statement elicits a very useful kind of response from classmates in the form of requests, offerings, elaborations, or clarifications that suggest to the speaker that he or she is on to something. These exchanges are crucial: listeners trying to understand the unfamiliar topics they hear about do so by likening them to ideas with which they are familiar—ideas that are apt to have arisen out of a year of work in a mix of disciplines different from the ones that inform the speaker. The connections thus made and articulated in the seminar are prototypes of what we mean by "bringing ideas and information from different disciplines to bear upon a topic." They are leads into fresh ways of reading and thinking about one's topic.

Expressed in what amounts to a seminar-specific argot, these leads are very frustrating because the nascent causal scenarios in which they are embedded correspond very little to what one might find through the topically oriented bibliographic searches that students have been pursuing. Eventually, most students realize that what they have generated may not appear in the usual places because no one else has conceptualized their topics in quite that way—that they may have come up with novel images of the structure and dynamics underlying their topics. They are then ready to recognize that a great deal may be known and presented in the literatures of fields that do not address their topic directly at all, but that do investigate the causal processes identified in their scenarios. The work they do in pursuit of this realization often puts them in the position of using again and better what they learned in the first two core courses. It is when this happens that we have a learning outcome that represents effective handling of the problems of access and integration.

Let me offer a rough example: At bottom, students seem to have a hard time realizing that research on processes implicated in the phenomena that interest them is research relevant to their topics, suitable for discussion in the literature review portions of their projects. In this regard, consider a student interested in what he describes as the way that "oppressive population policies of Western governments destroy indigenous cultures." Pressed by his classmates on obvious enough issues—which policies, which governments, what specifically does he mean by "destroys cultures"—he has plain enough responses about the United States in certain Latin American countries where indigenous peoples begin to lose their reproductive élan. To queries about why he thinks this happens, he mentions that the people involved begin to feel badly about themselves—as if they shouldn't reproduce because they and their way of life are not valuable. Somebody mentions that this sounds a little like stuff she's been reading on self-concept and self-esteem and how socialization establishes identity—stuff that the speaker has maybe heard of in one of the earlier core courses, but that got lost in the shuffle because most of his course selections were in the domain of political economy and development studies. So he goes to search for what's been mentioned and comes back later with the complaint that he can't find any research on this subject. What he means is that he can't find such research associated with his topical thrust—"oppressive population policies of Western governments destroy indigenous cultures." What hasn't yet become clear is that he might find all kinds of relevant material by looking for research on how self-esteem varies and trying on his own to match the conditions under which self-esteem fluctuates with the conditions that obtain when oppressive policies are put into effect. It is almost as if he doesn't realize that he and his classmates have come up with something original and that he has now to work on making connections to sustain it.

Eventually, the students get it. And, interestingly, they get it not by anyone "teaching" it to them, not even by anyone making examples of it available. Instead, they get it by being obliged to pay attention to each other's travails in seminars, in which setting they begin to offer each other suggestions based on what they know generally about each other's topics. It is a kind of small miracle.

SECOND INNOVATION—FROM INTEREST TO PROGRAM

Our second innovation has to do with generating new degree-granting programs. It grows out of the first innovation when significant numbers of students assemble very similar sets of topically related courses from the same array of departments. The numbers reflect widely felt needs for unavailable patterns of instruction that surface at about the same time among students at large, faculty in several departments, and, not infrequently, members of the wider community. This is the process of meeting new curricular demands.

Filling such demands does sometimes require entirely new course offerings. But often these demands can be served, at least initially, by regrouping existing courses. Complicated interactions enter with these rearrangements. Courses offered in different departments that appear to be about the same things often do not go together very well because of basic conceptual, methodological, and empirical disagreements. Barriers materialize out of considerations of turf, resources, reward structures, and the like. How to get around these barriers is an old problem in universities. We have used our program to contribute to its solution in two now obvious ways: We encourage our students to use the core-satellite structure to pursue fresh arrangements of existing courses. We have encouraged faculty from several departments to use the same structure as a means of pursuing a common concern with interested students—a means of seeing whether a basis for meeting some new curricular demand exists before facing the larger tasks of formal implementation. Many of our university's more innovative instructional developments began this way—starting as elective course patterns, later becoming freestanding minors, and, sometimes, growing to degree-granting departments and programs. Women studies, urban studies, criminal justice, information science, gerontology, employment and labor studies, public administration, religious studies, critical social thought, and world development studies are examples that have developed since the late sixties, almost all of which started as a topical focus in our major. Those that did not were born with members of our faculty acting as midwives.

Certainly there is more to all of this than just the good effects of our curriculum design. Especially relevant are visionary deans and faculty willing to play the midwife role. But these folks are much more likely to be effective if the front-end costs of learning to cooperate across fields have been paid more or less unselfconsciously by faculty and students while simply pursuing shared interests. This last is what the design facilitates.

LAST THOUGHT

An interesting final fact lends substance to this claim: None of the new programs, all of which are avowedly interdisciplinary, has displayed anything like the innovative élan of what my friend and colleague Ray Miller, who more than anyone I know has played the midwife role, calls Mother Social Science. One reason for this is that none has intended to sustain continuously fresh patterns of study for its students. On the contrary, they have tended to be topically focused and committed to taking particular ideological, technical-professional, or advocacy stances on their respective topics. As a result, they have tended to prescribe their students' course of study in much the same way that any discipline does—socializing their majors, so to speak, into the substantively prescribed frame of their "community." In this they have dismissed the aim of promoting innovation and, with it, a basic means of developing formulations of our subject matter that are complementary with respect to the necessarily partial knowledges that specialization generates. This lapse does leave room for programs of the sort I have described here. But it represents a denial of a most important reason for taking up the interdisciplinary persuasion in the first place.

Alas.

NOTES

1. Much of the information contained in this chapter is presented in greater detail in "Review of the Program in Social Science (Interdisciplinary Studies): A Self-Study, Spring 1992," prepared by the faculty of that program as part of the regular review process at San Francisco State University.

2. For an example of the working out of these requirements, see Bailis, "The Social Sciences."

3. For a discussion of holism in this connection, see Bailis, "Against."

WORKS CITED

Bailis, Stanley. "Against and For Holism: Review and Rejoinder to D.C. Phillips' *Holistic Thought in Social Science*." *Issues* (1984–85): 17–41.

———. "The Social Sciences in American Studies: An Integrative Conception." *American Quarterly* (August 1974): 202–24.

Boulding, Kenneth. *The Image*. Ann Arbor: University of Michigan Press, 1956.

Dimont, Max. *Jews, God and History*. New York: Signet, 1962.

Herkovits, M. J., D. T. Campbell, and M. H. Segall. *A Cross-Cultural Study of Perception*. Indianapolis, IN: Bobbs-Merrill, 1969.

Homans, G. C. *Human Behavior, Its Elementary Forms.* New York: Harcourt, Brace and World, 1961.

Homans, G. C. *Social Behavior: Its Elementary Forms.* New York: Harcourt, 1961.

Kuhn, Alfred. *The Study of Society: A Unified Approach.* Homewood, IL: Irwin/Dorsey Press, 1963.

Kuhn, T. A. *The Structure of Scientific Revolutions.* Chicago: University of Chicago Press, 1962.

Mann, C. C. "Can Metaanalysis Make Policy?" *Science* 266 (11 November 1994): 960–62.

Neurath, Otto. "Foundations of Social Sciences." *The International Encyclopedia of Unified Science.* 2.1 Chicago: University of Chicago Press, 1941.

Wilson, E. O. *Concilience: The Unity of Knowledge.* New York: Knopf, 1998.

CHAPTER 2

Enhancing Interdisciplinarity
Through Team Teaching

Jay Wentworth and James R. Davis

Interdisciplinary courses take many forms and appear in diverse parts of the curriculum (Davis 155). Interdisciplinary teaching can be accomplished, of course, by one person, prepared in two or more disciplines, teaching an interdisciplinary course alone, but a more common arrangement is team teaching.

Although team teaching is often used in interdisciplinary courses, is widely praised, and is growing in popularity, Donald Richards has warned that "team-taught courses that lay a claim to interdisciplinarity often fail to achieve their objectives precisely because the individual members of the instructional team themselves never really begin to understand their common concerns in a fashion that may properly be called interdisciplinary" (127). He also says, "my own evolving conviction is that team teaching is a poor vehicle for interdisciplinary undergraduate education" (127). While we accept the warning, we believe that team teaching, done well, does foster interdisciplinary aims and is both appropriate and exciting for many types of instruction.

If a course is only *multi*disciplinary, involving the sequential presentation of topics drawn from separate disciplines, it will not meet the aims of *inter*disciplinarity, which emphasizes conceptual and instructional integration. Many team-taught courses do begin as multidisciplinary because the teachers usually come from different disciplines or significantly different subdisciplines. They often face difficulties with integrating both substance and process that sometimes keep a course from moving beyond being simply multidisciplinary. Thus, we will address the question of how a course may become truly interdisciplinary by discussing how faculty can prepare to teach interdisciplinary team-taught courses (planning, integrating the team, and integrating content) and how they can function more effectively as an integrated team in the classroom. In other words, we will demonstrate how learning can become more interdisciplinary with the aid of team teaching. But, first, we must contend with the question: What can properly be called *interdisciplinary*?

William H. Newell, Executive Director of the Association for Integrative Studies, has long held that interdisciplinary studies should be defined in terms of integration. He and William Green wrote in 1982 that interdisciplinary studies could be defined "as inquiries which critically draw upon two or more disciplines and which lead to an *integration* of disciplinary insights" (24; emphasis ours). Newell and Julie Klein wrote that interdisciplinary studies "draws on disciplinary perspectives and *integrates* their insights through construction of a more comprehensive perspective" (3; emphasis ours). However, Newell acknowledges that Richards "makes a convincing case that synthesis [integration] should be a goal, not the *sine qua non* of interdisciplinarity" (vii).

What is achievable, in any interdisciplinary course, is the habit of seeing issues or topics from multiple perspectives. Teachers can help students become wary of or dissatisfied with any single formulation of a problem or any single-cause explanation of an event, topic, or theme, and can move students patiently toward integration or new conceptualization in spite of the improbability of any "final" synthesis that is "right." This habit, then, doesn't mean students or teachers will "know" the fullness of a topic, but it means they will move toward it knowing they don't and probably can't know everything about a topic. Through this process students discover the need for further learning, and they develop respect for different views. Richards calls this providing students with "a more enriched view of the issue, or topic, at hand" (125). Ursula Hübenthal says that the goal of "interdisciplinary thought" is *explaining a specific phenomenon in its totality*, in other words with all the attributes that are ascribed to it" (429; emphasis in original) from whatever discipline attributions may come. While this goal is appropriate for interdisciplinary work, we do best to accept that it is probably not wholly achievable. That we must make decisions, take positions, and act means that we always do these things provisionally, as works in progress by finite beings; still, decisions, positions and actions are perhaps better off done with the goal of a full understanding and the "more enriched view" that interdisciplinary work can provide. As students develop the habit of interdisciplinarity, the search for integration can be intensified. In the variety of circumstances of team teaching, interdisciplinarity is best achieved by consciously considering what it means to team members and how it will affect goals and practices in the course.

As part of achieving self-consciousness, we might consider some problems associated with team teaching. Julie Klein cites the following:

1. lack of "sufficient time for collaborative work"
2. "lack of training in group dynamics"
3. "problems with overlapping roles"
4. "territorial and status conflicts"
5. "a tendency for certain disciplines to dominate the process"
6. "and . . . insufficient funding and inadequate logistics." (142)

We would add that the fact of having to change one's cherished ways of doing things, which may be enriching, is also difficult; competition may develop among participating teachers or one or more may dominate or try to dominate; and the continuous challenge of teaming can be wearing.

However, we suggest that there are some distinct *opportunities* as well:

1. a wider variety of design, teaching, and assessment methods to draw on and thus more balance in the overall approach;
2. a wider knowledge base for students to draw on;
3. a wider personality base from which students can find compatibility (complaints that "the teacher didn't like me" are fewer);
4. an often increased sense of collegiality for teachers;
5. a more self-conscious approach to teaching, learning, and assessment processes;
6. an atmosphere of risk and experimentation that tends to generate involvement and, thus, learning;
7. and, as Klein notes, "more accuracy in assessment" (142).

We will examine what teachers can do to address problems and maximize opportunities to heighten interdisciplinary outcomes through team teaching.

PLANNING FOR INTEGRATION

Teachers tell students: It helps to do your homework. The same is true for collaborative teaching. All of the classroom roles described here work best when members of the team have also taken care of their other collaborative roles for the course: planning, team integration, content integration, and evaluation of student learning.

Planning begins with some overall concept for the course, some larger purpose or direction that creates a need for collaboration. Most interdisciplinary courses begin with a great idea. If you wish to do team teaching and are looking for an idea, there are some categories you can explore: themes, topics, and comparisons. *Themes* are recurring ideas or motifs and are exemplified by such titles as "Coming of Age" (which might include psychology, literature, anthropology, philosophy, religion, economics[1]) or "The Idea of the Romantic" (music, art, architecture, literature, philosophy, history) or "Women in Advertising" (marketing, psychology, women's studies, art). *Topics* are focused subjects for discussion and include such courses as "Particles" (physics, chemistry, biology, math, computer science); "Creativity" (art, music, theatre, dance, creative writing, psychology, biology, philosophy); or "Cultural Studies" (anthropology, literature, history, economics, political science, geography). *Comparisons* are explorations of similarities and differences and suggest such courses as "Einstein, Jung, and Joyce" (physics, psychology, literature, history, philosophy); "Shakespeare's England and Hugo's Paris" (history, literature, French, economics); or "Rousseau, Montessori, and Piaget" (education, philosophy, literature, psychology, history). Sometimes ideas just hit someone, or students suggest courses they would like to take (one course that came about this way was a course on "Myth and Dreams," in which psychology, literature, philosophy, anthropology, and religion were involved although the team had only two teachers). However the idea emerges, colleagues with different kinds of expertise need to be assembled to make the course work.

The next phase of development involves identifying those colleagues, testing their expertise and interest, and persuading them to be a part of the course. (Established courses sometimes have members assigned, and although this is often less than ideal, team members with appropriate backgrounds can learn to collaborate.) Sometimes graduate teaching assistants or advanced student co-teachers can be invited to be part of the course, in which case clarity about their roles also needs to be established. Student collaborators can make a strong contribution to a team-taught course through insights about current student attitudes and through feedback about how the course is being perceived. Students also often add an element of excitement to the team and usually learn a great deal about teaching and learning. In any case, the ideal team-taught course begins with a great idea and colleagues who are excited about the concept of the course.

Although the course may have begun with a great idea, the idea will need elaboration. During the planning process, the concept for the course will probably undergo significant change. Planning includes all of the elements that go into any course: statements of objectives and learning outcomes; choices about depth, breadth, scope, and sequence; decisions about the use of time; agreements about assignments and grades; and selection of topics and teaching strategies—all of which eventually come to be expressed in a syllabus (either before the course is taught, while the course is being taught, or after the course has been taught once—depending on the disposition of the faculty).

Planning also includes considering the minutiae that, when ignored, have sunk many a wonderful collaborative idea. *How many students will be in the course?* The most common solution is to agree on a number of students per faculty member—say the average student/faculty ratio at the school. The best solution is sometimes found in residential colleges and honors programs where the small class size is built into the charter of the program and the extra expense is budgeted. Another solution may come from a dean or chair who is willing to let a team teach with only the normal number of students in the department's lower level major courses (twenty to thirty, say) if, for example, over a three-year period each teacher adds, say, three hours to her or his total load or gives up a portion of scheduled release time. *How much credit will be given?* Three- to six-hour team-taught courses are common, often with cross-listing in several departments. *Which department gets the student or faculty credit hours?* Usually the department gets whatever the faculty/student ratio assigns each teacher. If the number of students is smaller than the average student/faculty ratio, credit may still be divided equally each time the course is taught or may be divided among the departments on a revolving basis.

Where will we get planning time? There are no real guidelines, but external grant sources are sometimes available if you have lead time. We suggest you talk with the chairs involved and enlist their help in getting resources from the dean(s). Often at least the lead person can get some release time, but keep in mind that time is a key factor in successful team teaching, so do your best to get the time you need. *If the class size is large, where will we find a space?* There are usually sufficient opportunities, if you check the whole institution; so your best bet is to go to the Strategic Planning Office, or its equivalent, to get ideas and to check space utilization charts. Look especially for odd times when large spaces might open up, and think of meeting at different times on different days. If the class is large, don't forget to schedule breakout space or find a way of dividing the large space. Try to find space that fits the type of learning activities to be used in the course. As in all aspects of team teaching, be creative!

The planning that results in an overall design and structure for the course is best supplemented by more detailed week-by-week and day-by-day planning. In weekly meetings, detailed plans for integrated teaching are hammered out and finalized, and the participants decide what is going to happen in class on a particular day. Without frequent communication about classroom roles (see later), faculty will revert to traditional practice, and the benefits of team teaching will be lost.

INTEGRATING THE "DREAM TEAM"

The world of sports has given us the concept of the dream team. Who would be on it? How would they play? Who could they beat? For team teaching, there is probably no "dream team," but there surely are some minimum ground rules for effective practice. Success depends on team members who have developed an appropriate level of comfort with each other and a high level of cohesion in their teamwork.

Unfortunately, a teaching team represents a kind of "anti-dream team." Instead of pulling together the best players of one sport, with similar skills, knowledge, and attitudes about the game, we intentionally bring together people whose methods of study, subject interests, values, and personalities may be quite different. Then we ask them to play together in a public arena, when most of their training and professional experience has taught them to "go it alone." It is as if we are bringing together one excellent player each from hockey, soccer, basketball, baseball, and football and asking them to invent a new sport. That's your interdisciplinary anti-dream team!

What will integrate a team? We will consider the following elements:

- Selecting faculty with appropriate characteristics
- Confronting personality differences
- Overcoming expertise
- Overcoming status
- Making meaning

Selecting faculty with appropriate characteristics. Certainly, selecting faculty who are willing to listen, learn, and change will make some aspects of team teaching much easier. Klein adds the following list of characteristics that have been found to promote interdisciplinary inquiry: "reliability, flexibility, patience, resilience, sensitivity to others, risk-taking, a thick skin, and a preference for diversity and new social roles" (183). For team teaching, we would add student-centeredness and emphasize the willingness to take intellectual risks with colleagues as well as classroom risks with students and colleagues.

Confronting personality differences. The opportunity to get to know each other as people is crucial. Storytelling, gathering socially, meeting in a variety of configurations and settings to discuss topics other than the course all help, but the interdisciplinary team needs members who are willing to recognize and deal with personality differences. Not all disagreements will be about academic matters; many have to do with personality traits, preferred modes of operation, and differing philosophies. The practice of living proves that differences in personality can cause problems, but team teaching confirms and magnifies that common experience. However, as Klein warns, the desire for congeniality may lead to an avoidance of conflict that, in the end, could make personality issues more difficult to resolve, so we are not advocating congeniality at any price but a congeniality that can support confrontation and exploration (127).

One approach to personality is to make certain aspects of it conscious. The Myers-Briggs Type Indicator (MBTI),[2] for example, is an instrument designed to show how preferences for certain ordinary ways of doing things affect human interactions. The preferences indicate whether energy tends to be used for internal or external concerns, how information is received, how decisions are made, and how much weight is given to information gathering or decision making. Because we use all the approaches outlined every day, but prefer a few, the instrument promotes internal integration by reminding us of other ways we do things and external complementarity by reminding us that the way the other person is doing something has advantages that our preferred approach lacks. Eventually, we may begin to prefer the approach best suited to the occasion rather than maintaining an absolute preference for any one approach.

The specific relevance here is that each set of preferences implies a different learning and teaching style. Once preferences are understood, a teaching team can assess its strengths and weaknesses, likely areas of conflict within the team, and ways of avoiding conflict and maximizing each teacher's contributions. It may also help the team think about teaching strategies because students will also have different learning styles and different needs (see, e.g., Lawrence). Of course, there is more to teaching/learning styles than can be covered in any single instrument, but the MBTI can be a useful starting place. Other such instruments, such as the Kolb Learning Style Inventory, may also be helpful. In any case, unaddressed personality differences can sink an otherwise well-built team, so be prepared to investigate and speak frankly about team-member personality differences.

Overcoming expertise. As faculty, we are trained to be experts—specialists in some domain. That domain is our turf, and we have been taught to respect (and tread lightly on) the turf of others. We know the rules and boundaries. In the collaboration that is required of a teaching team, however, the participants must loosen the boundaries, break the rules, dare to venture onto another's turf, and become welcoming tour guides for their own turf. The boundaries are subtle, and the new ground is often unfamiliar territory. People who work in the humanities, the social sciences, the sciences, and the professions all have their stereotypes of each other, perhaps even deep-seated prejudices.

A useful approach to overcoming expertise is to have some frank discussions among team members about how they do their work with the explicit, shared goal of becoming aware of differences and appreciating commonalities. A key commonality, often overlooked, is the fact that every discipline engages in scholarly work in a broadly scientific way, although "experiments" in the humanities may involve such things as reading and rereading a work to confirm a hypothesis or plunging into the archives for more evidence. All scholars, though sometimes in different ways, conduct literature searches, look for gaps in knowledge and understanding, seek new problems to investigate, develop hunches and hypotheses, gather evidence, draw conclusions, and present those conclusions for public scrutiny. Similarly, all scholars are creative and tell stories. A scientist can tell about leaps of insight just as a poet can, and both have narratives to tie together the information they discover. The poet and the chemist both have a craft, but on an interdisciplinary team, they may need to put forth considerable effort to overcome their expertise. The effort will permit greater respect for each other as scholars, make team members more eager learners, and support the goal of an appropriate, well-supported integration of methods, content, and principles where possible and a carefully articulated statement of differences where larger, integrating frameworks cannot yet be found.

Overcoming expertise may involve changing one's idea about the expert. On an interdisciplinary team, expertise is still honored, but it is democratized through sharing. As sharing of knowledge takes place, new expertise is developed by newcomers to the turf, but the expert also learns more about his or her own field from having to explain it and make it understandable to colleagues from other fields who ask quite different questions than students might. When enough sharing has taken place, the new turf no longer seems so foreign, and the expert no longer seems so exalted. Eventually, sharing expertise makes it possible for every team member to lead a discussion or respond to a presentation about any aspect of the course. Thus, we suggest that the most important expertise any faculty member brings to an interdisciplinary course is not their expertise as a subject matter specialist but as an expert perpetual learner. It is this skill and attitude that leads any researcher across disciplinary boundaries (Klein 183) and enables team members to play many different roles and enter freely into the experience of team teaching as true colleagues.

Overcoming status. Sometimes team member differences translate into power differences that create morale problems. As Julie Klein warns, "[i]nterdisciplinary teams . . . are status systems that reflect external hierarchies and disciplinary chauvinism" (127). Clearly, to be interdisciplinary, team members must be willing to suspend any sense of the superiority of their own discipline's principles, methods, goals, and subject matter even though that sense is so often validated by one's immediate colleagues and one's own experience. If suspension of superiority can be accomplished, the team can begin to move toward the fullness and integration that characterize interdisciplinarity. Some members of the team may hold tenure and higher rank and may be well-known scholars, while others are new assistant professors or adjunct faculty. Some members of the team may be more popular, more humorous, more approachable, or more interesting. Some may be males and some females, and unconscious patriarchal attitudes and practices are no less damaging for being unconscious. All these differences are possible sources of stress and should be acknowledged in the team-building process.

Students are quick to spot differences among team members and sometimes will "play games" that exploit those differences. A team that works well together acknowledges and discusses differences and will be more likely to spot the games and refuse to play. In one game, which might be called "Mommy and Daddy," students exploit the gender differences on the team and treat faculty according to traditional gender roles. A game we might call "You're My Favorite" is used by students to scapegoat the teacher with perceived weaknesses by appealing to the other teacher's need to feel appreciated. Another game that someone called "Let's You and Him Fight" pits one teacher against another and draws out perceived latent hostilities or expressed differences. Game playing is a threat to the cohesiveness of the team and needs to be addressed by discussing it within the team and exposing it to the students for what it is. In general, the team must develop a collaborative, mutually supportive environment as a foundation for taking on integrative roles in the classroom, and democratizing the faculty and inviting students into the collaboration by exposing games are two important steps to take.

Making meaning. Meaning-making is the payoff of team integration. It happens every time an intellectual insight strikes the group, a personal difficulty is overcome in the group context, the course develops into something more complex than any member had been able to envision before, or the team sees the light go on in a student's eyes. To give examples would require contextualizing, but we don't have to do that because every teacher, who enjoys teaching, experiences these moments. However, in the team context, the experience is amplified by the sharing of them. Experiencing meaning together is the glue that bonds the team, and when the team sees these moments, they know they have, on that occasion at least, succeeded.

INTEGRATING CONTENT

In a team-taught course, the interdisciplinary aspects should be made explicit, discussed, and agreed on among the faculty. Are we trying for a synthesis? Are we trying to teach interdisciplinarity explicitly? Are we trying to teach processes? Are we trying to give the richest possible view of the topic, theme, or comparison? All of these? To illustrate this aspect of the planning process, consider the problem of synthesis or integration.

In a sense, a topic, theme, or comparison that requires several disciplines to explicate adequately creates a new interdisciplinary "field" of inquiry. Since it is a new field, it may require creating metaphors, vocabulary, concepts, and principles that apply to the field. The new field might also invite "borrowing," that is, taking a metaphor, concept, set of principles, research data, or the like from one discipline and applying it to another in hopes of enlarging, enriching, and/or clarifying one or both disciplines. However, all integrative methods are somewhat perilous. For example, Julie Klein has offered the following six problems that can arise when we borrow material from one discipline to apply in another:

1. distortion and misunderstanding of borrowed materials;
2. use of data, methods, concepts, and theories out of context;
3. use of borrowings out of favor in their original context . . . ;
4. 'illusions of certainty' about phenomena treated with caution or skepticism in their original disciplines;
5. overreliance on one particular theory or perspective; and
6. a tendency to dismiss contradictory tests, evidence, and explanations. (88)

A team with these problems in mind will work more productively together although "progress" may be slow; however, what does come together is likely to stay together. Furthermore, these problems help show why, even as interdisciplinarians, we are well off to heed evolutionary biologist and essayist Stephen Jay Gould's comment that "interdisciplinary unification represents a grand and worthy goal of intellectual life, but greater understanding can often be won by principled separation and mutual respect, based on clear definitions and distinctions among truly disparate processes, rather than by false unions forged with superficial similarities and papered over by a common terminology" (32). Yes, patience in the expectation of integration is far better than creating false connections, and genuine, carefully prepared integration is difficult. While borrowing isn't the only way integration takes place, it has, we hope, illustrated what the team has to contend with in its own deliberations about content. What can we do to integrate content, if that is our explicit goal?

We can help students *define a conceptual framework*, such as a model, that integrates the disciplinary aspects of a course into a larger whole. An example would be a course on "Minority Women Writers"[3] in which the final task students worked on was attempting to create a model of self-identity that encompassed all the identity issues that the authors studied in the course had described. Another example would be a comparative cultures course, in which students would be asked to develop a model of culture that would embrace the variety of forms studied. Synthesis could also be achieved by *integrative action* in an interdisciplinary group. For example, a group of senior seminar students from different majors can select a problem, use everyone's expertise to get as broad and deep a view of the problem as possible, generate a proposal for action, and either carry it out or present it to a body that has the power to carry it out. Many kinds of service learning courses or components have much to offer as integrative action when they are conceptualized, discussed, and analyzed as interdisciplinary.

Another possibility would be a *creative integration* of material digested from various sources. For example, a performance art class works with teachers from music, theatre, dance, art, and creative writing. Student syntheses consist of a variety of performances, which use and modify the various media at their disposal (requiring the development of new skills and a transformed aesthetic). As Suzi Gablik and others have shown, artistic responses to social problems can actually help solve those problems, and that is integration of a high order—although not what we usually think of as integration. But interdisciplinary team teaching isn't about "what we usually think."

The term *"meta-goals"* refers to the larger learning outcomes that transcend immediate course objectives, and this concept is useful for thinking about the classroom aspect of content integration. For example, a team teaching non-Western cultures might have the meta-goal of giving students some experience of the more collective (less individualistic) nature of non-Western cultures. Thus, they might put students in shifting groups of three to do most of the assignments. Such a design will drive the students crazy, but they will learn to work together more effectively and, in the end, the meta-goal can be explained and discussed. A team teaching utopian communities might divide students into project groups to design their own ideal society but include the rule that all members of the group have to agree that each member would be willing to live in that society. The rule would facilitate the meta-goal of an experience of reaching consensus—especially on values—a process that actually illustrates what utopia is all about. A course on life-span development might have as its meta-goal the cultivation of more student responsibility for learning, so, as the course proceeds, the team may begin as lecturer/experts, then become discussion leaders, co-learners, and finish in the role of resources.

Having a clear idea of exactly how the disciplinary sources are to be integrated and an explicit understanding of course meta-goals provides a basis for developing new roles for faculty in the classroom.

CLASSROOM ROLES FOR TEAM TEACHERS

Even teams that function well in planning a course and integrating the content are sometimes puzzled about what to do when they enter the classroom. They frequently divide up the teaching task, assigning themselves to certain classes or units, thus engaging in what might be called serial teaching rather than integrated teaching. They teach what they have always taught, in the way they have always taught it. Sometimes they even choose not to attend the class when they have no major responsibility; and when they do attend, they are not quite sure what they are supposed to do. What can be more awkward than sitting in a class, wanting to contribute, but not knowing how?

We will discuss ten specific roles a teacher, who is not "presenting," can play as part of a team to bring about greater collaboration in the classroom and more nearly approximate a process we would call integrated teaching. Even in a team-taught class, the presenter will have the central role and can do all the things he or she has done in any other class, provided the presentation is varied and well done, but in a team setting, what the presenter does can be much enhanced when the other team members take on one or more of the following supplementary roles:

1. *Model Learner.* A simple role for a nonpresenting faculty member is to become a model learner, that is, to show students how to learn by the way you, as a teacher, learn. Being a model learner includes respecting the presenter by having read all assignments on time, doing extra research or reading, taking notes on assignments and presentations, asking questions in a respectful way, offering alternative ideas or interpretations for genuine discussion, listening carefully to the presenter and students, and accepting

guidance from the presenter. A model learner does not dominate or engage in an exclusive dialogue with the presenter, play "one-upmanship" games, or rely on technical vocabulary or teacherly authority to maintain his or her position.

Being a model learner can be hard for some teachers, so this role or process should be discussed, understood, and agreed on before the class begins. On the other hand, this role modeling is extremely valuable to students and can be fun, even a relief, to the faculty member who is, in fact, learning new material. Once you relax and accept the role, being a student again becomes an enjoyable part of the course. In addition, being a model learner can change a faculty member's relationship with students and with colleagues. Most teachers playing the role of a model learner will find that students respect their willingness to share their vulnerability, risk a "wrong" answer, and show ignorance. Furthermore, colleague-presenters who are listened to, asked acute questions, and discover that their material is interesting to faculty in other disciplines enjoy the experience and become more willing themselves to learn and grow.

The role of model learner promotes interdisciplinarity because the attitude of the model learner is receptive, open, and curious, and it stimulates the interactions necessary for "fullness" and integration. The model learner is giving up expertise without giving up knowledge, which he or she can respectfully bring to bear on the topic being presented. The model learner's questions and contributions will show the multidimensionality of the topic. If, instead, all teachers in the team do their best to maintain their status as "experts" in their field and resist learning the other teachers' fields, little integration will take place—either in the teachers' conception of the course or in the minds of the students; instead of fullness, the students will see fragmentation.

2. *Observer.* In a team, the presenter is free to concentrate on content while a nonpresenting teacher can simply observe the process, keep track of time, note communication patterns, and offer a rundown of the process elements to the presenter after class so that the process can be improved. For example, the observing teacher can note nonparticipating students so ways can be found to include them in the next class, identify any gender biases or preferences that show up in the presenting teacher's routine, observe how much silence the presenter allows after asking a question, or describe when and possibly why the students get restless during a particular activity. All these observations offered in a constructive way can lead to better teaching, and that reward bonds the team further. The observer role is a help to the teaching team and to students if entered into in the right spirit. Just the friendly warning, "We've only got ten minutes left," can be a

help, but the observation that "Susan was close to tears when you were dis-cussing women's roles among the Maya" could uncover a serious issue for Susan and cement the connection of the subject to her personal experi-ence. Systematic observation is often valuable when planning for the next class, week, or unit. Because interdisciplinary teaching involves integra-tion at many levels, having team members available to observe that process can be valuable.

3. *Co-Lecturer.* When a class calls for a presentation, explanation, or for-mal lecture, team members may wish to join forces in a co-lecture or dia-logue.[4] The subject in an interdisciplinary course often involves differing perspectives and what better way is there to represent these viewpoints than by having faculty present them in the same class period? Sometimes the perspectives represent complementary viewpoints, but at other times differences run deep and provoke intense discussion. The psychologist on the team, for example, may suggest that sociologists are so caught up in the importance of social trends that they fail to account for individual differ-ences, whereas the sociologist will point out that what psychologists as-sume to be individual differences are really part of larger social trends. This kind of disagreement is not easily resolved, but it is the very essence of in-terdisciplinary dialogue with the hope of a rich, both/and synthesis.

Having two team members present their views on a particular topic within the same class period may bring into focus the actual nature and ex-tent of disagreement, the grounds for argument, and the differing uses and types of evidence. The broad outlines of the discussion may be discussed be-fore the lecture, but there is something to be said for letting the conversa-tion emerge spontaneously so that students can see real disagreement, the passion behind it, and the way that differences can be resolved by hard work and good will. In the best of circumstances, lightning will strike, and students will see or even participate in the moment of integrative insight.

4. *Panel Member.* Sometimes a subject involves multiple viewpoints or levels of expertise, and a panel may be appropriate. The panel may consist of three or more team members, in which case the panel could discuss inte-grated concepts and processes related to the topic at hand. The panel may also be made up of selected team members and certain invited guests who will do best by having talked beforehand about interdisciplinarity in terms of process, fullness, and integration. In a course designed to help students work with children having special needs, it might be valuable to assemble a panel consisting of a school psychologist, social worker, pediatrician, teacher, and special educator to discuss what they do and how they work as a team. In this case, one of the regular members of the teaching team may play a critical role as moderator of the panel. Panels usually function to sug-

gest fullness, but the danger is the return of expertise in a negative way and a subsequent lack of interaction with the students. If the panel members have planned their method (e.g., a dialogic presentation rather than a serial one) and discussed contents so everyone is familiar with the ideas and evidence, they can perhaps offer an interactive presentation that fosters integration and other interdisciplinary goals through demonstration.

5. *Discussion Leader.* Many team-taught courses have arrangements for breakout groups that sometimes provide interesting opportunities for inquiry not always available in a larger class. If you use breakout groups, you may feel uncomfortable when the material under consideration raises a question for which you have no authoritative answer. However, this offers an opportunity to facilitate genuine inquiry. Your role shifts from expert about the topic to expert about the process of inquiry. Let's say the task is to provide interpretations of an assigned short story. Whatever your own discipline, you can bring it to bear on a story. This will broaden the students' view, and if you have prepared with the literature person on the team, you will be able to work at some level on the literary aspects of the problem and demonstrate respect for the material and the applicability of multiple perspectives. You can also demonstrate how to compile evidence to support particular interpretations that can then be brought back to the main group for further discussion with the presenting teacher, who may provide extra evidence that supports or contradicts the discussion group's conclusions. Asking "real" questions, that is, questions to which you, as the teacher, don't have an authoritative answer, may be hard at first, yet this is a place where you can show that answers to questions are earned, not magic, and that questions may be as important as answers. This kind of teacher risk-taking suggests that it is fine to be ignorant—but not fine to cherish or deny that ignorance. If the team has three or more teachers, a comparison of the group's results is often fun and instructive because comparison makes it easier to see biases, types of questions raised, mistaken presuppositions, and false information.

6. *Co-Discussion Leader.* Sometimes a discussion is best with the entire class assembled. If so, the discussion can be led by more than one facilitator, each bringing his or her unique questions to the inquiry. For example, in an interdisciplinary course on ethics and values, one might wish to debate the feasibility of bringing a controversial speaker, such as a neo-Nazi, to the campus. The request raises the value of free speech, but also the university's commitment to protection of minorities from harassment and discrimination. As co-discussion leader, it may be your assigned role to ask questions and push for recommendations on one side of this dilemma, whereas your colleague may be assigned the task of seeing that the other set of values is

not ignored. If the discussion generates a clear question, we suggest having students argue the side they do not believe so they can practice listening, stating the values inherent on each side, and then trying to find solutions that preserve some values from both sides (in this case, free speech and respect for diversity).

7. *Case Co-Facilitator*. Problem-solving and decision-making skills are often cultivated through cases. Many teachers, particularly in the fields of law, business, and health sciences, use cases when teaching alone, but cases can be greatly enriched through co-facilitation. Cases are usually already multidimensional and often require interdisciplinary perspectives. A business case about service quality improvement, for example, may require perspectives from management, marketing, and accounting, but a psychologist and an attorney might add interesting dimensions. A case on new product development may draw on expertise from engineering, materials science, and marketing, but would benefit from an ethicist or child psychologist. Having more than one facilitator or a team of facilitators available increases the likelihood that more levels of the case will get explored and in more depth. Co-facilitators may take turns, focusing first on one aspect of the case and then another, or they may work in tandem, responding spontaneously to issues that students generate about the case.

8. *Group Facilitator*. Group processes are often used for exploring opinions, attitudes, and beliefs—what educators call the affective domain, but which might more simply be called matters of the heart. Sometimes a team-taught class can be broken into smaller groups with each member of the team taking on the role of group facilitator. A class session on right-to-life issues might begin with a carefully facilitated exploration of how participants feel about such issues and how their attitudes may have developed, or students can be led in storytelling about right-to-life incidents known to them. Having one team member to facilitate each group has its advantages for such a topic. At other times, the class may be divided into even smaller "leaderless" groups,[5] where the instructors for the course design group instruments, compose the groups, and keep an eye on the process but neither facilitate the groups nor appoint leaders. The instructor's role in this case is to help the groups succeed in their task and to elicit and help interpret the meaning of the activity at the end. When such groups are used, the instructional team members may each play different roles—such as developing the instrument, assigning the groups, and interpreting the activity—or they may work collaboratively on all aspects of the activity.

9. *Gadfly*. In some instances, one team member may be assigned or take on the special role of gadfly. The gadfly has license to poke fun, raise irreverent questions, or suggest unthinkable outcomes—all for the purpose of

moving the activity at hand along in a more creative and confrontational way. Socrates was perhaps the Western gadfly prototype, but there are also precedents in Shakespeare's fools and the "clowns" of the Hopi tradition who question ritual behavior and unexamined assumptions. This irreverent role for a teacher, though potentially useful, is also risky; it needs to be discussed carefully by members new to a team, but can be done more spontaneously with old friends once everyone knows what is intended. An instructor handing back a batch of papers in a course on Zen Buddhism tore up a student's paper, handing him the pieces, then blew his nose on the next paper, and tossed the third in the wastebasket. The class was in an uproar, but soon the team of instructors had crafted a lively discussion of the Zen principle of immediacy. Why had the papers been written, and what value might have come from that experience if the paper had been lost or went unread?

The gadfly role is perhaps not for everyone, or every team, but variations of it may prove useful in certain settings. A milder and more familiar form of the gadfly is devil's advocate. This role is safer—since most people announce that they are "playing devil's advocate"—and useful when one is teaching alone. In a team-taught course, by contrast, there are many opportunities for honest disagreement, so a devil's advocate is less often necessary than the gadfly.

10. *Resource*. One goal of any class can be to empower students—that is, to return students to an awareness of their power. As mentioned in our discussion of meta-goals, a teaching team can slowly offer and expect more responsibility from students so that both student and teacher roles change during the course. The teachers can go from authority to guide to model learner to resource. As resource, they would only answer questions of a certain type or suggest where answers could be found, but would not provide substance, structure, or judgment.

In a team-taught course, many roles can occur at once. Sometimes it is useful just to have an extra hand available as a roving resource. One teacher is able to stand by, troubleshoot, and respond to the unexpected, while other members of the team are busy with their agreed-on roles for the day. Sometimes the help provided can be as mundane as finding another projector bulb or setting up the PowerPoint. A roving team member is especially useful in a laboratory or studio situation where students need feedback on their efforts: a new idea when they are stuck, encouragement when they are frustrated, or simply reinforcement and affirmation for doing something well. A roving resource is also especially valuable for field trips and other experience-based learning adventures. Sometimes teachers become a valuable resource to groups of students as advisors for a project and a panel, or in an experiment to see how different groups respond to a particular problem or prompt. If the teachers do not discuss ahead of time what the outcome might be, the way the groups function can then become a legitimate topic of large group discussion and learning. If the class explores the reasons why they went in different or similar ways, what each group found or missed, and how they might cover the topic more completely by combining resources, questions, methods, and insights, they will have become more interdisciplinary.

As you can tell from the previous list, we believe that classrooms should be stimulating places where many strategies are employed and many roles are taken both by teachers and students. This is true for the one-teacher classroom, but can be more fully realized in interdisciplinary, team-taught courses. The bottom line, of course, is that integrated teaching contributes to fullness and integrative learning. What teachers do either facilitates or diminishes integrative learning. Why go to all the trouble of developing interdisciplinary courses if each teacher only intends to come to class to lecture, one at a time, on his or her specialty? Why would we expect students to go to the trouble to accomplish what we ourselves are not willing to attempt? Integrative courses deserve integrated teaching.

EVALUATING STUDENT LEARNING

Practical reasons alone provide sufficient motive for team collaboration to establish clear guidelines about assessment of student work.[6] In one course we know about, the students knew that a common assignment was to be graded by faculty section leaders, so four creative but lazy students got together and handed in one paper to their different section leaders. That self-same paper earned, respectively, an A, B, C, and D from the different section leaders. The students were caught, but the faculty members were embarrassed. How could they have graded the paper so differently, they asked. They now establish clear criteria for every assignment and exchange samples of student work with each other to maintain consistency.

Beyond these practical reasons, however, are other, perhaps more important reasons, for collaboration on evaluation. If one of the main purposes of interdisciplinary teaching is to make connections, where otherwise connections are not being made, then the central purpose of evaluation ought to be to assess this integrative process in the work of students. Becoming explicit about evaluation is simply another way of gaining clarity about the integrative processes of the course. Once again, knowing the larger scheme for integration provides a basis for selecting appropriate roles for integrative teaching.

Ideally, every assignment should be read by all teachers, but that is not always practical. One idea to make it more practical is to run the class in groups some or all of the time so that the writing is a coordinated effort yielding from ten to twenty papers rather than, say, sixty papers requiring sixty separate grades. Even if the same number of pages is read, the need to decide fewer grades is helpful, and the fewer grades are more easily negotiated. Another idea is, for grading purposes only, to divide the class into as many groups as there are instructors, then rotate grading such that every student is graded by every instructor at least once (more often if possible). A third idea is to create a set of grade criteria for papers and projects before the class begins. These may or may not be shared with the students (we prefer sharing) and may range from a rough hierarchy of important characteristics to a rather detailed grid. Some groups prefer to wait until there are actual student products before them to decide how grading will occur. This is fine, but at some point, clear communication about criteria must take place with students and within the team. Criteria may sometimes change as the team develops and the class progresses.

Well-structured student self-evaluations can be a way of getting information about individual and group performance in any course; however, in a team-taught course, it can also provide a focus for faculty grade discussions, particularly if students have been working together on group projects. If each teacher has read a particular writing assignment or exam and given it a tentative grade, looking at a set of student self-evaluations can help settle team disagreements and make coming to a common decision easier. On the self-evaluation instrument, have students:

- Estimate the time they spent on each activity (reading, writing, doing research, doing projects, etc.).
- Describe how they read each book (skim, average, carefully, with notes), what percent of the book they read, whether they read it on time for the first discussion as well as their writing method, their research process, and their group process.
- Rank order (by the student's own idea of the quality of participation) the members of their work group and comment on why the ranking is this way (allow students to bracket members of approximately even contribution and allow them to suggest grades *if they wish*).
- Respond to grading criteria, tell anything extra they did for the course that the teacher might not be aware of or any circumstances that affected their performance, and tell why each grade (or just the final grade) they suggest should not be higher or lower.
- Sign the self-report form.
- Fill out the form in silence and privacy.

Self-evaluation offers a range of information from members of a group, thereby giving a kind of truth index. Rank ordering of peers is especially onerous to students, but for teachers, it is an excellent guide to student contributions outside class. For example, if a person ranks himself second and everyone else ranks him last, we are probably justified in doubting his word—just as we would be if a student were to rank herself last while others rank her second! Our experience is that women are more likely than men to undervalue themselves when assigning grades, so we recommend caution. Discussion after everyone has read the evaluations is usually lively, focused, and surprisingly convergent. It is a good practice to talk with students whose self-assessment is more than one letter grade off the assessment of the instructors.

CONCLUSION

To make team teaching interdisciplinary, the team must decide what it means by "interdisciplinarity" for its own purposes—which may be aimed first at sharing knowledge, then comparing knowledge, and finally combining knowledge in various ways. Then it must decide what interdisciplinarity will mean for teaching purposes—which may be urging toward habits of interdiscplinarity, emphasizing the fullness of a topic, guiding development of self-conscious interdisciplinarity, and promoting the integration that comes from sophisticated knowledge of several disciplines influencing each other to solve problems or illuminate ideas. For us as teachers, the integration, finally, that interests us most is that which happens inside the student, changing the student, healing, creating new opportunities, building self-esteem, recognizing unsuspected abilities and interests, developing new views of the world and new commitment. It doesn't *require* interdisciplinarity or team teaching to foster personal integration in a student, but appropriate choices by risk-taking faculty, who have shared power (status and expertise), confronted issues of personality, and learned to collaborate in the classroom, should provide students exciting, integrative educational experiences—despite the many demands the enterprise will make on the time, patience, and resources of even the most committed teachers.

NOTES

1. The list of disciplines is meant to be suggestive rather than exhaustive. We've learned that combinations of disciplines that seem odd are actually fine

because of the people involved—their interpersonal skills, willingness to learn new material, avocational interests, and so on.

2. The instrument has to be administered by a professional, but it is available through the psychological services unit at most higher education institutions. Three useful books are Bates and Kiersey's *Please Understand Me* and Lawrence's *People Types and Tiger Stripes* and *Looking at Type and Learning Styles*. Some people object to the MBTI on the grounds that they are complex human beings and not bound by a particular set of preferences. However, the objection is based on a misunderstanding of the instrument's assumptions and intent. The designers assumed (as did Jung) that everyone uses all the functions every day! So we do adapt; we are flexible, complex beings. The point of the MBTI is that despite our ability to use all the functions, we prefer some to others, and that fact has implications for many behaviors—including teaching and learning. The MBTI preference styles should not be treated as boxes or labels; they are properly used to help understand oneself and others without prejudice. The MBTI does not include all the dimensions of personality nor everything that is important to consider about teaching or learning styles, but it can be helpful, especially in concert with other approaches.

3. Taught by Dr. Edelma Huntley at Appalachian State University.

4. A debate might also work if it were used to define the factors on each side of a controversy as preparation for using the results to arrive at a creative solution, especially one that honors the best of both sides. See point 6, Co-Discussion Leader.

5. The word "leaderless" is probably a misnomer for such groups because leaders do usually emerge from among the participants. However, there are times when a group works in a collaborative way in which the duties of leadership are shared. This situation always seems to feel magical and is highly valued by participants. We hope that teaching teams can sometimes reach such a level of integration.

6. Please see Chapter 13 in this volume for more information on assessing interdisciplinary learning and teaching.

WORKS CITED

Bates, M., and D. W. Keirsey. *Please Understand Me*. Del Mar, CA: Prometheus Nemesis Book Company, 1978.

Davis, James R. *Interdisciplinary Courses and Team Teaching: New Arrangements for Learning*. Phoenix: Oryx Press, 1995.

Gablik, Suzi. *The Reenchantment of Art*. New York: Thames and Hudson, 1991.

Gould, Stephen J. "What Does the Dreaded "E" Word *Mean*, Anyway?" *Natural History* 109 (February 2000): 28–44.

Hübenthal, Ursula. "Interdisciplinary Thought." Newell, *Interdisciplinarity* 427–44.

Klein, Julie T. *Interdisciplinarity: History, Theory, and Practice*. Detroit: Wayne State University Press, 1990.

Klein, Julie T., and William H. Newell, W. H. "Advancing Interdisciplinary Studies." Newell, *Interdisciplinarity* 3–22.

Lawrence, G. *People Types and Tiger Stripes*. 3rd ed. Gainesville: Center for Applications of Psychological Type, 1993.

———. *Looking at Type and Learning Styles*. Gainesville: Center for Applications of Psychological Type, 1997.

Newell, W. H. "Guest Editor's Introduction." *The Journal of General Education* 45 (1996): v–viii.

———, ed. *Interdisciplinarity: Essays from the Literature*. New York: College Entrance Examination Board, 1998.

———. "Professionalizing Interdisciplinarity: Literature Review and Research Agenda." Newell, *Interdisciplinarity* 529–63.

———. "The Theory of Interdisciplinary Studies." National Conference of the Association for Integrative Studies, Naperville, IL, September 29, 1999.

Newell, W. H., and William J. Green. "Defining and Teaching Interdisciplinary Studies." Newell, *Interdisciplinarity* 23–34.

Richards, D. G. "The Meaning and Relevance of Synthesis in Interdisciplinary Studies." *The Journal of General Education* 45 (1996): 114–28.

CHAPTER 3

Writing in Interdisciplinary Courses

Coaching Integrative Thinking

Marcia Bundy Seabury

INTRODUCTION: WAC AND IDS

I magine an interdisciplinary arts course composed of students from engineering, business, education, the health professions, and various arts and sciences, all enrolled to meet a general education requirement. Many of them have never been to an opera, a symphony concert, or an art museum. Their team of instructors, faculty from art, music, and literature, assigns them not only to make forays into firsthand experiences with the arts but to write about them and draw connections, as they gain an understanding of the European-wide cultural movement known as Romanticism. Indeed the students write continually as they process weekly multimedia experiences of revolution, nature, and individualism.

Interdisciplinary study for students across a university shares a related heritage with writing across the curriculum: Both can trace their roots to ancient times but took on increased importance in American higher education during the 1970s and 1980s in response to widespread concerns about fragmentation of the curriculum and limitations of students' ability to think and express themselves. Some universities have explicitly linked these directions of change: at my own, for example, all baccalaureate students are required to take at least four interdisciplinary courses, each of which explicitly works to develop two or more "essential skills" such as written communication.[1]

Now, twenty to thirty years later, both writing across the curriculum (WAC) and interdisciplinary studies (IDS) have proven themselves durable features of the American higher education scene. Among multiple indicators of their continued importance, a recent Boyer report (1998) criticizes the fragmentation of undergraduate education at America's research universities and includes among its ten key recommendations "remove barriers to interdisciplinary education," specifically including lower-division courses as well as study in the major, and "link communication skills with course work."

But despite juxtaposition of these movements in programs, recommendations, and widespread individual courses, and despite the growing literatures of both WAC and IDS, there has been little discussion of intersections between the movements and what these might mean for strengthening undergraduate education.[2] The literature of the former has often ignored the latter. Publications, conference presentations, and bibliographical entries frequently refer to WAC as an interdisciplinary movement, but typically meant is that its concerns are important *within* multiple disciplines. Writing becomes more central within diverse courses, faculty across the disciplines share concerns and ideas about writing, but discourse that crosses those disciplines is likely not on the agenda. While Elaine Maimon argues the importance of the A for "across" in WAC, entailing "forming conceptually interrelated communities" ("Teaching" 390–91), and Joseph Harris urges that students learn to deal with conflicting "claims and interests that extend beyond the borders of their own safe houses, neighborhoods, disciplines, or communities" (124), WAC research and practice still usually assume students are working within one of the prevailing divisions of knowledge.

The literature of IDS can hardly ignore writing, for the kinds of goals typically cited for interdisciplinary education such as building students' integrative thinking cannot be adequately practiced or assessed through short-answer tests and end-of-semester term papers. Articles tend to contain passing mention of student projects for particular interdisciplinary courses rather than reflective commentary on interdisciplinary teaching and learning in relation to composition theory and practice. Numerous articles explore the interface between composition and another discipline (e.g., see Fiscella and Kimmel). Faculty members describe paired composition and engineering courses, or a single course integrating principles of composition and biology, possibly team taught. These articles and teaching arrangements do not address writing within a wide variety of courses that feature multiple disciplinary perspectives on a common topic. One article that does so (Haynes) focuses on a four-year sequence of writing courses ushering students into the discourse community of interdisciplinary studies. Also needed is further analysis of what is possible within the time frame of a semester and with students and faculty having "homes" in the disciplines.

This chapter offers some thoughts about such writing-intensive courses, focusing on general education as the largest category of interdisciplinary courses now being taught in this country (Edwards, "Are"). "Writing intensive" designates the central assumptions of the writing across the curriculum movement: not just increased quantity of writing but ongoing writing, with coaching of the process rather than simply expectations of a product; ongoing feedback from the instructor and likely from other students as well; and opportunities for revision—not just editing but genuine rethinking in response to feedback.[3] These assumptions of frequency, coaching, and revision seem to be widely agreed on as the essentials, as evidenced in their presence on Web pages offering guidelines for writing-intensive courses at universities across the country, as well as in my own university's guidelines. A number of other practices typically accompany them, such as sequences of assignments, one piece building on another, and writing for varied purposes and audiences.

But writing-intensive courses that cross disciplinary boundaries obviously need to go beyond the two most frequently discussed approaches in writing-intensive courses: writing informally as a mode of discovery, to think through the issues and approaches of a particular discipline ("writing to learn"), or learning to use the accepted genres of a discipline ("writing in the disciplines"). And when practiced in combination, writing across the curriculum and interdisciplinary studies present not only related but compounded challenges. Faculty and students who engage these can reap compounded rewards as well. A flexible, fluid, recursive model for combining WAC and IDS can help students to become active thinkers drawing the fruitful connections that interdisciplinary study promises.

CHALLENGES OF IMPLEMENTING WRITING-INTENSIVE INTERDISCIPLINARY COURSES

Concerns about Expertise

Asking experienced faculty to change practices, either to incorporate writing more integrally into their courses or to explore connections across disciplines, can yield similar concerns, skepticism, even resistance—and understandable resistance at that. These practices push many faculty outside their relatively comfortable habits and routines. One concern is whether faculty not trained in writing or in interdisciplinary inquiry can teach those approaches with the requisite authority. Either practice may force a faculty member to learn new approaches and to make the invisible visible—that is, to consider questions of disciplinary practice that have been taken for granted: what *does* one prioritize, in specific, to help students see and practice some of what it means to think and write like an economist, biologist, or historian?

Indeed the challenge is greater than many faculty at first realize, since both composition/rhetoric and interdisciplinary studies have increasingly developed traditions of their own, with their own concepts, methodologies, and literatures. Faculty across the disciplines will not likely become expert in either area. The question—as Austin Doherty et al. similarly ask with regard to the literatures of intellectual skill building (182–83)—then becomes how much expertise would be necessary, pragmatically, to make a difference for students. Without some conscious awareness of the accumulated wisdom of WAC, for example, faculty incorporating writing may simply assign more of it or feel obligated to join the "grammar police"; and without awareness of the accumulated wisdom of IDS, an interdisciplinary course easily remains stuck in "serial disciplinarity," expecting synthesis from students without offering sufficient practice and coaching.

Combining writing-intensive and interdisciplinary approaches adds new dimensions to the issue of expertise. In good writing-intensive disciplinary courses, faculty coach students to do as they do: try out the varied kinds of writing, with varied audiences and purposes, produced by a practitioner. In writing-intensive interdisciplinary courses, faculty may be coaching students to write in ways they do *not* write: analysis in other disciplines plus analysis crossing disciplines. Clearly a team-taught course has advantages here, allowing faculty to learn directly from their colleagues, frame assignments together, and share and discuss writing samples by students and themselves.

Related to concerns about expertise are concerns about time demands on faculty from each of the approaches: Many faculty argue that they simply do not have time to read quantities of student writing, or to learn material outside their discipline plus work as part of an interdisciplinary team. Combining WAC and IDS compounds these concerns. Programs with writing-intensive interdisciplinary courses, like their counterparts in WAC or IDS more broadly, will be successful only to the extent that planners meet the concerns in theoretical, practical, and administrative ways, adapting the myriad suggestions in the professional literature of both areas to the local context (e.g., see McLeod and Soven; Newell, ed.).

Concerns about "Coverage"

A part of the breaking out of "business as usual" via WAC or IDS may be that faculty need to rethink unexplored assumptions about "coverage." Faculty express concern that moving away from traditional models via WAC will "take time away from content and thus lower standards" (Russell, *Writing* 293); indeed, fear over coverage has been deemed "the most resilient enemy of WAC" (Maimon, Preface xiii), even as skeptics of IDS continue to fear that interdisciplinary courses will lack sufficient disciplinary depth. Active learning advocates have effectively critiqued the dominance of the coverage metaphor, noting that faculty's "covering" a lot of territory may bear little correlation to what students have learned. Both WAC and IDS are premised on the assumption that they are not simply adding something to existing practice but transforming that practice. New goals and new classroom procedures come into play, as a course examines a perhaps more focused topic but students gain time to work through ideas for themselves and/or explore connections across disciplines.

In courses both writing intensive and interdisciplinary, even experienced faculty will need to cope with the time crunch posed by the demands of multiple disciplines and multiple writings: the nagging feeling that there is a lot to do and not a lot of time to do it in. Conscientious faculty are particularly vulnerable here. But if too much of this feeling gets conveyed to students, even by rushing through guidelines for an assignment, students can feel dragged on a whirlwind interdisciplinary journey more overwhelming than enlightening. Teaching teams need to be particularly vigilant about not overwhelming students, as conscientious faculty pool their separate ideas of what assignments are essential.

The Need to Coach a Process

Another example of the related challenges posed by WAC and IDS, compounded when the approaches are combined, involves the issue of coaching a process. Assignments such as those discussed later in this chapter may sometimes in and of themselves yield good results, but integrative thinking is a process that needs ongoing guidance. Assigning the process and even modeling it are not enough to help it "happen" with any sort of the frequency or depth faculty would want. Carolyn Haynes notes that the workshop approaches advocated by the process theorists of composition should help to encourage integrative thinking (36). Indeed they do, as faculty at my university have discovered over the fourteen years of our program.

The need to coach a process, definitional in WAC, needs more emphasis in IDS. The metaphor can help to balance the "presentational" language that too often dominates (faculty work out an interdisciplinary understanding of an issue or problem and then "convey" it to students [e.g., Richards 127]). Discussions of coaching, and explicit analysis of the metaphor, have appeared numerous times in the composition literature of recent decades (some of which I survey in my own contribution, Seabury, "Sports"). The metaphor and model bring into focus that instruction in both writing and integrative thinking entails trial and error, learning by doing, the awkwardness and frustration of altering habits and stretching/playing in new ways, the need for ongoing practice, and the benefits of feedback during the process. In- and out-of-class coaching needs multiply in a writing-intensive interdisciplinary course: as James Davis notes, in an interdisciplinary course, tasks at a particular level in Bloom's taxonomy of educational objectives are typically more complex than if they were framed within a particular discipline (55). In their course evaluations, both faculty and students repeatedly single out individual conferences as especially helpful toward the goal of students' dealing integratively with course materials and concepts. Chapter 9 in this volume discusses the complementary practice of peer review.

Criteria and models can assist the coaching process. A writing-intensive course within a discipline coaches students in their successive approximations of a disciplinary voice, as they learn acceptable evidence, tone, and argument structure. But in an interdisciplinary course, as noted previously, faculty may be feeling their way into new discourses along with students and thus may possess and provide more limited awareness of criteria for success. A team-taught format helps by allowing students to learn directly from faculty trained in diverse disciplines (albeit still often not experienced in discourses that attempt to synthesize disciplinary perspectives). Students can be encouraged or assigned to interview faculty in other disciplines, not only to gather perspectives on the issues at hand but to get specific advice on thinking and writing processes. Guest experts who work in discipline-crossing public spheres can help to define the writing challenge—for example, how they would evaluate a proposal.

Accompanying the challenge of criteria can be a lack of models. My own team has been on the lookout, not always successfully, for accessible models of the kind of interart analysis we hope for from students. We have learned to save, distribute, and discuss models of successful student writings from past semesters, although amidst the busy pace of a semester we sometimes neglect to do so.

Differences Across Sections of a Team-Taught Course

The team-taught, or at least multisectioned, structure of many interdisciplinary courses can lead to further complications, since within a teaching team, faculty may not agree on how to handle writing in the course. Some may simply resist the demands of assigning frequent writing. Some may be comfortable assigning open-ended major projects, for example, with students writing "about" a major Romantic figure in the arts, while others object that such assignments yield occasional brilliance but more often unreflective "reporting," not to mention downloads from the Web.

Many teams try to follow "best practice" recommended in the "Guide to Interdisciplinary Syllabus Preparation" (Association for Integrative Studies and Institute in Integrative Studies) by negotiating common exams and projects across sections, but sometimes agreement especially on the latter may be impossible. A result: Students who come to class accountable for what they are to have read via five-minute in-class writings as discussion starters and whose essay projects demand higher-order thinking may object that other sections are "easier." Such differences can become divisive—for example, when one instructor requires students to attend labs and write up formal lab reports while another hopes to inspire rather than require. Even given the excellence of faculty and productive differences in teaching styles, agreement across sections on writing does help. Faculty workshops such as those discussed later increase its likelihood; a last resort may well be to allow sections to diverge rather than to sacrifice some faculty's effective uses of writing for the sake of compromise.

Sustaining Commitment

As WAC and IDS programs continue beyond their early years, problems of sustaining individual faculty commitment emerge. The gravitational pull back to old modes can be strong: It is easier not to cope with the myriad problems of getting students to write good journals or researched arguments and simply abandon the project altogether; it is easier to teach what your chair asks you to teach than try to get released once again to join an interdisciplinary team and then do all the actual work of teaching the course. Both writing-intensive teaching and interdisciplinary teaching can be "invisible" service that does take some additional time and energy (even if WAC techniques and interdisciplinary collaboration help out) but receives few tangible rewards. Great satisfaction may result but not much credit.

These faculty issues often mirror larger programmatic ones. Both WAC and IDS have become widespread, as witness such surveys as Susan McLeod's of WAC programs and Alan Edwards's (*Interdisciplinary*) of interdisciplinary programs. Both now have professional associations and conferences specifically dedicated to their concerns. But the problems of sustaining the programs are similar and substantial, as one hears clearly at such conferences. Programs in both areas are often begun with grant support but must be sustained after that money has run out, sustained as units cutting horizontally across the power structures and budgetary structures of the institution. This challenge becomes particularly acute during tough economic times, when departments are fighting hard for faculty lines if not for their very survival.

Indeed David Russell's detailed analysis of the difficulties of sustaining WAC programs applies in many ways to IDS as well: "WAC challenges deeply held institutional attitudes toward writing, learning, and teaching: attitudes that are reinforced by the differentiated structure of knowledge and education"; "WAC efforts easily fall victim to the institutional inertia of academia's differentiated, hierarchical structure." He concludes that in today's American university "there is thus no permanent defense against the slow erosion of programs [WAC or other interdepartmental] under the pressure of well-defined departmental interests" (*Writing* 292, 296, 298).[4] Thus, institutions planning to implement writing-interdisciplinary courses successfully will need to pay particular heed to the multiple and similar strategies devised by WAC and IDS advocates to counter their invisibility, including categories on P&T forms to acknowledge these contributions, increased weight put on teaching portfolios in which these activities can be highlighted, summer stipends, travel funding, and other rewards and incentives. Programs encouraging such across-the-curriculum endeavors need a single locus of authority: a program director supported by a faculty committee, an independent budget, and a strong voice in broader policy and budget matters through direct reporting to an upper-level administrator.

Addressing Pedagogical Concerns via Faculty Workshops

One of the distinguishing features of the WAC movement, important both in creating and in sustaining a program, has been faculty workshops. These bring faculty from across a college or university together to discuss shared issues of teaching and learning rather than the more usual ones of university politics. A key to WAC has been that it involves new possibilities not just for students but for faculty as well, as a new culture of faculty as learners emerges. The workshops are typically nonhierarchical (Maimon, "Teaching" 383–86), with faculty learning from each other. A similar process has characterized IDS, as faculty come together to discuss topics and pedagogies across the boundaries of departments and colleges.

If we learn from this shared history, we realize that institutions cannot effectively implement writing in interdisciplinary courses and maintain its importance by directive. Focused workshops[5] can address such questions as these: What kinds of writing are we assigning in our interdisciplinary

courses? Which have worked well, which have not? What are the goals of
these assignments? To what extent and how are we encouraging students to
synthesize perspectives from different disciplines? How are we sequencing
assignments, if at all? What kinds and extents of structure do they have? To
what extent and how are we coaching the writing process? And what commonalties emerge across courses on such issues? The following section offers thoughts on some of these issues, working from the more general
questions to examples of assignments.

TEACHING ISSUES AND OPTIONS

Consciously Encouraging Integration via WAC and IDS

How, asks this volume's general editor, can we ensure that students engaged
in the approaches under discussion move toward synthesis and integration?
Quite simply, we can't. As critical thinking expert Stephen Brookfield
notes, "*there is no standard model of facilitating critical thinking . . .* no one way
to instructional enlightenment." It is possible to devise a variety of productive pedagogical approaches, but the kinds of thinking for which one hopes
"will frequently come unexpectedly to individuals" (233, 244).

But as WAC workshop participants have discovered, increased consciousness on faculty's part of what we are asking of students, along with going on to coach the process, can increase the chances that the desired
learning will occur. Aren't we already conscious, given all the time we
spend designing assignments? Not necessarily. Even within our own disciplines we often do not take a step back from our assignments to reflect on
the kinds of thinking we are asking of students. When I told an experienced
colleague I was working on a project about writing-intensive courses, she
responded, "Well, that'll be a short article. Have them write! What's the
mystery?" In workshops at my university where faculty brought in photo-
copies of assignments they use, some of these ran for a couple pages of intended help but confused workshop colleagues, not to mention students.
Upon discussion, faculty can reflect on the kinds of thinking they hope to
see, break down the skills needed to accomplish these results, and better articulate the assignment or sometimes redesign it altogether.

Similarly, faculty teaching interdisciplinary courses are more likely to
become passionate about their subject matter and how much it comes to
mean to their students than to take the time to step back and reflect on the
kinds of integration they are asking of students, which can seem at a
too-far-removed level of abstraction. Whether we are just moving from our
own discipline into interdisciplinary teaching or have been doing it for

some time, however, we would benefit from some reflection on what we are asking students to integrate and how we are helping them toward that end.

But Is That Always the "End?"

A further question arises with the general editor's framing challenge previously cited: Is integration and synthesis indeed the end toward which students should steadily be moving in an interdisciplinary course? "Moving toward synthesis" embodies a metaphor that deserves unpacking. It suggests a graph-like progression whereby students gradually move from lower forms of thinking on up to more holistic, abstract thinking, ending in the upper-right quadrant of the page.[6] "Toward" involves a destination, a goal, an end. We hope students will "reach" a holistic understanding.

But as I have argued elsewhere ("Finding" 99–100), the "goal" may be *not a position but a motion*: students' facility with moving among levels of abstraction and generalization. Integrative thinking means not just bringing together diverse data, diverse disciplinary perspectives in order to reach an overarching synthesis but also using and testing such a synthesis in relation to the more specific and concrete. John Dewey offers some underpinnings here: He warns that educational methods priding themselves exclusively on either analysis or synthesis are "incompatible with normal operations of judgment"; abstract thinking represents "*an* end, not *the* end" of the thinking process (130, 227). As linguist S. I. Hayakawa puts it, good thinking involves the "constant interplay of higher-level and lower-level abstractions, and the constant interplay of the verbal levels with the nonverbal ('object') levels" (162). Composition expert Ann Berthoff similarly speaks of a natural dialectic of mind, "a dialectic of sorting and gathering, of particularizing and generalizing" (105).

Thus, as we create assignments to encourage integrative thinking, the process and goal may be to build a synthesis but may also be to apply, evaluate, or break down a synthesis. Productive interdisciplinary assignments will ask students to move among levels of abstraction and generalization in order to accomplish specific purposes.

Sequences/Spirals

Some of the additional questions we face when designing writing-intensive interdisciplinary courses cut to the core of both WAC and IDS. They involve finding workable balances among sometimes competing, sometimes complementary goods, balances that will vary depending on the goals of a particular course and the students and faculty in it. These issues are provocative but often lie buried beneath a faculty team's negotiations about the selection and organization of issues and materials in an interdisciplinary course. They are hidden as well in the aforementioned "Guide to Interdisciplinary Syllabus Preparation."

Much composition scholarship, for example, has discussed progressions of assignments, as students first attempt more basic cognitive challenges and then move on to analysis, comparison, evaluation, and so forth; in the interdisciplinary literature, Haynes likewise emphasizes progressions, which make good sense within a semester as well as over her four-year time frame. But as commonsensical as carefully sequenced writing sounds, it may not always make sense pedagogically in an interdisciplinary general education course (or disciplinary general education course either, for that matter), where many students may simply not *care* enough at first to bother putting much effort into learning particular kinds of disciplinary analysis. Overheard from a student trying to walk out the back door as my music colleague raised the issue of chord progressions in Beethoven: "I never listen to this kind of stuff." Faculty may need to be figurative as well as literal exit-blockers of easy outs in interdisciplinary courses. Rather than assigning students to work patiently through disciplinary discourse conventions toward integration, writing-intensive interdisciplinary courses may well need to use recursive strategies allowing students to spiral in their understanding: asking some "big questions" and trying some integration in week one and then revisiting those issues/modes along the way as they increase their awareness of the disciplinary discourses involved. Students meet related challenges again and again but with increased ability to handle them.

Spontaneity/Structure

Faculty hope that both WAC and IDS will offer students a medium for exercising their creativity, trying out ideas, and making personal connections with the subject matter at hand, at the same time that they become aware of and practice some of the genres of writing used within the academy and beyond. A tall order. But especially true of interdisciplinary thinking as composition scholars have discovered of writing, courses need to give students a mixture of opportunities by which thinking can grow. Students will cope with the complex demands of interdisciplinary courses in different ways and need multiple modes of learning and expressing learning. Thus, in a writing-intensive interdisciplinary course, many of the assignments may be more exploratory, out of which perhaps some epiphanies will emerge—or perhaps some fruitful chaos ("I thought of a wild connection, but I'm not sure if it makes sense . . ."). Other assignments may be more structured but "creative" as well: indeed one of the concepts faculty and students have jointly discovered in our course on creativity in the arts, as noted later, is how often creativity blossoms within limits of one sort or another.

Too much emphasis on either spontaneity or structure can inhibit the growth possible through WAC, IDS, or a combination. And one point of agreement in WAC that applies to IDS as well is that some choice along the way amid the varying topics, genres, audiences, and purposes of a course's assignments gives students an important voice in their own learning process—especially needed in required general-education courses. In the process of assignments of various kinds, faculty can encourage or require students to follow Peter Elbow's suggestions for "cooking" in the writing process (40–53)—allowing different, even conflicting materials into the mental "pot" together to simmer and to transform each other (e.g., by talking with people, encouraging contradictions in thinking, or freewriting and stepping back to reflect)—a metaphor and model well suited to interdisciplinary work.

Writing to Learn (in an Interdisciplinary Context)/Writing in the Disciplines (and Across)

Should writing in an interdisciplinary course focus on writing-to-learn activities, adapting to the interdisciplinary context activities such as journal responses aimed to help students make sense of new material for themselves, to explore and discover? Or should it build more on the writing-in-the-disciplines approaches, providing practice with the modes of disciplinary discourse used to communicate with others, but going on to bring them to bear, in combination, on the subject at hand? This choice of emphasis is obviously related to the previous issue of spontaneity/structure but cannot simply be conflated with it, since some writing-to-learn exercises might be fairly structured (e.g., a guided journal) while some exercises in the genres of disciplinary/interdisciplinary discourse might be fairly open ("write an informal memo to the leader of your interdisciplinary project . . ."). Writing-to-learn has been defined as more suited to general education; learning genres, to advanced or specialized courses (Anson 773). Amid the arguments within composition studies about the relative merits of these approaches, frequently termed one of the major conflicts in the field, many scholars are objecting that the framing of the discussion has emphasized false dichotomies, the supposed poles of which are actually intertwined (e.g., Kirscht et al.; Maimon, "Teaching"; Russell, "Writing"; McLeod and Maimon). But given the time constraints of any given fourteen-week semester, priorities do need to be set. It is certainly possible to include some of both, for example both short, informal responses plus proposals to a public agency.

Coaching/Interrogating Disciplinary Discourses

The issue of whether faculty should be guiding students to learn academic discourses and/or to interrogate them, raised in WAC scholarship, is fundamental to IDS. It involves both theoretical stances and practical complications. The coaching metaphor discussed earlier, which sounds unproblematic in conception although always challenging in practice, could imply the underlying assumption that there is a "game" or games, with established "rules," in which the novice is invited to participate. But this conception of academic discourse has been called into question in the composition literature as falsely suggesting that disciplines are closed, static, and monolithic and as encouraging in students "both conformity and submission" (Spellmayer 266). A response that comes naturally to me from my work with Goya, Beethoven, Wordsworth, and other Romantics (and that Maimon has also made repeatedly with regard to WAC) is that effective rebels typically do not spring ex nihilo; they have learned the conventions and then employ, modify, or move beyond them for their own purposes. Charles Bazerman argues that explicitly "teaching students the rhetoric of disciplines . . . holds what is taught up for inspection," which can enlighten rather than oppress.

The juxtaposition of disciplines in interdisciplinary study goes a long way toward helping students to see a discipline as offering *ways* of seeing, not *the* way. Much interdisciplinary literature includes as axiomatic that students need to go on to become conscious of and explore similarities and differences, assumptions, limitations of various disciplinary perspectives: to "problematize" the disciplines. But how much is it possible to do in a semester of general education with students inexperienced in the disciplinary discourses at hand? Some, indeed. Following class readings, guest speakers, and debates on hunger in a particular region, students write a policy recommendation in which they juxtapose and weigh perspectives on economic development, concerns about maintaining the local culture, and more. At a recent writing-across-the curriculum conference, however, an experienced humanities professor claimed he was lucky just to get students to discover and write with clarity about some common threads across the course readings. Even that can involve looking critically at disciplines. In the Romanticism course, students discuss and then write about ways in which feminist perspectives reveal aspects of specific works across the arts that have been overlooked by more traditional modes of disciplinary analysis.

Sample Assignments

This final section offers some examples of productive kinds of interdisciplinary assignments, focusing particularly on ones encouraging the motion among levels of abstraction and generalization that characterizes effective thinking within and across disciplines.

William Newell's overview of the interdisciplinary literature ("Professionalizing") distinguishes four techniques of achieving synthesis: dialectical thinking (working with conflicting perspectives, resulting either in a nonresolved dialectic or a reconciliation of the differing paradigms), metaphorical thinking, building a metalanguage (agreeing on a vocabulary going beyond that of the everyday), and developing a common ground. The related list here of productive kinds of interdisciplinary student writing includes references to approaches Newell cites but also adds several other important ways students can work with integrative thinking, since that does not always involve building a synthesis. It may, for example, involve taking holistic understanding built during the course and communicating it to others, applying it in new situations, or critiquing it. I will draw on work by colleagues at my university (Seabury, ed.).[7] In their chapters on how interdisciplinary courses help to build students' integrative skills, a number of them discuss writing assignments. What does looking across these examples, plus some others from colleagues in our program, reveal about kinds of integration and synthesis we might ask of our students?

First, I should perhaps say the obvious that many effective assignments in interdisciplinary courses may be discipline centered. The results may later become part of other assignments featuring synthesis. Our course on "Epidemics and AIDS" is rigorous enough in laboratory science to meet a four-credit requirement, but instead of analyzing cells as a scientific exercise, students do it in relation to a major social problem. They distinguish serum from a person with an immunodeficiency from normal and control samples and summarize their results in a traditional lab report. In another of the course's labs, within the discipline of epidemiology, students chart the spread of an epidemic. A subsequent project, discussed later, integrates knowledge built in these and other disciplinary writing assignments as students communicate the many-faceted understanding they have gained.

But to say the obvious about the use of single-discipline assignments is also to say that many interdisciplinary courses simply select from assignments typically given in the constituent disciplines. The following are among the wide range of possibilities for interdisciplinary assignments encouraging students to practice integrative thinking.

1. *Action/reflection.* Active learning, in Charles Bonwell and James Eison's widely quoted definition, entails students "doing things and thinking about the things they are doing" (2), an apt place to begin this discussion. These assignments start with action, *doing* something new in relation to the issue or problem in focus: students in a hunger course work in a soup

kitchen; students in a course asking "What Is School?" tutor in an after-school program. As they reflect on what they have experienced, whether in journals, letters to the editor, or various kinds of academic analysis, they can be encouraged to make connections with class discussions and readings. Thus, many students enter naturally into integrative thinking: The firsthand experience helps to break down one-dimensional views about causes for hunger or poor performance in school. Students begin to realize the complexity of the problems and may connect psychological, sociological, economic, health, and other factors.

Assignments can specifically ask students to discuss the new experience in relation to course concepts. In a course on "Creativity: The Dynamics of Artistic Expression," students go to a performance, exhibit, or other "live" art and then write a critical paper about it that incorporates principles from at least two course workshops. In a course on "Sources of Power," students use the university as their lab: they meet with guests from various parts of the university community and write about the discussions in terms of analytical frameworks such as Dennis Wrong's "forms of power" and Peter Bachrach and Morton Baratz's "nondecision-making."

2. *Reconstrual.* These assignments ask students to assimilate new material into their evolving understanding: to reconstrue the more concrete, the more abstract, and their evolving connections. Students not only add new insights but also readjust their understanding, re-seeing what has come before. As Arthur Applebee discusses in *Curriculum as Conversation,* this process is key to critical thinking (77). Journals are a frequent mode for encouraging this thinking, as students puzzle through new data, methods, and concepts and then look back at what light they shed on earlier learning. Students in the "Creativity" course, in a workshop with one of the university's leading artists, are asked to use only three shapes for a design. In their journals they often express resistance to the limits: if the course is about creativity, why can't they do whatever they want? Questioning of the guest presenter has led to discussion of the new issue of the role of limits in creative processes: the generative tension found across the disciplines between structure and freedom. Students have then reflected in their journals on whether/how limits have played a role in previous workshops focusing on other disciplines.

In a wide variety of interdisciplinary courses and assignments, as students write about what connections they see in themes and techniques with works studied earlier, they gradually build a concept. The process of developing a synthesis thus is not necessarily a late-in-the-semester result of earlier stages of developing disciplinary thinking. It can begin from week one, as students in my own course, for example, write what similarities they note among a particular Romantic poem, painting, and musical composition. Similar comparative assignments later in the semester may show greater sophistication, but the integrative thinking begins from the outset. This process of reconstrual may also lead students to *unbuild* concepts. As they see images of nature in works by Turner and Mary Shelley, they may write about the limitations of their generalizations about Romantic views of nature built on the basis of Constable and Wordsworth.

These assignments particularly demand the coaching discussed earlier. Repeated urgings often do not suffice to get students to comment and connect rather than simply report. Models, collaborative in-class experiments, conferences, and multiple drafts ("how does this relate to . . .") help to provide the needed nudge, especially for the less motivated.

3. *Application of a synthesis.* Students can take a discipline-crossing concept or method with which they have worked in class and explore it in writing within a new realm. Students thus search for and develop a new range of applicability of the concept or method. Amid all the discussion in the composition literature about differences among the disciplinary discourse communities students enter as they traverse a university, it is worth remembering Barbara Walvoord and Lucille McCarthy's classroom research, which revealed that across the disciplines they studied "students were asked to apply discipline-based categories, concepts, or methods *to new data and new situations*"; the teachers "held, with Peter Elbow (1986), that what constitutes 'real learning' is the ability to apply discipline-based concepts to a wide range of situations and to relate those concepts to the students' own knowledge and experience" (7, 8). This approach is likewise effective in an interdisciplinary classroom, helping students to apply *interdisciplinary* categories, concepts, or methods to new data and new situations and relate those concepts to their own experience.

The new field of applicability may well be within students' intended major; thus, they have the opportunity to link general education with the major. In a course on "Seeing Through Symmetry," students write a project, due in several stages throughout the semester, in which they apply what they have learned about symmetry to another field, ranging from the stock market to metaphysics to music. Such a process may lead not just to application of known categories but to discovery of new ones: new aspects of the concept, seeing the concept in unpredicted ways. In the "Creativity" course, some students elect the option to write an essay based on an interview with someone in their intended field about whether and how creativity functions within it. Students see that creativity in the arts unexpectedly connects with the activities of practicing professionals in engineering or marketing.

4. *Creation of a product embodying a synthesis, with accompanying comment.* Students can create a product that embodies a synthesis: for example, of materials from multiple disciplines concerning a particular culture under study, or a multimedia work of art. Nonverbal modes of learning and expressing learning are primary here, deserving of a chapter in themselves, but students can also build writing and thinking skills as they put into words some comment about the kind of synthesis they have attempted. In a course on "Ethnic Roots and Urban Arts," students create various squares to be displayed in the class's ethnic arts quilt, based on an early "Ethnic Me" assignment and then on reactions to specific African American and Puerto Rican readings and experiences, and also compose a commentary for the class about these squares. In the "Creativity" course, students work individually or as a group on a final creative artistic project integrating at least two disciplines, embodying a particular thematic idea, and synthesizing ideas explored in earlier workshops and journal entries, then write a commentary on what they have done.

5. *Written communication of a synthesis.* As a course proceeds, students gradually increase their holistic understanding of the issue or problem at hand and can communicate that understanding to others, making it into something new. In the "Epidemics and AIDS" course, students study scientific, psychosocial, ethical, and cultural aspects of AIDS. In a laboratory assignment in the second half of the course, they engage in some kind of public activity such as conducting a public health campaign to teach others within the university community or beyond about AIDS, high-risk behaviors, and/or discrimination. Students have created pamphlets and distributed them to middle-school children, created a book (text, pictures, production) for grade-school children, and published editorials in the campus newspaper. In the process of conveying the integrative understanding they have built, they need to consider not just what to convey, drawing on multiple disciplinary perspectives, but how to convey it, considering issues of age level, possible constraints from school or parents, techniques of persuasion, and so forth. These projects also may integrate general education with students' major (e.g., in education, communication, the arts).

In the "What Is School?" course, students may write letters to the editor or to their local school board taking a position on issues currently in public discussion, such as school vouchers or ability grouping—issues on which insights from multiple disciplines can be brought to bear and on which thoughtful argument from citizens and taxpayers is important at varying levels of expertise. Many of our courses assign such letters and may give extra credit when students mail them and even get them published (which does happen with good frequency).

6. *"Zoom lens/wide-angle lens."* These assignments guide students to look closely at a phenomenon using a particular disciplinary approach, then pull back to put what they have seen in relationship to other phenomena and/or approaches. The integrative thinking is built on first looking closely. Thus, these assignments structure in movement among levels of abstraction and generalization. They block the easy outs of "dead-level abstracting," a term Hayakawa borrows from Wendell Johnson (Hayakawa 161): skimming over the landscape without engaging closely with anything in it, or looking only at the details and losing sight of the larger picture. In our "Romanticism" course, such assignments may include a guided analysis of a painting, using techniques practiced in class, and then commentary and connections.

7. *Eclectic data gathering/eclectic data given.* These assignments pose a question (or ask students to construct such a question) that meets Julie Thompson Klein and William Newell's definition of the root of interdisciplinary inquiry: It "is too broad or complex to be dealt with adequately by a single discipline or profession" (393). Students thus must draw on materials of multiple kinds in order to address the question. One section of a course in our "Discovering America" series is taught in the university's Museum of American Political Life, where students are surrounded by a rich variety of primary materials to use for their projects. These projects—for example, a transcript of an imaginary debate between a variety of key figures on slavery or on the role of women, or, moving outside museum sources, exploration of the relation between data on juvenile delinquency during the 1950s and Hollywood portrayals—lead students to draw on materials ranging from political tracts, social essays, and memoirs to cartoons, popular fiction, film, and advertising.

Or such a course and its writing assignments may be structured in the form of case studies. Another "Discovering America" instructor has been composing a series of cases for students built on key decision points in American history. He describes his case exhibits as including "primary materials (diplomatic correspondence, presidential and cabinet member memoirs, committee reports, decrypted radio transmissions, participant recall, and so on), cartographic aids, and other resources (demographic, military, cultural, anthropological, sociological, scientific, and economic charts, diagrams, and tabular data calculations and summaries)" (Canedy 197). Using a carefully constructed approach to the case study drawn from its roots in business schools, he choreographs students' work with the materials he has assembled, as they work not just toward an understanding of complexity but toward decision-point.

Dialectical thinking such as Newell describes comes into play throughout both approaches described here, as students deal with the diverse data. In the former examples, the end point may often be a focus on differences; in the latter, a decision based on weighing and reconciling as far as possible the diverse perspectives.

8. *Playing with metaphor.* These assignments ask students to make leaps: not to build a concept by successive abstraction and generalization, not to move stepwise toward synthesis, but to try out the unexpected, play with figurative language, make discoveries. Students leap across disciplinary materials, methods, concepts, and see what happens. The importance of seeing likenesses where no likeness was perceived before has been affirmed by poets and scientists alike; given the eloquence and provocativeness of their comments, I include a few here. As Robert Frost puts it,

> I have wanted in late years to go further and further in making metaphor the whole of thinking. . . . We still ask [students] in college to think . . . but we seldom tell them what thinking means; we seldom tell that it is just putting this and that together; it is just saying one thing in terms of another. To tell them is to set their feet on the first rung of a ladder the top of which sticks through the sky. (332, 336)

Scientist Jacob Bronowski comments,

> A man becomes creative, whether he is an artist or a scientist, when he finds a new unity in the variety of nature. He does so by finding a likeness between things which were not thought alike before, and this gives him a sense at the same time of richness and of understanding. The creative mind is a mind that looks for unexpected likenesses. This is not a mechanical procedure, and I believe that it engages the whole personality in science as in the arts. . . . To my mind, it is a mistake to think of creative activity as something unusual. I hold that the creative activity is normal to all living things. Creation is the finding of order in what was disorderly. (12, 16)

Composition expert Peter Elbow discusses in detail the metaphoric process as an "ideal strategy for inventing concepts":

> It is mostly poets and children who are given to saying that things remind them of seemingly unrelated things and they don't know why. . . . [People have] been taught too often that it's cuckoo to think two apparently unrelated things are the same and not know how or why—so they've stopped doing it. . . . Therefore, when most people think of metaphor, they think of traditional metaphors . . . [that don't] tell us anything we didn't know. . . . But the capacity is in us all . . . and the more unexpected and difficult-to-explain the feeling, the greater the

payload. . . . [It's a] wild, idiosyncratic, and nonlogical quality. . . . But to get the benefit of this basic capacity, a person must practice it, learn to develop trust in it. . . . The qualities of *play* and *fooling around* must be helped to flourish. (25–30)

Faculty can encourage metaphoric thinking in journals, design a variety of course-specific experiments in metaphor, and provide models; students take it from there and frequently enjoy it. A simple example I have used is to ask students to write in response to the prompts: "What is a teacher like? What is a student like?" For the "What Is School?" course, in preparation for guest workshop leaders from multiple disciplines, course members can share results from this experiment and explore underlying assumptions within the metaphors they have chosen: from the realm of the arts (teacher as performer, as conductor, or as potter, molding students?); sports (teacher as coach?); religion (teacher as missionary?); horticulture (teacher as planter of seeds, and as nurturer of a process?); business (teacher as boss, or teacher as seller, student as consumer?); or perhaps jurisprudence (teacher as judge and jury combined?). Obviously the implications for students of their previously unexplored metaphors are enormous, as they grapple with the multidimensioned course focus and with their own attitudes toward school.

Or students may talk about two or more things in terms of a third thing, as they take an excursion in interdisciplinarity. The travel metaphor here is deliberate: Students in recent offerings of the "Creativity" course have tried a writing assignment discussing their course "journey": "What kind of journey has it been for you so far? What have the various stops along the way been like?" Thus they are challenged to integrate and conceptualize multiple experiences in terms of something else. As preparation for this assignment, students engage in a class workshop on metaphorical thinking and explore the extended metaphor in Frost's poem "Mother to Son" ("Life for me ain't been no crystal stair . . .").

9. *Translation.* Assignments can ask students to take a work in one discipline and try it out in another. As students in a course on "Literature and Film of Other Cultures" learn more about both literary and film techniques, they may write about how a particular story could be filmed. As students in the "Romanticism" course study *Frankenstein*, they discover that their paperback does not look like that of the student next to them as editions have changed and apparently so fast that the caption on the inside cover of the newer edition still identifies the previous image. They consider what resonances particular choices set up and then write a memo to a publisher recommending a Romantic painting for the cover of a "Rime of the Ancient Mariner" edition and arguing their choice.

10. *Asking good questions*. An appropriate note on which to end this list is question asking: frequent and in writing as well as aloud. Disciplines entail modes of inquiry, interdisciplinary study entails modes of inquiry, and inquiry means question asking. An instructor of two of our courses dealing with unfamiliar cultures plus multiple genres finds "thinking aloud" about the concerns of the courses to be essential for students to cope with their multifaceted nature. The questions—written in five minutes at the beginning or end of class, in an e-mail, or perhaps explored more fully in a journal—encourage students to put into words their struggles and queries and efforts to connect. The questions can then feed into class discussion and perhaps further writings. What kinds of questions are we engendering in students through all of our innovative interdisciplinary courses (that they may well be too unsure to ask in class)? Further, what kinds of questions do the disciplines involved ask, in relation to the subject matter at hand?[8] How do these questions compare? And here is a question for the instructors: Do we always want students to come to synthesis or do we also want them to ask good—and often messy—questions, and explore how others' questions are framed?

CONCLUSION: HOW ELSE?

After thirty years of working with student writing, and over a third of that time with interdisciplinary studies as well, I am tempted to end this chapter with a simple "how else?" How else can you teach a good interdisciplinary course than by having students write? How else can you help students to become active players in interdisciplinary inquiry instead of passive absorbers of supposedly fascinating interdisciplinary insights? But let's have a little dose of reality here. The very structure of the interdisciplinary program in which I teach modifies that message: The courses may focus on oral rather than written communication, and on other skills such as social interaction. Many of the courses rely heavily on a rich variety of group presentations, debates, role plays, and so forth to encourage integrative thinking. Other essays in this volume persuasively discuss integration and synthesis achieved through other modes.

Writing does form a key part of the approaches many of those essays describe, though, such as technology-assisted learning. Writing will be a key learning strategy in most interdisciplinary courses. In one of the founding documents of the WAC movement, "Writing as a Mode of Learning," Janet Emig argues the differences between written and spoken language and advocates the learning that takes place only through struggling to put ideas into written form. She cites the work of Vygotsky, Luria, and Bruner indicating that "higher cognitive functions, such as analysis and synthesis, seem to develop most fully only with the support system of verbal language—particularly, it seems, of written language" (122). And Berthoff reminds us that "one of the best ways to teach your subject is by teaching writing," "the chief means of making meanings and thus of laying hold on the speculative instruments of one discipline or another" (113, 123)—statements true of interdisciplinary work as of disciplinary. She argues persuasively for seeing writing not as a separable "component" in a course occupied with other business but as central to that business.

Writing-intensive interdisciplinary courses, while often stretching both faculty and students beyond their comfort zones, yield student thinking that impels faculty in my hallway to call out to each other to share it, whether an excerpt from a student journal or course commentary or a major project. Considering the wide variety of approaches they describe, and the wider variety of courses to which this teaching approach applies, I should close with Christine Farris and Raymond Smith's reminder about writing-intensive teaching: "the way to keep writing tied to thinking and learning and to changes in teaching is to deal with it as locally and as discipline- and professor-specifically as possible" (85). But amid the enormous variety are some common goals. If we fully engage the challenges of writing-intensive interdisciplinary teaching from the beginning of students' college careers, by the time they enter their majors we know that they have already struggled explicitly, within particular courses, with the complementary and conflicting demands of diverse disciplinary discourses, rather than that struggle remaining implicit and unexplored as they negotiate the demands of different courses. Students will have worked through, in writing, complex issues of their society, from hunger to power to the role of the arts, issues too important be relegated to "experts." And they will often have directly engaged—for example, through letters to the editor or to senators and representatives—the challenge of entering the realm of informed public debate about those vital issues.

NOTES

1. Other designated "essential skills" in our program include oral communication, critical thinking and problem solving, values identification and responsible decision making, social interaction, and responsibility for civic life.

2. Among the handful of articles explicitly focusing on writing in interdisciplinary courses, beyond those mentioned in the text, are: Cooper, with examples from a graduate rhetoric course; Minock, focusing on using rhetorical concepts during establishment of WAC in an interdisciplinary program; and my own

("Writing," revisited with a more interdisciplinary second half as "Finding"), dealing with a general education context. Davis's discussion of interdisciplinary outcomes (55–58) could easily become the basis for useful writing assignments. Some recent articles discussing metaphors for teaching and learning, while not centering on issues of interdisciplinarity, offer useful insights: Clark advocates conceiving of rhetoric as travel, while Kleinsasser et al. advocate teacher as border-crosser, part of which may entail crossing disciplinary borders.

3. For an overview of assumptions and issues of writing-intensive teaching, see Farris and Smith; for comment on the particular challenges of writing-intensive teaching in general education, see Thaiss. Writing-intensive interdisciplinary courses today employ many techniques of collaborative learning and technology-assisted learning such as peer critiques, group projects, student e-mails with peers and faculty, and online discussions, but since these issues form the focus of chapter 5 in this volume, I concentrate elsewhere for this occasion. Another aspect of this topic is how writing-intensive interdisciplinary courses differ according to their position and sequence within students' undergraduate education. Is a course closely related to students' major or not? Are the students first-years or seniors? In the interdisciplinary teaching my colleagues and I do, we have found that nonmajors typically are equally at sea writing about a painting and a symphony whether they are freshmen or seniors; thus, for this occasion I assume students who are novices to the disciplines at hand, regardless of the students' level. Writing in an upper-level interdisciplinary course related to students' major would entail other assumptions: that students have developed some awareness of the discourse of their field and are now putting that discourse in conversation with other discourses on a topic of common concern, a rhetorical situation that likewise much deserves further attention.

4. And Walvoord's list of dangers to WAC similarly echoes IDS at every item: "lack of full institutional support, the high cost of some WAC programs, the compartmentalized structure of academia, counterproductive attitudes and assumptions about writing and learning in the university, research and service demands on faculty, faculty workload, the faculty reward system, current emphasis on quantification and testing in the academy, lack of an appropriate theoretical and research base for WAC, and leader retirement or burnout" (58). This article warrants close study for the light it sheds on challenges and strategies for IDS.

5. A series I helped to organize at our university a few years ago drew twenty-five people—a good percentage of the sixty full-time faculty teaching in the program, given multiple conflicting meetings of departments and colleges. Many claimed their sense of being ill equipped to teach writing in interdisciplinary courses brought them to the workshops.

6. Williams uses this graph/quadrant image to discuss prevailing models of the progression of student thinking by theorists such as Piaget, Perry, and Kohlberg, and argues the advantages of alternative metaphors, in particular that of community.

7. That volume contains further detail on some of the examples cited in this chapter. The faculty who designed the assignments deserve credit here: Ralph Aloisi, Karen Barrett, Margaret Ciarcia, Jill Dix Ghnassia, and others for "Epidemics and AIDS"; Charles R. Canedy, III, and also Thomas Grant, for "Discovering America"; A. Cheryl Curtis, Anthony T. Rauche, and S. Edward Weinswig for "Ethnic Roots and Urban Arts"; Robert Fried, Holly DiBella Mc-Carthy, and Doug Dix for "What Is School?"; Jill Dix Ghnassia for "Romanticism in the Arts"; Laurence I. Gould for "Seeing Through Symmetry"; Virginia Hale for "Literature and Film of Other Cultures"; Jane Horvath for "Sources of Power"; John Roderick, and also John Seabury, for "Creativity: The Dynamics of Artistic Expression"; and Harald Sandström for "The Caribbean Mosaic and also Cultures and Transnational Corporations."

8. Cf. Postman on such question asking as basic to study of any discipline (153–56) and basic as well to interdisciplinary study. Postman also offers support for metaphor as basic to study of a discipline—all the more so to interdisciplinary study.

WORKS CITED

Anson, Chris M. "Writing Across the Curriculum." *Encyclopedia of Rhetoric and Composition: Communication from Ancient Times to the Information Age*. Ed. Theresa Enos. New York: Garland, 1996. 773–74.

Applebee, Arthur N. *Curriculum as Conversation: Transforming Traditions of Teaching and Learning*. Chicago: University of Chicago Press, 1996.

Association for Integrative Studies and Institute in Integrative Studies. "Guide to Interdisciplinary Syllabus Preparation." *Journal of General Education* 45, no. 2 (1996): 170–73.

Bazerman, Charles. "From Cultural Criticism to Disciplinary Participation: Living with Powerful Words." *Writing, Teaching, and Learning in the Disciplines*. Eds. Anne Herrington and Charles Moran. New York: MLA, 1992. 61–68.

Berthoff, Ann. *The Making of Meaning: Metaphors, Models, and Maxims for Writing Teachers*. Upper Montclair, NJ: Boynton, 1981.

Bonwell, Charles C., and James A. Eison. *Active Learning: Creating Excitement in the Classroom*. ASHE-ERIC Higher Education Report No. 1. Washington, DC: George Washington University, School of Education and Human Development, 1991.

Boyer Commission on Educating Undergraduates in the Research University. *Reinventing Undergraduate Education: A Blueprint for America's Research Universities*. 1998. 8 January 1999. http://notes.cc.sunysb.edu/Pres/boyer.nsf.

Bronowski, Jacob. *A Sense of the Future: Essays in Natural Philosophy*. Cambridge: MIT Press, 1977.

Brookfield, Stephen D. *Developing Critical Thinkers: Challenging Adults to Explore Alternative Ways of Thinking and Acting.* San Francisco: Jossey-Bass, 1987.

Canedy, Charles R., 3rd. "A Business School Case Method, Clio, and Interdisciplinarity." Seabury, *Interdisciplinary General Education* 189–206.

Clark, Gregory. "Writing as Travel, or Rhetoric on the Road." *College Composition and Communication* 49, no. 1 (1998): 9–23.

Cooper, Marilyn M. "Dialogic Learning Across Disciplines." *Journal of Advanced Composition* 14, no. 2 (1994): 531–46.

Davis, James R. *Interdisciplinary Courses and Team Teaching: New Arrangements for Learning.* Phoenix: American Council on Education and Oryx, 1995.

Dewey, John. *How We Think: A Restatement of the Relation of Reflective Thinking to the Educative Process.* Boston: D. C. Heath, 1933.

Doherty, Austin, James Chenevert, Rhoda R. Miller, James L. Roth, and Leona C. Truchan. "Developing Intellectual Skills." *Handbook of the Undergraduate Curriculum.* Eds. Jerry G. Gaff and James L. Ratcliff. San Francisco: Jossey-Bass, 1997. 170–89.

Edwards, Alan F., Jr. "Are Interdisciplinary Studies Still Alive and Well? Summary Findings from the New Undergraduate Interdisciplinary Studies Program Directory." *Association for Integrative Studies Newsletter* 18, no. 4 (1996): 1–3.

———. *Interdisciplinary Undergraduate Programs: A Directory.* 2nd ed. Acton, MA: Copley, 1996.

Elbow, Peter. *Embracing Contraries: Explorations in Learning and Teaching.* New York: Oxford University Press, 1986.

Emig, Janet. "Writing as a Mode of Learning." *College Composition and Communication* 28 (1977): 122–28.

Farris, Christine, and Raymond Smith. "Writing-Intensive Courses: Tools for Curricular Change." *Writing Across the Curriculum: A Guide to Developing Programs.* Ed. Susan H. McLeod and Margot Soven. Newbury Park, CA: Sage, 1992. 71–86.

Fiscella, Joan B., and Stacey E. Kimmel. *Interdisciplinary Education: A Guide to Resources.* New York: College Entrance Examination Board, 1999.

Frost, Robert. "Education by Poetry: A Meditative Monologue." *Robert Frost: Poetry and Prose.* Eds. Edward Connery Lathem and Lawrence Thompson. New York: Holt, Rinehart and Winston, 1972. 329–40.

Harris, Joseph. *A Teaching Subject: Composition Since 1966.* Upper Saddle River, NJ: Prentice-Hall, 1997.

Hayakawa, S. I. *Language in Thought and Action.* 3rd ed. New York: Harcourt Brace Jovanovich, 1972.

Haynes, Carolyn. "Interdisciplinary Writing and the Undergraduate Experience: A Four-Year Writing Plan Proposal." *Issues in Integrative Studies* 14 (1996): 29–57.

Kirscht, Judy, Rhonda Levine, and John Reiff. "Evolving Paradigms: WAC and the Rhetoric of Inquiry." *College Composition and Communication* 45, no. 3 (1994): 369–80.

Klein, Julie Thompson, and William H. Newell. "Advancing Interdisciplinary Studies." *Handbook of the Undergraduate Curriculum*. Eds. Jerry G. Gaff and James R. Ratcliff. San Francisco: Jossey-Bass, 1997. 393–415.

Kleinsasser, Audrey M., Norma Decker Collins, and Jane Nelson. "Writing in the Disciplines: Teacher as Gatekeeper and as Border Crosser." *Journal of General Education* 43, no. 2 (1994): 117–33.

Maimon, Elaine P. Preface. *Writing Across the Curriculum: A Guide to Developing Programs*. Eds. Susan H. McLeod and Margot Soven. Newbury Park, CA: Sage, 1992. ix–xiv.

———. "Teaching 'Across the Curriculum.'" *Handbook of the Undergraduate Curriculum*. Eds. Jerry G. Gaff and James R. Ratcliff. San Francisco: Jossey-Bass, 1997. 377–92.

McLeod, Susan. "Writing Across the Curriculum: The Second Stage, and Beyond." *College Composition and Communication* 40, no. 3 (1989): 337–43.

McLeod, Susan, and Elaine Maimon. "Clearing the Air: WAC Myths and Realities." *College English* 62, no. 5 (2000): 573–83.

McLeod, Susan H., and Margot Soven, eds. *Writing Across the Curriculum: A Guide to Developing Programs*. Newbury Park, CA: Sage, 1992.

Minock, Mary. "A(n) (Un)Certain Synergy: Rhetoric, Hermeneutics, and Transdisciplinary Conversations about Writing." *College Composition and Communication* 47, no. 4 (1996): 502–22.

Newell, William H. "Professionalizing Interdisciplinarity: Literature Review and Research Agenda." Newell, *Interdisciplinarity* 529–63.

Newell, William H., ed. *Interdisciplinarity: Essays from the Literature*. New York: College Entrance Examination Board, 1998.

Postman, Neil. *Teaching as a Conserving Activity*. New York: Delacorte, 1979.

Richards, Donald G. "The Meaning and Relevance of 'Synthesis' in Interdisciplinary Studies." *Journal of General Education* 45, no. 2 (1996): 114–128.

Russell, David R. *Writing in the Academic Disciplines, 1870–1990: A Curricular History*. Carbondale: Southern Illinois University Press, 1991.

———. "Writing in and across Curriculums and Disciplines: Where Multiple Cultures and Intelligences Meet." Fourth National Writing Across the Curriculum Conference, Cornell University, Ithaca, NY, June 5, 1999.

Seabury, Marcia Bundy. "Finding a Voice Across the Disciplines." Seabury, *Interdisciplinary General Education* 89–103.

———. "Sports Talk: The Coaching Metaphor in Action." *Maryland English Journal* 25, no. 1 (1990): 55–64.

———. "Writing and Interdisciplinary Learning." *Perspectives: The Journal of the Association for General and Liberal Studies* 26, no. 2 (1996): 40–54.

Seabury, Marcia Bundy, ed. *Interdisciplinary General Education: Questioning Outside the Lines*. New York: College Entrance Examination Board, 1999.

Spellmayer, Kurt. "A Common Ground: The Essay in the Academy." *College English* 51 (1989): 262–76.

Thaiss, Christopher. "WAC and General Education Courses." *Writing Across the Curriculum: A Guide to Developing Programs*. Ed. Susan H. McLeod and Margot Soven. Newbury Park, CA: Sage, 1992. 87–109.

Walvoord, Barbara E. "The Future of WAC." *College English* 58, no. 1 (1996): 58–79.

Walvoord, Barbara E., and Lucille P. McCarthy. *Thinking and Writing in College: A Naturalistic Study of Students in Four Disciplines*. Urbana, IL: National Council of Teachers of English, 1991.

Williams, Joseph M. Afterword. "Two Ways of Thinking about Growth: The Problem of Finding the Right Metaphor." *Thinking, Reasoning, and Writing*. Ed. Elaine P. Maimon, Barbara F. Nodine, and Finbarr W. O'Connor. New York: Longman, 1989. 245–55.

PART II

Innovative Approaches to
Interdisciplinary Teaching

CHAPTER 4

Teaching on the Edge

Interdisciplinary Teaching in Learning Communities

Valerie Bystrom

Because of the compartmentalization and departmentalization of colleges today as well as the complicated and varied nature of students' lives, students often experience learning in an isolated, fragmented manner. In 1998, the Boyer Commission noted that universities are "so complex, so multifaceted, and often so fragmented that, short of a major crisis, they can rarely focus their attention on a single agenda. We believe that the state of undergraduate education is in such a crisis, an issue of such magnitude and volatility, that universities must galvanize themselves to respond" (37). Among its ten recommendations, the commission called for postsecondary educators to cultivate a sense of community.

Advocating community in higher education, however, is hardly a new concept. Over a century ago, John Dewey criticized schools for their focus on individualized learning:

> I believe that much of present education fails because it neglects this fundamental principle of the school as a form of community life. It conceives the school as a place where certain information is to be given, where certain lessons are to be learned, or where certain habits are to be formed. The value of these is conceived as lying largely in the remote future; the child must do these things for the sake of something else he is to do; they are mere preparation. As a result they do not be-

come part of the life experience of the child and so are not truly educative. (My *Pedagogic Creed* 8)

According to Dewey, schools encourage inflexible teaching to individual
and passive students instead of flexible teaching based on the sharing of
ideas. In describing the role of the ideal teacher, he writes:

> I do not know what the greater maturity of the teacher and teacher's
> greater knowledge of the world, of subject-matters and of individuals,
> is for unless the teacher can arrange conditions that are conducive to
> community activity and to organization which exercises control over
> individual impulses by the mere fact that all are engaged in communal
> projects. . . . The planning must be flexible enough to permit free play
> for individuality of experience and firm enough to give direction to-
> wards continuous development of power. (*Experience* 58)

Drawing on Dewey, a host of educators no longer suppose their business
to know the world and to make small deposits of knowledge in students. To
understand knowledge as not simply discovered, stored, or conveyed, but
made through sharing means that teaching is less about simply conveying
information and more about providing the time and space for students to
make, exchange, and evaluate knowledge. Toward this end, many have
gone so far as to create learning communities or intentionally developed
communities that promote and maximize learning. The phrase "learning
communities" has been used to refer to several different kinds of innovative
learning environments. Some, for example, use it to refer to any class engaged in collaborative work and active learning, whereas others use it to
describe residential colleges.

Although both of the approaches may have value, neither necessarily
addresses the issue of interdisciplinarity and curricular coherence through
purposeful links among courses in different disciplines and collaboration
among instructors. By interdisciplinary learning communities, I mean a
course of study designed by two or more faculty that includes work in different disciplines integrated around a particular issue or theme. Such a definition has important implications. I argue that even if one changes the
pedagogy of a course in, say, the English Romantic poets from lecture to a
most varied and successful sequence of collaborative activities, and even
though students demonstrate their knowledge in brilliant research papers,
lively discussion groups, parodies, student-created exams (usually harder
than we would dare set)—still, it is English 313. There it is, a tidy box as
noted in the course catalogue and stored in the closet where students put
their college experience—Psych 101 top shelf to the right, Japanese Drama
second shelf in the back.

Learning communities, as I use the term, however, assume that the human construction of knowledge may be vast and complex, a finally indescribable cathedral with zillions of parts, with vaults, buttresses, and dazzling windows, amazing in its aspects but connected, linked, and, if not available to anyone in its totality, still not itself offerable in several hundred, or million, tidy boxes for easy storage. Interdisciplinary studies courses let the knowledge out of the boxes, so that students set to building connections, buttresses, windows. The box of English Romantic poets might be integrated with the contents of any number of history boxes—the Industrial Revolution, the rise of the working class, or the French Revolution. Students in environmental studies could stand to read the Romantic poets, too, and so could students in art class. We can imagine integrating the Romantic poets in various ways to explore particular issues: What is a revolution? What is the nature of nature? What is the use of human imagination? Coherent, thematic interdisciplinary programs of study are more likely to shape how a student lives, how she thinks, how she understands, how she addresses issues. What students take away from such a program cannot be boxed up.

Interdisciplinary learning communities, then, have numerous benefits for students. Whereas more traditional education offers students a collection of courses, interdisciplinary learning communities provide coherent academic programs that reflect the distribution of knowledge in the real world and the ways people must confront and solve problems. The benefits to teachers, however, are not so obvious, yet teachers up and join these interdisciplinary, community-based programs. Their friends wonder why. Why would someone immersed in her subject, deeply involved in the scholarly dialogue, and confident of her well-crafted courses leave the academic mainstream? The answers no doubt vary. College faculty members who welcome interdisciplinary work may question the way knowledge is institutionalized and may want to provide their students with a more coherent and useful academic experience. Or they may be closet generalists abounding with intellectual curiosity. Or, particularly teachers of introductory courses, they may be driven by sheer boredom, the specter of one class after another of English composition, Sociology 110, Chemistry 100, or even Shakespeare's tragedies stretching clear to the horizon of retirement. Whatever the initial motives, once launched into an interdisciplinary program, faculty members enjoy as many benefits as students. They find themselves swept up in teaching and learning and having the time of their lives.

In the following chapter, I describe different interdisciplinary learning communities developed and adapted by faculty members and administrators in Washington State to fit the needs of their institutions, enumerating, though not exhaustively, their benefits to students and especially to teachers, and supporting the proposition that important and successful curricular change can begin with an individual or a few like-minded teachers. Moreover, rather than simply listing the various types of interdisciplinary learning communities, I will offer an interdisciplinary typology for these communities, beginning with the simplest to implement (linked courses and customized links) and progressing to the most complex forms of interdisciplinary learning communities (fully integrated links, coordinated programs, and team-taught, integrated programs). I will end by discussing an even more arching and ambitious learning community—the consortium—and one specific example of it—the Washington Center for Improving the Quality of Undergraduate Education—where faculty from across the nation come together to learn and collaborate on how to achieve learning communities in their home institutions.

LINKING CLASSES

As noted earlier, learning communities come in a variety of shapes and sizes. The most popular model, the linked class, is nearly infinitely variable. Most simply, classes are linked. That is, a number of students, usually twenty-five, sign up for the same classes. Although schools have adapted linked classes in many ways, the initial motive remains interdisciplinary, the desire to provide coherent courses of study, to deepen a student's understanding of the differences and similarities among the assumptions, methods, and characteristic inquiries of the disciplines and their bearing on one another.

Many faculty members in Washington have heard this story from Patrick Hill about an undergraduate he knew:

> She was taking a course in behaviorism from 10:00 to 1:00 and a course in existentialism from 1:00 to 4:00. And she was pulling A's in both courses. In the behaviorism course—this was pure Skinner—she was learning about the predictability of human behavior and of the illusory character of consciousness and intentions and certainly of their insignificance in explaining human behavior. In the philosophy course, which was focused on the early Sartre, she was learning that we are ultimately free, even to the point of being able to define the meaning of our pasts.
>
> I asked her which course was right. She said, "What do you mean?" I said, "If you had to choose between the two courses, which one would you choose?" She said, "I like the psychology teacher better." I said, "That's not what I'm asking. Which one is correct? Which one is cor-

rect about the nature of our human being?" And she said, "I'm getting
A's in both courses." (Hill, "The Rationale" 3–4)

This conversation took place at the University of New York, Stony Brook,
in the late 1970s, and, responding to what it reflected, the "atomization of
the curriculum" and the privatization of academic experience, Hill and his
colleagues proposed the Federated Learning Community or FLC (Hill,
"Communities of Learners" 107).

In a Stony Brook FLC, about twenty-five students registered for the
same three carefully selected and thematically resonant classes. In the FLC
"Technology, Values and Society," several groups of twenty-five students
took philosophy, history, and engineering in the first semester and chemistry, sociology, and literature the second. Hill explains that the "act of feder-
ation" made courses "come alive for the students," partly because professors
had lively exchanges (Hill, "Communities" 114). For instance, after one
professor distributed a Monsanta pamphlet on the role of chemicals in everyday life, an excited federated colleague wrote a refutation and requested
it be distributed to the class. Given such exchanges, Hill notes, "students
cannot avoid refashioning their view of expertise" ("Communities" 116).
Every week, each small group met in a program seminar to explore not only
connections but also profound differences among the concepts, assumptions, methods, and even facts presented in the various courses.[1] A typical
seminar writing assignment asked students to develop a theme of their own
devising or discovery, using multiple disciplinary perspectives and resources.

To support their efforts, a faculty member, freed from his regular teaching, traveled along with the students, attending lectures and reading the
texts. He experienced, along with the students, the interaction among the
disciplines and "taught" the program seminar, modeling interdisciplinary
reflection. In his role as master learner, he also wrote papers and studied for
tests, interacting collegially with students, offering advice to someone
stalled on an essay, for instance, and, in turn, accepting help with differen-
tial equations. As the courses unfolded, he kept his colleagues in the feder-
ation abreast of the students' responses. As he collaborated with
overworked students, relived bewilderment, or re-mastered the art of taking notes while tuned out, the master learner experienced comforting and
discomforting things about pedagogy that he could take to heart and include in the frequent faculty discussions. Later, with a fresh perspective on
his own discipline and on the lives of his students, the master learner returned to his regular assignment to apply what he learned through the experience.

At the University of Oregon and at the University of Washington, an incoming student may enroll in a Northwest version of the FLC. This version is called the FIG, the Freshman Interest Group. FIGs were developed at Oregon by advisers who recognized just how alienating a student's first-year experience can be. Rather than allow entering students to flounder in the huge course catalogue, advisers assemble several apt programs of study and, during the summer before their first year, incoming students are invited to select one. At the UW, a student might select a comparative culture link, "Eastern and Western Traditions," which includes the literature and culture of ancient and classical China, the history of the ancient world, and English composition. "Ecosystems" includes forest and society, composition, and a survey of oceanography. Thus, each FIG encourages an interdisciplinary exploration of a theme. As with the FLC groups, students in a FIG section move together from one large class to another, a community within the sea of anonymity. They also meet once a week with a peer advisor, an experienced student trained to lead a FIG. The weekly FIG meeting keeps to a fairly strict schedule of projects and assignments including faculty or guest speakers and written reflections. Interdisciplinary insights are encouraged by the curricular structure and may be generated by the students, but the faculty members and peer advisors make no special attempt to help students develop them.[2] Including composition in the link, however, offers more possibility of interdisciplinary writing assignments. Primarily, these learning communities help students in their very first quarter establish a community in an academic context.[3] Students love FIGs. Each year more are offered—60 at UW for fall 1996, 115 for fall 2000.

Both FLCs and FIGs restructure—or perhaps purposefully structure—a student's program of study to invite independent interdisciplinary thinking and provoke awareness that on specific issues professors in different disciplines may make different and even contradictory claims. In the Stony Brook model, program seminar assignments make interdisciplinary investigations a central piece of a student's academic work. Both models encourage a sense of intellectual community among students. Alexander Astin suggests that the students' interactions with each other have the most far-reaching effects on their learning and development and that second in importance is the amount of interaction between individual students and faculty members. The Stony Brook federated plan directly promotes both kinds of interactions. Although the less expensive FIGs promote meaningful interactions among students, interactions between students and teachers are not so inevitable. Anecdote has it that students gain confidence by participating in FIGs, and thus more readily visit professors' offices and ask questions in large classes. Further, although the faculty members involved are free to make something of the interdisciplinary opportunity they offer, FIGs are not designed to promote faculty development or cross campus conversation and collegiality; they have little impact on the enormous university schedule of classes, and almost none on the routines of departments, disciplines, and faculty members. More purposeful restructuring of the university curriculum to promote interdisciplinary insights, student-teacher interaction, and faculty development remains too formidable.

The good news is that organizing more thoroughgoing interdisciplinary learning communities is not so formidable at smaller colleges with smaller classes and that a handful of teachers may initiate them. Especially at community colleges, learning communities serve the needs of students who outside of class may have few opportunities for meaningful interactions with each other or with their teachers as well as the needs of students who commute, hold down jobs, and often have families. Learning communities also help students who enter college tentatively. Perhaps the first in a family to go to college, or having years ago graduated high school with poor grades, a student may feel suspicious of education. Others may feel insecure because they are recent immigrants or international students. Of course, some students are quite confident but are bound for somewhere else; like travelers through hub airports, they transit the first two years of college to get prerequisites out of the way. In addition, for this wide array of students, teachers are (or feel) obliged to provide the prerequisites, replaceable, re-producible (Something 110) courses eminently transferable to other state institutions. Fat, standard textbooks assure everyone that students get what they need. Part-time teachers, especially, who often commute from school to school, feel just as standard and replaceable as the courses. In response to these conditions, faculty members and administrators pursue the many benefits of learning communities.

Hundreds of teachers in Washington have developed learning communities by the simple expedient of linking classes. A handy version includes a skills course, perhaps English 101, and a content course, but just as easily a history class could link with an art, a philosophy with an economics.[4] The logistics are easy and cost free but must be handled well before the quarter or semester begins. Basically, students who enroll for the link must enroll in both courses. Thus, with the blessing or active support of a key administrator, the faculty members inform the advisors, the registrar, and/or the computer-handling registration data that students who sign up for the English course must sign up for the content course also. The necessary information and instructions for the students must be in the college schedule. If at all possible, the classes should meet in the same room during succeeding hours (e.g., composition at nine and oceanography at ten), and both faculty members should be available for both hours.

Well in advance of teaching the link, the faculty members plan and reorganize their syllabi and schedules of assignments so that students will not only meet the objectives of each course but will gain the most benefit from taking the two courses in conjunction. As a beginning, the teachers may propose smart changes so that the assignments in the two classes complement each other; for instance, students will study Meso-American art while reading the documents of conquest in the Americas. They may reorganize course materials so that assignments in a composition class dovetail nicely with the schedule of readings in cultural anthropology and include ethnography as a composition assignment. Some tricky logistical issues may arise. The optimal arrangement requires every student to register for both classes. Although small classes may be the rule, however, an anthropology class often carries a higher enrollment (forty students) than a composition class (twenty-five students). The teachers may decide only to make changes that do not trouble the smooth course of anthropology students not in the link. Or, they may split the difference, in a way reassuring to administrators who worry about costs, and each accept thirty-two students. And they can more thoroughly integrate their courses.

In the course of their discussions, fundamental questions may come up, questions that faculty members seldom discuss with colleagues. (What are you teaching, and why and how?) They may exchange books and visit each other's classes. Perhaps the anthropology teacher felt bruised by a high school English class, and the English teacher has doubts about ethnocentric prowling in other people's cultures. They may talk about their disciplines and about their working assumptions. To the extent that they can foresee and accommodate, the faculty members plan the interdisciplinary work. They consider possible lectures, guest speakers, films, and workshops.

Using this approach, even graying faculty members are encouraged to adopt alternative teaching methods, to reconsider their coffee-stained lectures (typed years ago on onion skin). In lieu of or in addition to lecturing, teachers engage the students in some active pursuit of knowledge, often in groups, to deepen their grasp, for instance, of the concept of anomie, of the social world of Jane Austen's *Pride and Prejudice*, or of the distinctions between the Marxian and the Hegelian dialectics. Invited beyond passivity and figuring out (with sufficient guidance) how to be effective as a group, students respond with unexpected insight and inventiveness. Of course, it doesn't take two teachers to innovate, but linking classes gives teachers the occasion and support to try innovations they might not usually risk.[5] Experience suggests that working together helps teachers conceive of and refine productive, challenging group assignments and workshops. In addition, as they discuss how to help students appreciate the different ground rules in art and history, or literature and anthropology, the faculty members must further clarify their own disciplinary and perhaps ideological assumptions. Innovative course work informed by these discussions goes on to promote learning that would not have come into focus in either stand-alone class.

Once the linked classes are under way, students get into the act, noticing frictions and harmonies unforeseen by the faculty planners. "Objectivity," a student points out, seems to be one thing in composition, another in anthropology, and problematic in both. "Objectivity" becomes the topic for a workshop. Or, perhaps an international student experienced in other intellectual traditions openly challenges certain assumptions, for instance, of anthropological investigation. And she finds the traditional rhetorical forms in English composition insufficient as vehicles for expressing her concerns. Can the argumentative paper suffice? Is the status of logic universally agreed on? The faculty members and students consider whether and how to explore the questions further. Perhaps they invite a philosopher to help clarify some epistemological issues. The faculty members may organize assignments that aid students in teasing out other unspoken beliefs and hidden premises typical in their culture, in their daily behavior. Approached seriously, linked classes can open interdisciplinary spaces and nurture what sprouts there. Even the usually tedious stuff of English composition can leaf out exotically.

By the time grades are turned in, exhausted but gratified students and faculty members have learned a lot. They have covered the important terrain of the two courses, including several boundaries and intersections, and together explored unmarked territory lying between. The tentative students and the confident ones have thought, listened, talked, read, wondered, critiqued, argued, edited—done intellectual work together for two hours a day; they feel connected with each other and to the processes of education. They look forward to the next quarter's classes.[6] The faculty members share ideas about how to make changes in their regular courses. Students and faculty members who normally go about their business as familiar strangers have new respect for each other as colleagues; some have established firm friendships. These gains for students and for faculty can happen in a simple link.

CUSTOMIZING A LINK

By making small changes or additions to a simple link, faculty members or administrators can respond to specific needs or desires. To further emphasize interdisciplinary reflection and student responsibility, and without adding much to their teaching loads, faculty members might offer a weekly integrative seminar. The teachers of an ethics/political science link at Chehalis Community College, for instance, set aside two class hours each week for seminar. Both faculty members attend the seminar, but early on, they lay groundwork that helps students move toward successful integrative discussions. The students go on to establish guidelines for seminar behavior and to take responsibility for the weekly agendas. The teachers act as seminar members, providing models of civil disagreement—which some students observe for the first time.

To provide a coherent program of study and a supportive intellectual community to incoming students at a very large urban institution, LaGuardia Community College requires enrollment in a multiple link called a "cluster." Along with composition, students take a course in the research paper, two other courses from science, social science, or the arts, and an integrating seminar hour. (The composition classes may also take on the aspect of an integrating seminar.) For instance, the cluster "Freedom and Seeing" includes composition, research paper writing, introduction to philosophy, and introduction to art. "Work, Labor and Business in American Literature" includes the English courses, an introduction to sociology, and a humanities course. Clusters resemble FLCs but with no master learner or a special need for one. The faculty members work together; they rewrite their syllabi in order to pursue themes, sequence presentations for coherence, and construct assignments that help students define the disciplinary perspectives and take advantage of the interdisciplinary possibilities. One of the faculty members might lead the integrating seminar, but any one of them could. When the cluster is under way, they meet for lunch once a week to monitor progress and discuss the inevitable necessary adjustments. Roberta Matthews reports that LaGuardia clusters positively affect student success and retention in a school with at-risk students (46–47). Even though teaching in a cluster requires more work, one LaGuardia faculty member says, "Teaching any course in a cluster is better than teaching it out of a cluster" (qtd. in Matthews 45).

At Lower Columbia College, entering students must take a "cornerstone" course, and graduating students must complete an integrative "capstone" course. Both courses have been designed as simple or multiple link learning communities. While the cornerstone stresses skills needed for success in college, capstone courses with themes like "The Order of Nature" and "Style and Revolution" encourage interdisciplinary reflection and allow students to demonstrate their capacity to integrate disciplinary methods and materials.

FULLY INTEGRATED LINKS

If faculty members planning a simple link really hit it off, they may toss their usual syllabi to the winds and change everything. They may decide to rearrange all the work around a common theme and/or a set of provocative questions that haunt their courses. While it adds considerably to their teaching loads, they may decide to team teach, both staying in the classroom for both hours. No longer need she teach the class during one hour and he the next. They plan those two hours to suit best the development of their theme, and many more of their innovative ideas can come to fruition in a two-hour block. In addition to or in place of textbooks, they may order significant texts that will help students explore the theme—*Sula, Civilization and its Discontents, The Structure of Scientific Revolutions*, so on. They may provide a selection of essays through a local copy center. As they talk about how they teach, new ideas for group assignments, lab assignments, experiments, workshops, Web searches, writing assignments, field trips, films, guest speakers, performances, and student presentations may come up.

Time is an issue. Preparing and planning may take a week, weeks, hundreds of hours. Preparing any new class takes time, too, of course. As technologies and epistemes change, so does the curriculum, and faculty members in many departments prepare courses unimaginable by their own professors. Even teaching an old chestnut for the first time takes hours and hours. Yet planning an integrated link involves more. A teacher must think about her own discipline in the light of someone else's and someone else's in the light of her own. The stakes are high. Are fundamental assumptions shared or in conflict? And what does one's discipline have to say for itself in a conversation with another—with inorganic chemistry? Where and how far can such a conversation go? Must words give way to math? Will one discourse dominate? Which is mightier, math or metaphor? What will help students discern and benefit from the differences? What will help students develop intuition in the lab? Although their teaching styles may vary, the two faculty members must decide about texts, assignments, and classroom methods. The fully integrated link can address questions generated when the disciplines are not taken for granted, and it may bear little resemblance to any course either faculty member has taught before. No amount of planning time may seem enough, and what there is must be used wisely.

Once the link is under way, the full panoply of team-teaching effects bears on the students' experiences. First, having authorities from two different disciplines in the room has a powerful effect. Often astounded that teachers don't always agree, students realize they themselves must discern, think critically, and make judgments—about Skinner and Sartre perhaps. Second, unnerving as it may be, for stretches of time in the classroom, one of the teachers is not an expert in the subject under discussion. Not entering as the bona fide expert takes some practice, and some teachers never get used to it. Admitting to being not a universal authority, however, places a faculty member differently in relation to the students, as is the case with the FLC master learner. This difference, the bridging of the distance between student and teacher, radically alters the students' experience of teachers, of teaching and learning. After one learning community, a student reported:

> I had an experience I had never had before. The teacher left the lectern and sat beside me. Instead of having teachers just tell me what I should know, they were there learning with us, being exposed to subjects from new perspectives. That way each teacher also became a student. It wasn't such a power structure anymore, but a learning environment, humanized, where everyone was learning. I learned that I have knowledge, that I have what it takes to pursue knowledge, to gain knowledge.

(In light of student responses like this one, some community colleges now require that students take one learning community course as part of the degree requirement.) Handled well, the politics of the team-taught class can put the inquiry, the disciplinary methods, the interdisciplinary exploration, even the quest to make knowledge, at the center of each person's concern. Surrounded by a deep investment in course materials, working hard with other students and their teachers, students develop a different attitude about education. Furthermore, teachers rediscover the great pleasure of learning from each other and from their students. As one teacher noted, while team teaching in learning communities, he gained the education he missed the first time around. Nancy Finley reports that at Seattle Central Community College many faculty were candidates for "burnout," but the "stimulation and support resulting from the team-teaching experience stopped a few from leaving the profession altogether" (52).

LARGER FULLY INTEGRATED LINKS (OR SMALL COORDINATED STUDIES)

Not only does planning take an extraordinary amount of time, so does staying abreast and responding as a term unfolds. Doing this in addition to teaching other classes overloads faculty members, and few can actually take the time to integrate a simple link fully. However, if enough students consistently enroll in two classes, something different can happen. That is, instead of twenty-five students meeting together, forty to fifty students can meet for two hours daily with both faculty members. For the faculty members, this will be (on the regular fifteen hours per week per quarter system) two-thirds of a teaching load. Each will teach only one other class. This means there will be more time in the teachers' schedules to work together on all aspects of the class. With more time, they can organize more thoroughly around a theme and a set of questions. Faculty members at Seattle Central have developed these recent fully integrated links: "Values and Violence: In Search of Authentic Liberation" (philosophy and literature, focusing on liberation ethics); "The Beat Goes On" (music and literature, focusing on the Beat Generation); "In Search of Community: Identity, Language, and Place" (anthropology, sociology, and literature, investigating the relation between identity and community); "Cultural Memory as Power" (literature and sociology); "Making Peace and Doing Justice" (psychology and philosophy, examining students' own participation in the social/political realm); and "Art and Anarchy in the Modern World" (social anthropology and modern art, finding a political vocabulary manifest in works of art).

Since the larger integrated link places fifty students in a classroom with two teachers, to regain or retain the benefits of small personal classes, breakout sessions or small seminars are part of the schedule. Such scheduling complexities require more cooperation among the faculty, administrators, and staff.[7] Seminars themselves are discussed at length in the following section.

FULLY INTEGRATED PROGRAMS OF STUDY OR COORDINATED STUDIES

If patterns of enrollment warrant it, a faculty team may propose a Coordinated Studies Program (CSP). One may think of a CSP as a fully integrated cluster. A CSP amounts to a full-time student's full course load and a faculty member's full teaching load. The usual arithmetic suggests that for each teacher on a team, twenty-five students should be enrolled in the CSP. If two faculty members teach the program, there will be fifty students; if three faculty members teach, there will be seventy-five students, and so on. The programs usually last one or two quarters, but may also run for a year. Because neither students nor teachers have other classroom obligations, CSPs offer the most in flexibility for planning and scheduling and require the most support from other members of the college community. Advisors may need to persuade students, for instance, that CSPs are real college.

The Evergreen State College first developed the CSP model adapted by faculty members around the state. Evergreen traces its lineage back to the exciting but short-lived Experimental College established by Alexander Meiklejohn at the University of Wisconsin in 1927. Meiklejohn believed that education should prepare people for citizenship and that the disciplines and discrete courses poorly prepared students to reflect on important issues. Richard Jones writes that the eighteen founding faculty at Evergreen read Joseph Tussman's *Experiment at Berkeley* and were most influenced by the

> *pedagogical* innovation which [Tussman and Meiklejohn] introduced in order to achieve their curricular objectives: substituting for the traditional format of separate teachers, teaching separate courses, in separated blocks of time, to separate students (who are separately combining different assortments of courses), a format in which *a team of teachers teach the same group of students, who are all studying the same things at the same time, over a prolonged period.* (Jones 22)

Evergreen, which accepted its first 1,000 students in 1971, still holds to this learning community model, especially for lower division students. The college does not have typical departments and has few "regular" courses. Rather, faculty members have responsibility for and latitude in establishing the curriculum. Typically but not necessarily, four faculty members from different disciplines plan a theme-centered, year-long CSP program for about eighty-five students. The weekly schedule can be organized just as the teachers see fit and can include lectures, workshops, book seminars, and other activities that promote students' learning. Everyone in the program may spend a week at a bird sanctuary or at the columnar basalt near the Columbia River.

Book seminars, however, are the key element of the model. Meiklejohn thought students should discuss Great Books. For most programs at Evergreen, the books are not textbooks but primary texts. Jones argues that most college students take classes that cover a large breadth of material:

> [S]tudents are thus required to ingest large bodies of ultimately useless information by preparing for careers which they will not pursue. At the same time they are denied, without their knowledge, the opportunity of devoting their college years to learning how to do the more important things that need to be done to information by an educated adult: choosing and finding it, weighing it, criticizing it, analyzing it, comparing it, reflecting on it, editing it, and then expressing what has been made of it by way of spoken and written language.
>
> By making book seminars the instructional centerpiece of a program, we turn the priorities diametrically around. Covering the book

is not nearly as important as doing something interesting and meaningful with it. (65–66)

Typically students discuss one book a week during two lengthy seminars.
While the teachers and students all meet together for lectures, for book
seminars, individual teachers meet with smaller assigned groups of students. Traditionally, the teacher steps out of the spotlight to facilitate
rather than dominate in book seminars.[8]

The teacher also assesses the work of students assigned to his seminar.
He reads and comments on his students' writing assignments, which include an extensive narrative self-evaluation. At the end of each term and
more completely at the end of a program, he also writes a narrative evaluation of all aspects of the work of each of his students. He and the student
discuss both evaluations in an individual conference. Their contents
agreed on, the two summative narrative evaluations, completed at the end
of a program, enter the student's official record/transcript. In addition,
each student writes a final evaluation for each faculty member in a program, and the faculty members write collegially to one another. These go
into the faculty member's file and are the subject of periodic review with a
dean.

Although the curriculum is not standard as at other state colleges, there
is continuity. For instance, faculty members at Evergreen plan and teach
regularly offered programs such as "Molecule to Organism," designed for
students who plan to attend medical school or a graduate school in life science. The year-long program includes human physiology, cellular and molecular biology, and organic chemistry and biochemistry. Another,
"Human Development," usually includes anthropology, psychology, and
the biology of human development and is designed for students wishing to
pursue psychological and social services. Within these and other regularly
offered programs, a faculty team may further develop an integrating theme.
For instance, the full title for the science program might be "Molecule to
Organism: Vital Stuff," and the focus might be on the biology and chemistry of food. Whatever the focus, particular theme, or central questions, the
students get solid disciplinary work within the interdisciplinary program.

Faculty teams may also organize programs in response to current issues.
The teachers and students in "The Millennium: On the Brink of the New
Age" questioned claims made by Robert D. Kaplan and others (e.g., in the
controversial 1994 *Atlantic* article, "The Coming Anarchy") that the categories and political structures of the nation-state are crumbling, whereas
others—ethnic, cultural, and religious—are emerging. Unrest in several
parts of the world, Kaplan explains, follows from the tension between the

dying nation-state and the emerging power structures. The central questions for "The Millennium" included: Is the nation-state really crumbling? Are we in a time of tension between political structures? Is it accurate to say that emergent forces cause the unrest and hatred?

To address such questions, the learning community undertook case studies including the Balkans, India, and the Middle East. The traditional frameworks of the disciplines provided methodology and concepts—history, of course, and ethnography—to evaluate claims that the unrest is created by centuries-old ethnic hatred. To evaluate disciplinary answers to the core questions, students had to understand discipline-based bias and to study not only history but also the methods and assumptions of history, not only ethnographies but what it means to do an ethnography. What is contained in the category "culture"—anything that could provoke this degree of hatred? Thus, "Millennium" and other strong coordinated studies programs explore the interesting tensions between their organizing core questions and the assumptions, conceptual frameworks, and methodologies of the disciplines.

Getting ready for programs like "The Millennium" requires no small amount of preparation. In addition to teaching in programs centered on the full range of Mediterranean cultures and histories, the anthropology teacher spent a sabbatical traveling in the Mediterranean countries. Because important research required knowing modern Greek, she studied modern Greek. She learned that for an Evergreen teacher, it's read, research, and teach, again and again.

Most faculty members at Evergreen hold steady to teaching in the discipline they studied in graduate school, although often their expertise not only expands within their own fields but extends to others. A political scientist may first study Camus while teaching in a coordinated studies program, read more in and about Camus, come to value how his plays express important political ideas, suggest Camus for the program he is planning, and offer to take primary responsibility for presentations on Camus's dramatic literature. Sometimes a faculty member's major interest changes. An historian of nineteenth-century America has become a competent naturalist; a biologist who once researched the inner-ear mechanisms that keep fish swimming upright now researches in two other areas: on the one hand, the mechanism of acupuncture and Jin Shin Jyutsu, a Japanese form of acupressure, and on the other, the geometrical proportions and numerology used by people laying out and constructing Gothic cathedrals.

Washington colleges adapting the Evergreen model have departments and course descriptions, and even in CSPs, faculty members must respect the standard curriculum in order to furnish a student's transcript with course numbers and grades. Balancing allegiances, faculty members may jettison textbooks but must still teach the essentials of each course credited in the program. After a good deal of discussion and inquiry, a faculty member may discover that not so much is absolutely essential. This realization is a major step toward theme- and issue-centered programs. The challenge then is to decide on appropriate texts and develop fresh ways to introduce anthropological concepts and methods without a textbook but using, perhaps, the *Mismeasure of Man* and *Tristes Tropiques*. Replacing anthologies with primary texts may seem familiar to humanities teachers, but abandoning the textbook has proven harder for those in the social and physical sciences and nearly impossible for math teachers. Even at Evergreen, the book seminar is not the most essential part of many science programs.

If faculty members make book seminars the centerpiece of a program, they must ready themselves to help students develop rich, productive book seminars. For many teachers, that seminar is the hardest and the most rewarding part of a program. Optimally and following Evergreen tradition, each week, faculty members first have their own seminar to discuss the current book. Sometimes the faculty discussion is a "fishbowl," observed by the students. Also, it is common that the faculty member most expert on the current text will give a preparatory lecture for everyone in the program—not to settle issues about a text but to help faculty members and students prepare to discuss it.

In addition to using the book seminar, many teachers of CSPs and other learning communities have variously adapted the Evergreen process of narrative student self-evaluations to help students claim and value their own learning. In addition to giving grades, many require an end-of-the-course reflection so that students review in some detail what they learned from the books they read, the lectures they heard, the discussions in seminar. The self-evaluation is often the occasion for new insights, new connections among the ideas they pondered. Further, even though the students have written essays that used different disciplinary approaches to develop a topic, in the self-evaluation they discuss what they learned writing the essay, what they learned about intersections of knowledge and modes of thinking and problem solving. This reflection may be of more long-term use and interest to the student and to the teacher than the original essay. Also useful is the student's reflection upon herself as student, the community, her own participation in it, and her support of and participation in the making of meaning and knowledge.

Working within the requirements of more traditional state institutions, faculty members have developed interesting CSPs. While fulfilling the general goals of learning communities, CSPs can serve a number of purposes. At Seattle Central Community College, "Body and Mind" is a one-quarter program taught regularly for students going into health care programs (pre-nursing, biotech, surgical tech, and respiratory therapy), but also for students wanting an interesting way to fulfill regular AA requirements. This program includes Zoology 113 (anatomy and physiology), a lab science, Psychology 110 (the standard introduction), and English 101. The human body and mind are viewed from different disciplinary perspectives, and the grueling work of memorizing body parts is balanced by book seminar discussions of essays by Lewis Thomas and novels by Doris Lessing and Mary Shelley. The program prepares students to pursue a number of careers and helps them succeed with difficult prerequisites. It builds community among the vocational students who will work together in upcoming quarters and gives them the opportunity to interact with students from the larger college population. The program also nurtures collegiality among faculty from three different college divisions.

A CSP may foreground provocative issues. For "Africa in the Imagination," course advertisement posters show several maps of Africa—including the Mercator and the Peters Projections. Underneath is the question, "Which is the real Africa?" In this program students are encouraged to review critically images of Africa that they have absorbed and reproduced uncritically—because of romantic films like *Out of Africa,* for instance. As faculty members introduce and use different current textual strategies (e.g., the influential poststructuralist methods of Edward Said's *Orientalism*), students come to recognize distorted images of Africa and the ways they are constructed in texts. Students read about Africa in texts from different disciplines (usually history, literature, and anthropology), written by Africans and by non-Africans. They consider the historical contexts in which the different Africas were constituted and also the disciplinary assumptions, even discipline-based biases, that inform them. Thus, students read anthropological texts to help understand the nature of certain African cultures, but at the same time question the assumptions and methods an anthropologist uses to do fieldwork. What is the connection between myths governing books like Ernest Hemingway's *The Green Hills of Africa* and decisions made by the IMF? What assumptions govern the study of a canonical text like Joseph Conrad's *The Heart of Darkness?* What does it mean, at the beginning of the twenty-first century, to speak of African nations?

Learning communities may target certain groups in the student population. Shortly after learning communities were established at Seattle Central Community College, Minnie Collins and Gilda Sheppard pointed out that African-American students were not registering for them. They wondered why. Perhaps students saw learning communities as fancy classes that might detour a student from steady progress toward his goals, Collins speculates, or that they were only for the "privileged," adds Sheppard. In response, Collins and Sheppard designed "Our Ways of Knowing," which may in different quarters include different disciplines—sociology, political science, anthropology, English—but is always organized to meet the needs of African-American students who are actively recruited. Many of them, explains Collins, haven't been satisfied educationally because institutions do a kind of colonizing; if students do not do things in a certain way, they are on the outside. The aim of "Our Ways of Knowing," she says, "is to make these students an inside," to show that their concerns are of concern to thinkers in different disciplines, are part of higher education.

"If you are in a course about Africa or African-American life, then someone on the team should be African-American," says Collins, "not because only African-Americans can teach the subject, but because community college students gravitate toward people of their own ethnic background, whom they perceive to be culturally connected to them." Having a young African American on the team helps, she says, because that person probably can make concepts clearer in cultural examples and language shared with the students. Sheppard, often the younger teacher, says it is important to know the students demographically. In order to teach sociology concepts, she says, she always uses references to popular culture. However, she adds, she wants to "choreograph difference"; when she discusses deviance and conformity, she discusses Mozart and bebop. The African-American emphasis in recruitment—on the faculty team, in the curriculum, and in the delivery of the curriculum—helps create a comfort zone in the college from which the students can bridge to other programs and courses. If offered every fall, during subsequent quarters, students will have the benefits of the network established in "Our Ways of Knowing." They may also feel encouraged to get off the beaten track and take innovative classes in the future.

Other programs respond to the communities they serve in other ways. A combination easily replicable to provide students with a deeper sense of place in any region is one like "A Billion Years of Washington History: Experiences in the Promised Land" (Northwest geology, anthropology of the Northwest, Washington State history, and freshman composition). Because the program is a student's entire schedule, the faculty members can routinely plan those extended field trips they've always dreamt of—to rock outcroppings, Hoover Dam, Hanford, archaeological digs, wilderness areas, and graveyards. Such programs also lend themselves to organization around a particular problem or set of problems facing a region: how to preserve remaining salmon runs, how to maintain the forest and lumber industries, how to improve the health of the Puget Sound ecosystem. Not only does focusing on such issues help students see the need for and value of different disciplinary approaches, but the practical focus engages even wary science teachers whose everyday aegis is "coverage." They recognize and want students to recognize that more data than scientific facts dictate public policy.

Vocational programs may gear themselves toward the practical needs of a region. At Grays Harbor Community College near the estuary formed by the Chehalis River and the Pacific Ocean, learning communities are part of the Natural Resource Technology Program and respond directly to local environmental conditions. In one of them, "Man, Machine, and Nature," led by Don Samuelson, students formed an environmental consulting firm and did a baseline survey of the college campus, which included a watershed. On the basis of their survey of resources—water, soil, trees, and so forth—and of a comprehensive recreation plan, the school received two different clean water grants (worth nearly $600,000) to build a model watershed. Also, in the summer of 1997, Grays Harbor Community College offered an institute (with ATE funding), organized as a learning community, for high school and community college instructors who wanted to use learning communities to develop natural resources programs. Later, when contacted by Samuelson, the teachers who had attended the institute expressed appreciation, and most reported significant classroom reforms.

TEAM TEACHING IN INTEGRATED PROGRAMS

Planning a fully integrated learning community may seem unsettling even if faculty members do not learn Greek or build watersheds. Many feel at sea, queasy about venturing from the safety of their syllabi.[9] Others may experience lightness of being. Having read and discussed many more books than they finally order, everyone on a team may feel overworked and frustrated. In the nick of time, the philosophy teacher decided he could develop ethical issues using *Crime and Punishment* and *The Poverty of Nations*. Then, the economics teacher wants every hour of class planned in advance, whereas the literature teacher thinks so much attention to detail is merely tedious. Yet they must reshape the curriculum, relying on their combined disciplinary knowledge and pedagogic know-how. Team members must also decide how to divide the labor of running a program. Who will take care of advertising; who will make up the book order? At Evergreen, team members sign a covenant that lists the responsibilities of each faculty member and describes how any disputes will be settled. Just how rewarding long planning sessions will be depends on the individuals, of course, and some teams simply do not work out. Planning sessions may be heady stuff, full of bang and shazam, insight and connections, and some snarl when disciplinary hackles rise. Or not.

Once a program is under way, newcomers may feel even queasier, deeply uncomfortable, teaching in front of other teachers. At the same time, for young or newly hired faculty members, learning communities can provide valuable models, mentors, and day-to-day support. They offer an extraordinary opportunity for discussing all the fascinating elements of a class in process, for interpreting, troubleshooting, second-guessing, enjoying, probing, rehashing, researching, rethinking, and revising. The most advantageous arrangement allows teaching teams a leisurely(!) lunch together each day or some time for conversation when the students have gone. Since teams tend to make the class itself a text to be explored, it is important to distinguish between nuts-and-bolts sessions and faculty seminar sessions so that the first doesn't crowd out the latter.

Even very experienced teachers get inspired while team teaching. Many have revolutionized their usual practices after a term in a learning community. Others have refined their techniques, picking up subtle things they have observed their colleagues do. It may be something simple, such as how to write things on the blackboard effectively rather than haphazardly or how to pace instruction in a computer lab. It may be something more complex like how to build effective workshops. Watching how another faculty member used groups to teach calculus prompted an Evergreen physics teacher to restructure an environmental issues program, formalizing group work and giving students problems so intellectually challenging that they needed others' help.

Teams also face the sobering fact that even hundreds of hours of reading, discussion, and planning before a program starts will not assure what happens. Team-taught interdisciplinary programs move on like breaking news. The literature teacher is not sure what the philosophy teacher will say in his lecture (or what questions the students will ask) that provokes response in the next day's literature presentation. Not everything can be prepared in advance of the actual unfolding of the program. It goes without saying that plenty of advance work is done, but skilled people leave some things undone because they know they must. Their careful plan says, "Tuesday, November 14, Ethics workshop—applying the models to *Crime and Punishment*," and sometime before the fourteenth someone (or more) must invent a workshop. In the light and dapples of early November, they may plan one different from anything they would have conceived in August.

By the end, even a carefully planned program may have become something quite different from what the team envisioned. It may change course abruptly in response to some national or international political event; it may change direction gradually as a result of an emphasis reoccurring in the seminars, the writing assignments, and the workshops. Old pros who are well aware that interesting things simply come up are less concerned when at the beginning they cannot quite see the end. They are willing to let the program launch without the destination crisply in focus. The sense of destination unknown occurs most often when a team decides to ignore the usual syllabi as much as possible and venture where the usual curriculum does not take them. They may pursue a theme or an issue without particular regard for what particular disciplines would have to say about it. Students may wonder just how to organize their notes. Is this history? One Evergreen faculty member calls these "adisciplinary" studies.[10] Other faculty members may wonder just how to escape the disciplines without being undisciplined and on just what methods and assumptions adisciplinary teachers base their work. Where is the taxonomy for the stuff that sprouts in the interdisciplinary spaces; and where the map of the adisciplinary wilds, and what of the status of knowledge there? Years after, students write to say what they are currently thinking.

Open-ended learning communities in which the subject itself as well as the means to pursue it are always in the process of becoming, of being constituted each week or day, are not for the undisciplined, unskilled, or faint of heart. It is extreme teaching, an extraordinary use of one's abilities in order to negotiate unforeseen terrain, handle the speed, and avoid disaster. An extremist learns about his limits, about the mountain and his equipment. But it is also a thrill to teach and learn—or ski—at the top of one's ability, intrepid with all one's training and expertise.

WASHINGTON CENTER

Faculty members at institutions in Washington State not only have the support of their immediate colleagues, but of intrepid colleagues around the state and across the country—thanks to a grassroots movement begun in 1984 when the academic deans, Barbara Leigh Smith at the Evergreen State College and Ronald Hamburg at Seattle Central Community College, agreed to a faculty exchange. The exchange initiated a statewide discussion of teaching and learning, formalized as the Washington Center for Improving the Quality of Undergraduate Education, now a consortium of two-year and four-year colleges, public and private, and the state's universities. A majority of the fifty-one member schools offers some part of the curriculum through interdisciplinary learning communities.

The inception of the Washington Center coincided with other important, often nationwide, teaching and learning initiatives in postsecondary education, and they, one after the other, focused the conversation among members of the consortium. Active and collaborative teaching and learning, assessment, minority student success, multicultural curriculum, and digital technology all have been part of the ongoing discussion among colleagues at schools in the Washington consortium. For fifteen years, the Washington Center has sponsored workshops, regional and national conferences, and annual planning retreats. For these, teachers arrived from across town, across the state, and across the country. Thanks in great part to the indefatigable Jean MacGregor, who was for many years the Center's Associate Director, very little innovation in postsecondary teaching and learning has escaped the notice of consortium members. The Center publishes a newsletter, maintains a Website (www.evergreen.edu/washcenter), and keeps adding to its library of books and articles on teaching, learning, and innovation in postsecondary education, including much written by staff and members of the consortium.[11]

Whatever the topic of the current workshop, conference, or retreat, it is difficult to exaggerate the pleasures of attending. Faculty members exchange ideas and thrive on each other's support. Further, because introducing interdisciplinary studies in any college requires the cooperation of administration and faculty, the Center routinely invites institutional teams so that administrators find themselves engaged by discussions of what works in the classroom, and faculty members contemplate the economics of instruction. Talking with teams from other schools, consortium members gain the long view, a vision of an educational enterprise reaching beyond their own classrooms, departments, and institutions.[12]

It is often after a Center conference (on a contact high) that a faculty member returns to campus eager to launch a learning community. He or she feels up to the task of finding colleagues to join in, of persuading an administrator to support the changes and ready the stage. Someone must contact the public relations officer and the academic advisors, make the case for learning communities, and enlist their help recruiting for the new program. Someone must make some posters, write a piece for the upcoming schedule, and set up a table to lure students during registration. These activities, this little revolution, may be transforming. In the development of learning communities, not only are some splendid teaching partnerships begun, but the extraordinary collegiality that learning communities engender schoolwide has changed the culture of education at several colleges. Within a teaching team, within an institution, and even among institutions nationwide, people involved in learning communities have a buoyant sense of shared enterprise. Even when a faculty member returns to the stand-alone classroom, work is never the same again.

CONCLUSION

The unprecedented gathering of the leaders of nations, the Millennium Summit of the United Nations, has made the front page of today's *New York Times*. Even in the face of long-standing animosities, they will discuss poverty, AIDS, genocide, hopes for peace, and other global issues and crises. Further into the *Times*, David Berreby reports on collaboration between social psychologists and neuroscientists. Psychologists studying emotions and group perceptions and neuroscientists scanning the brain are together improving our understanding of how people of one "race" categorize people of another. In another article, George Johnson reports on the invention of a hypothetical ultimate laptop, which processes information at the maximum possible speed before it becomes an informational black hole. "Work like this exemplifies a fruitful new convergence of theoretical physics, computer science, and mathematics," says Gregory Chaitin, a mathematics of information specialist at IBM; "Interdisciplinary research of this kind would have been unthinkable a few years ago" (qtd. in Johnson D9).

Beyond preparing students for life beyond college, learning communities result in improved GPA, retention, and student satisfaction (Gabelnick et al.; MacGregor; Matthews). A careful study conducted at William Rainey Harper Community College as well as a research study supported by the National Center for Teaching, Learning, and Assessment found that students' improvements were significantly greater for the more integrated varieties than for the lesser ones. Coordinated studies groups, for example, showed more positive change than the customized links, which in turn showed more positive change than their freshman interest groups (Tinto, Goodsell-Love and Russo).

Learning communities prepare students for the interdisciplinary age. It is to their advantage that faculty members at colleges and universities find the work satisfying.

NOTES

1. As described by Hill, the FLC also includes a "core course," a three-hour class held once a month in which each of the faculty members addresses the same theme or question, modeling the interdisciplinary approach.

2. Several articles in Levine discuss the roles of student advisors in these and other FIGs.

3. See Tokuno and Campbell for statistics on student retention and development.

4. The Interdisciplinary Writing Program at the University of Washington offers students in any one of several large content classes the chance to enroll in a

linked composition section. Typically, about 10 percent in a class of 200 opts for the link. The two teachers discuss the writing assignments, which usually support the disciplinary approach of the larger class.

5. Goodsell et al. is a good starting point and includes a bibliography as well as contacts for teachers who want to develop more active and collaborative classrooms.

6. See Tinto et al., another of many studies on the positive effects of learning communities on retention (and student development).

7. For a brief and useful discussion of the nuts and bolts of starting up, see Elliott and Decker.

8. Jones goes on, "Helping the students convert this reversal of priorities into consonant changes in attitudes, expectations and study habits is the seminar's prevailing responsibility. In a first-year program consisting of high-school graduates it can take upwards of the whole year for most of the students to make this conversion. Until the conversion occurs, nothing else that goes on much matters" (66).

9. A faculty member with deep convictions about the authority of her disciplinary knowledge may refuse interdisciplinary work altogether. For those willing but tentative, it can help to read the extensive literature on interdisciplinary teaching. At Miami of Ohio, William H. Newell offers a workshop for people who are about to join interdisciplinary programs to help them cross the boundaries. See Newell and Downes, Armstrong, Strommer, and Evenbeck et al.

10. For thoughtful discussion of the distinctions among disciplinary, multidisciplinary, transdisciplinary, and adisciplinary approaches, see Newell and Green.

11. For a key book on learning communities, see Gabelnick et al. A new edition is forthcoming. The Center library also includes many pamphlet resources for teachers undertaking seminars.

12. With support from the PEW Charitable Trust, Jean MacGregor has been working on a national learning community project to develop connections among institutions in other parts of the country. Other centers have been established, e.g., the California Learning Community Consortium (*www.learningcommunity. org/*) supports learning community efforts in schools at all levels in the state. It is located at the Hutchins Center (www.sonoma.edu/hutchins) at the Hutchins School of Liberal Arts at Sonoma State University. Delta College in Michigan in conjunction with William Rainey Harper College is also building a network.

WORKS CITED

Astin, Alexander W. *What Matters in College: Four Critical Years Revisited.* San Francisco: Jossey-Bass, 1993.

Bereby, David. "How, But Not Why, the Brain Distinguished Race." *The New York Times* 5 September 2000: D3.

Boyer Commision on Educating Undergraduates in the Research University. *Reinventing Undergraduate Education: A Blueprint for America's Research Universities.* Stony Brook: State University of New York at Stony Brook, 1998.

Dewey, John. *Experience and Education.* London: Collier Books.

———. *My Pedagogic Creed.* New York: E. L. Kellogg, 1897.

Elliott, Jeanine L., and Emily Decker. "Garnering the Fundamental Resources for Learning Communities." *Learning Communities: New Structures, New Partnerships for Learning.* Ed. Jodi H. Levine. Monograph No. 26. Columbia: University of South Carolina, National Resource Center for the First-Year Experience and Students in Transition, 1999. 19–28.

Evenbeck, Scott E., Barbara Jackson, and John McGrew. "Faculty Development in Learning Communities: The Role of Reflection and Reframing." *Learning Communities: New Structures, New Partnerships for Learning.* Ed. Jodi H. Levine. Monograph No. 26. Columbia: University of South Carolina, National Resource Center for the First-Year Experience and Students in Transition, 1999. 51–58.

Finley, Nancy J. "Meeting Expectations by Making New Connections: Curricular Reform at Seattle Central." *Educational Record: The Magazine of Higher Education* 71, no. 4 (Fall 1990): 50–53.

Gabelnick, Faith, Jean MacGregor, Roberta S. Matthews, and Barbara Leigh Smith. "Learning Communities: Building Connections Among Disciplines, Students, and Faculty." *New Directions in Teaching and Learning,* No. 41. San Francisco: Jossey-Bass, 1990.

Goodsell, Anne, Michelle Maher, and Vincent Tinto, with Barbara Leigh Smith and Jean MacGregor. *Collaborative Learning: A Sourcebook for Higher Education.* University Park, PA: National Center on Postsecondary Teaching, Learning, and Assessment, 1992.

Hill, Patrick J. "Communities of Learners: Curriculum as the Infrastructure of Academic Communities." *Opposition to the Core Curriculum: Alternative Models of Undergraduate Education.* Eds. James W. Hall and Barbara Kevles. Westport, CT: Greenwood Press, 1982. 107–33.

———. "The Rationale for Learning Communities." Paper presented at the Inaugural Conference of the Washington Center for Improving the Quality of Undergraduate Education, Olympia, WA, 1985.

Johnson, George. "The Ultimate Apocalyptic Laptop." *The New York Times* 5 September 2000: D1+.

Jones, Richard. *Experiment at Evergreen.* Cambridge, MA: Schenkman, 1981.

Levine, Jodi H., ed. *Learning Communities: New Structures, New Partnerships for Learning.* Monograph No. 26. Columbia: University of South Carolina, National Resource Center for the First-Year Experience and Students in Transition, 1999.

MacGregor, Jean. "What Differences Do Learning Communities Make?" *Washington Center News* 6, no. 1 (Fall 1991): 4–9.

Matthews, Roberta S. "Learning Communities in the Community College." *AACJC Journal* (October/November 1986): 44–47.

Meiklejohn, Alexander. *The Experimental College*. New York: Harper and Row, 1932.

Newell, William H., and William J. Green. "Defining and Teaching Interdisciplinary Studies." *Improving College and University Teaching* 30, no. 1 (Winter 1982): 23–30.

———, and Peg Downes. "Overcoming Disciplinary Boundaries." *Liberal Education* 80, no. 1 (Winter 1994): 24–26.

Strommer, Diane W. "Teaching and Learning in a Learning Community." *Learning Communities: New Structures, New Partnerships for Learning*. Ed. Jodi H. Levine. Monograph No. 26. Columbia: University of South Carolina, National Resource Center for the First-Year Experience and Students in Transition, 1999. 39–49.

Tinto, Vincent, Anne Goodsell-Love, and Pat Russo. "Building Learning Communities for New College Students: A Summary of Research Finding of the Collaborative Learning Project," Syracuse University, National Center on Postsecondary Teaching, Learning and Assessment, 1994.

Tokuno, Kenneth A., and Frederick L. Campbell. "Freshman Interest Groups at the University of Washington: Effects on Retention and Scholarship." *Journal of the Freshman Year Experience* 5 (1992): 7–22.

Tussman, Joseph. *Experiment at Berkeley*. London: Oxford University Press, 1969.

CHAPTER 5

"Good and Ill Together"

Interdisciplinary Teaching with Technology

Robert M. Bender

INTRODUCTION

That we are in the midst of a massive technological transformation is undisputed. Like it or not, technology is transforming the landscape of higher education. In "Changing Landscape: From Cottage Monopoly to Competitive Industry," Barry Munitz comments:

> We are suddenly confronting an extraordinary range of full- and part-time, on-site and at-distance, in-person and machine-driven teaching and learning experiences that constitute an array of quality training previously unknown anywhere in the world. (12)

Some may object to the reference here to "training," but clearly an increased emphasis on knowledge useful for specific purposes is widespread in higher education. Moreover, it is clear that the shift toward technology has already occurred. The "new" technologies, as they were called just a few years ago, have had a profound impact on faculty, the "producers" in the "knowledge industry," as well on "consumers," empowering students as never before. *Dancing with the Devil: Information Technology and the New Competition in Higher Education*, an important collection of essays that describes many of the changes that *already have occurred* and speculates on what lies ahead, offers some useful information.

This technological transformation not only has the power to challenge and change notions of disciplinarity and interdisciplinarity, but it already has altered the way integrative work is conducted. For example, the Human Genome Project could not be carried out without extensive use of computers. Similarly, the Perseus project at Tufts University (http://www.perseus. tufts.edu/) has brought together a range of resources for the study of antiquity that few students and researchers could have hoped to examine even in the recent past. There is, however, a curious omission of any discussion of computer technology in the literature of interdisciplinary study. The recent collection, *Interdisciplinarity: Essays from the Literature*, is an interesting case in point. In his excellent review essay, "Professionalizing Interdisciplinarity," William H. Newell makes no mention of information technology, nor is there any reference to technology or its use in the entire volume (529–63).

What makes this omission particularly odd is that many interdisciplinary practitioners and scholars in fields such as Women's Studies and Peace Studies are doing their integrative work with technology and recording their findings online. The Center for Women and Information Technology at the University of Maryland, Baltimore Country (http://www.umbc. edu/cwit/), the Virginia Tech Women's Studies Directory of Online Learning Modules (http://www.cis.vt.edu/ws/wsmodules/moduledirectory. html), and the Women's International Electronic University (http://www. wvu.edu/~womnsu/) are just three sites that support interdisciplinary inquiry and direct people to a variety of resources. INCORE, a conflict resolution program housed at the University of Ulster, maintains an active Website (http://www. incore.ulst.ac.uk/) for the dissemination of its interdisciplinary research and additionally offers an "International Information WWW Service on Conflict Resolution and Ethnicity." Yet in otherwise excellent essays in *Interdisciplinarity*, written in the mid-1990s and late 1980s respectively, by Julie Thompson Klein on "Women," and by Richard Ned Lebow on "Interdisciplinary Research and the Future of Peace and Security Studies," there is no mention of the work being done with information technology.

Despite its glaring omission in interdisciplinary professional literature, technology can advance the best hallmarks of interdisciplinary teaching. Technology can be useful in achieving the educational outcomes so often cited in the interdisciplinary literature:

> an appreciation for perspectives other than one's own; an ability to evaluate the testimony of experts; tolerance of ambiguity; increased sensitivity to ethical issues; an ability to synthesize or integrate; enlarged perspectives or horizons, more creative, original, or unconven-

tional thinking; increased humility or listening skills; and sensitivity
to disciplinary, political, or religious bias. (Newell, "Designing" 35)

Indeed, the use of technology is conspicuous in the practice of many of the
approaches to teaching discussed in this book—collaborative learning,
lifelong learning, performance-based teaching, learning communities,
team teaching, writing-intensive teaching, and inquiry-based teaching.
Technology alone, of course, will not assure success in any of these endeavors, nor is the use of technology in teaching without difficulties. To take a
cue from Shakespeare, "The web of our life is of a mingled yarn, good and ill
together" (*AWW* 4.3).

The key point that must be made about the use of technology in teaching is that pedagogy is more important than any of the technical problems
that have to be addressed. Technology alone never will improve teaching.
It is all too easy, for example, to get caught up in software that creates busy
Web pages. Rather than incorporate technology for its glitz and glamour,
instructors should use it to facilitate their learning objectives for students.
The first question to ask is: What is it I want students to learn during my
course, and what do I want them to take away with them at the end of the
course? Once these objectives are identified, then it is time to determine
the best means to achieve these goals. Some of the goals may best be
achieved through computer technology; others may not necessitate the use
of technology at all. This chapter will explore some of the ways I have integrated technology into my classes in order to advance interdisciplinary
learning. Before considering specific uses of technology, however, there are
some insights to be gained by exploring why technology must be addressed
in conversations about pedagogy.

Among the growing number of studies that have examined online education in a balanced way, a report based on a year-long seminar conducted
at the University of Illinois in 1998–1999 is one of the most impressive.
Faculty members from all three campuses, at Chicago, Springfield, and Ur-
bana-Champaign, were brought together to discuss technology and teaching. Organizers of the seminar intentionally sought a balance of faculty
who were "skeptical" and "converted," but all the faculty members were interested in the improvement of pedagogy. "Online teaching and learning,"
the authors of the report observed, "occurs in a range of modes . . . : 1) sup-
plemental or adjunct, 2) mixed, and 3) wholly online" ("Teaching at an
Internet Distance"). Their conclusions offer insight into the learning experience as well as some cautionary thoughts about the feasibility of administrative takeover:

> The seminar concluded that online teaching and learning can be done
> with high quality if new approaches are employed which compensate

for the limitations of technology, and if professors make the effort to create and maintain the human touch of attentiveness to their students. Online courses may be appropriate for both traditional and non-traditional students; they can be used in undergraduate education, continuing education, and in advanced degree programs. The seminar participants thought, however, that it would be inappropriate to provide an entire undergraduate degree program online. Participants concluded that the ongoing physical and even emotional interaction between teacher and students, and among students themselves, was an integral part of a university education.

Because high quality online teaching is time and labor intensive, it is not likely to be the income source envisioned by some administrators. Teaching the same number of students online at the same level of quality as in the classroom requires more time and money. ("Teaching at an Internet Distance")

There are skeptics, of course, who tend to see administrative plots in the infusion of technology into higher education. David F. Noble has launched a major attack. In "Digital Diploma Mills: The Automation of Higher Education," he claims,

[U]niversities are not simply undergoing a technological transformation. Beneath that change, and camouflaged by it, lies another: the commercialization of higher education. For here as elsewhere technology is but a vehicle and a disarming disguise.

The problems Noble identifies here, and elsewhere, were with us long before the arrival of technology. Richard Lanham brilliantly defines this attack on technology as part of one of the great debates of Western culture—the "rhetorical/philosophical distinction" that involved opposing "theories of motive, human selfhood, and human society":

When people talk about the baneful influence of electronic technology, often they are really talking about something quite different, about a cultural debate technology has reintroduced. The deepest debates . . . about the computer . . . are usually variations on the long-standing debate between the rhetoricians and the philosophers. Since the premises of the two camps differ radically, the contenders always talk past each other. (203)

Noble would remedy the problems of higher education by doing away with computers—not a very likely prospect. Lanham instead would ask us to understand the ways in which computers can help with education. The focus, then, is not on the technology for its own sake, but rather on the ways in which we can use technology to enhance teaching and achieve integrative goals.

BEGINNING STEPS

Some form of technology presently is being used in untold thousands of courses. In June 2000, WebCT, one of the largest providers of course management software, reported that their program alone accounted for more than six million student accounts at over 1,400 institutions in fifty-five countries. The basic classroom formats for the use of technology include:

1. Courses in which students access computer technology outside of class (using bulletin boards, electronic discussion lists, e-mail, CD-ROMS containing lectures, or other supporting material, most recently Video on Demand, whereby students are able to access video files on a server).
2. Courses in which some computer technology is brought into the classroom (such as PowerPoint, screens that display the course Website or other sites on the Internet).
3. Web-based courses with face-to-face interaction (taught in computer labs or in a more "traditional" classroom with students using laptops connected to a wireless network).
4. Distance learning courses (using all these technologies plus two-way video or teleconferencing and other kinds of Web-based support).

The sheer variety of practices now in use can be dismaying to the uninitiated as well as the initiated, to the neophyte as well as the "early adopter." What is clear is that to integrate technology successfully into teaching, faculty must learn to incorporate it in comfortable ways that advance their pedagogy and are not guided by technical concerns. My intent in this chapter is not to catalog all the ways in which technology is being or can be used to enhance student learning, but rather to present a number of strategies that I have used to address specific interdisciplinary concerns in teaching.

In this discussion, I also want to stress a sense of process. More than a decade ago, Apple Computer, Inc. began the Apple Classrooms of Tomorrow (ACOT) project "with the assumption that computers might change the classroom" ("Teacher-Centered"). Apple provided a number of K–12 schools with computers for every student in selected classes for classroom and home use and conducted faculty workshops to train the participating teachers. There was extensive assessment of this project, including a great deal of classroom observation by a variety of visitors. It soon became clear that change did not come easily:

> When we met with ACOT teachers they would describe what they were doing in their classrooms and what they anticipated they would do next. However, when we visited their classrooms, what we observed was often very different from what they had described. There seemed to be a gap between the teachers' espoused beliefs about their practice and their practice in action. What we came to realize is that change occurs differently for each teacher.

On the basis of their research, Apple was able to identify a number of stages that "teachers went through as they integrated the computer into their practice," including Entry, Adoption, Adaptation, Appropriation, Invention. *Entry* is that early stage in which a teacher simply dives into something new. *Adoption* carries with it the sense of a more conscious use of a particular program, shortly after which a seasoned teacher finds that some *Adaptation*, or a personalized use of an application, is necessary. In this process, there may be some *Appropriation* of work that others have done. Ultimately, the instruction arrives at the stage of *Invention*, in which the use of technology seamlessly becomes part of one's approach to teaching; in effect, its use becomes naturalized. This is not necessarily a linear process; nor is it ever really complete. Given the speed with which technology is changing, along with present concerns for innovation in education, we all are likely to repeat this process again and again, jumping in each time at various stages.

In many ways, the process by which faculty move into interdisciplinary research and teaching mirrors the process by which we become comfortable with technology. Julie Thompson Klein observes, "Interdisciplinarity is neither a subject matter nor a body of content. It is a process for achieving an integrative synthesis, a process that usually begins with a problem, question, topic, or issue" (*Interdisciplinarity* 108). Klein goes on to comment "there is no absolute linear progression," and then defines a number of steps in the process:

1a. *defining* the problem [question, topic, issue];
  b. *determining* all knowledge needs, including appropriate disciplinary representatives and consultants, as well as relevant models, traditions, and literatures;
  c. *developing* an integrative framework and appropriate questions to be investigated;
2a. *specifying* particular studies to be undertaken;
  b. *engaging* in "role negotiation" (in teamwork);
  c. *gathering* all current knowledge and *searching* for new information;

d. *resolving* disciplinary conflicts by working toward a common vocabulary (and focusing on reciprocal learning in teamwork);

e. *building* and *maintaining* communication through integrative techniques;

3a. *collating* all contributions and evaluating their adequacy, relevancy, and adaptability;

b. *integrating* the individual pieces to determine a pattern of mutual relatedness and relevancy;

c. *confirming* or *disconfirming* the proposed solution [answer]; and

d. *deciding* about future management or disposition of the task/project/patient/curriculum. (188–89)

We might conclude that using technology for teaching is yet another process for exploring and engaging in integrative work in the classroom. Not only should instructors think of technology as a tool for investigating interdisciplinary problems (e.g., technology seems especially relevant for the 2c and 3a steps), but they might also consider using some of the relevant steps in the process of integration that Klein outlines as a means of incorporating technology into their teaching. In other words, define the problem as how to use technology in the classroom (step 1a) and then follow all of the other necessary steps to address it.

What follows is a description of how I addressed the problem of using technology in teaching. In particular, I discuss my initial use of a listserv to expand class discussion, more extensive experiments with a variety of pedagogical approaches to problem solving, and finally the creation of a paperless, Web-based classroom in which student-centered learning achieved a number of integrative goals. In every instance, I will explore ways in which face-to-face teaching can be enhanced with the use of technology, as well as a number of challenges and concerns this use of technology poses for interdisciplinary teaching.

SPECIFIC TECHNOLOGIES

Using a Listserv to Extend Discussion

My entry point: In the fall of 1993, I first used an electronic discussion list for a course in modern drama with the rather vague notion that it might enhance discussion. Having become involved with a number of professional discussion lists in the late 1980s, I assumed that setting up a class discussion list might be rewarding and, in any event, would lead to some heated debate. I provided no instruction for the use of e-mail and gave no specific e-mail assignments. Without prior notice in the course schedule, I announced on the first day of class that all students would be required to post messages to an electronic discussion list and provided them with a number of user-friendly print documents. Then I asked them to log on and submit a brief autobiographical statement. I also mentioned something about our subsequently being able to discuss performative aspects of self in class and online as a way of exploring drama. It was encouraging, and, on reflection, more than a little surprising that more than half the students followed my directives over the next two days. Of course, nearly half of the twenty-four students did not. I tried to remedy this problem by scheduling sessions in a computer lab for the second week of school.

Eventually, just seventeen of the original twenty-four students managed to post the autobiographical note to the discussion list. After a couple of weeks, I no longer hounded the others to do so. At this point, only twenty-one students remained in the course, about half of whom remained incredibly active participants in the online component. When, about midway through the course, I showed the students how to review the list to discover how many messages each subscriber had sent, many of them increased their participation in hopes of sending the most messages, despite my never having encouraged such competition. Even this partial participation had an enormous impact on the conduct of the class. Students who were sending messages regularly arrived in class ready to continue their intense, online discussion of a particular play or of a particular approach to that play. I would allow them to continue their debate for a short while, usually until one of the students not engaged in the online discussion would ask what was going on. Then one of the list participants would provide some exposition, which often enough would be "corrected" by another of the online participants.

What impressed me most was the range of knowledge these students brought to their study of modern drama. Comparisons with film, of course, were omnipresent, but having taught this course over a period of ten years, I had never found students so eager to discuss other vantage points. A reading of Synge's *Riders to the Sea* provoked an extensive discussion of ethnography; Brecht's *Life of Galileo* raised political issues that carried over to the discussion of plays by Shepard and Fugard and sparked serious questions about Beckett's apparent disregard of politics. In their solitude in front of a computer, students were far more willing than they were in class to offer their own opinions and apply knowledge they had acquired elsewhere to the study of drama. I also was impressed with how carefully many of them composed their messages. In terms of the integrative process as defined by Klein, these students were "*engaging* in 'role negotiation,'" with the result that they began "*integrating* the individual pieces to determine a pattern of mutual relatedness and relevancy" (*Interdisciplinarity* 189).

Students also appeared more willing to offer personal information and insights to their classmates. Early on, a twenty-eight-year-old woman, who considered herself much older than the others, announced in her autobiographical note that she was a lesbian and had been wanting to make this known to her classmates for years. Her comments prompted a few students in their mid-twenties, and not yet in graduate school, to reveal their age. It also helped to focus attention on sexual orientation, a central issue in many modern plays.

From this first experience, I learned a number of important lessons: instruction in computer use is essential, and the work must "count." My conclusion (then and since) is that the problems relating to teaching with technology are pedagogical, not technical. Providing basic instruction in the use of technology is important, but still more important is for students to understand the ways in which technology can enhance their learning experience and facilitate their achievement of clearly defined course goals. On reflection, it was also clear to me that the listserv had helped to achieve a number of interdisciplinary goals: the students certainly were exposed to perspectives other than their own (whether or not they gained an appreciation for those perspectives was unclear); they certainly cultivated a sensitivity to gender issues; and many learned to listen to—or at least read—the opinions of others more thoughtfully than they had in other courses. In discussing "Models of the [Integrative] Process," Klein notes that students often are able to move beyond "clarification" to "resolution," by focusing

> on a more thorough integration of the different perspectives identified by definitions of "salient concepts" in the participating disciplines. Students can challenge their conclusions by combining inputs from more than one discipline and working towards a more comprehensive understanding of the problem at hand. (*Interdisciplinarity* 191–92)

I believe that, through the listserv, students were able to move toward combining different viewpoints and arriving at a fuller understanding of the course material.

Using a Listserv to Enhance Journal Writing

Journal writing is a useful tool for courses in which students do a substantial amount of writing. Journals provide an unstructured space in which students can record their "thoughts," engage in pre-writing, and explore topics of interest without having to pay attention to rules of grammar, spelling, and all those "things" that they claim as impediments to their "free expression." In courses designed to empower students, journals can also be useful for raising consciousness. The steps in the integrative process all require a certain amount of self-awareness, an ability to make conscious choices, and an ability to reflect on the process. As Klein and Newell observe in "Advancing Interdisciplinary Studies," "Achieving synthesis requires proactive attention to process," which is precisely what journal writing should achieve (15).

The usual problem with journals is that many students consider them to be "private space" and are reluctant to share their thoughts with others. My previous attempts to de-center journal writing had proved cumbersome and not particularly successful. I had asked students to keep their journals in loose-leaf notebooks, and then transfer the notebooks from one writer to another. I also required students in a number of interdisciplinary studies courses to keep a paper journal "together," exchanging their writing on a weekly basis. Because this process was so cumbersome, I asked another class to record their entries on a diskette that could be passed from one student to another. This latter attempt was a short-lived disaster. Although my students had not mastered diskette management, they were all too adept at spreading viruses, leaving diskettes to melt in overheated cars, and simply misplacing them.

My success in using the listserv in the drama course to provide a more integrative experience for at least some of the students prompted me to use the same technology for journal writing in an interdisciplinary studies senior seminar in winter 1992. The seminar was originally designed as a vehicle for students to complete a required capstone project. In addition, I had traditionally focused the course on gender studies and had always asked them to keep a journal in which they recorded observations about gender differences. Although the course had always been a success, I encountered the usual difficulties with the journals; students wrote for and to me rather than for themselves and each other.

In 1994, I decided to have the students use the listserv to keep a collective "electronic" journal (see Bender 38–43). Judging from student comments, this project was a great success. Even in a small class—just fifteen students—there are always students who are reluctant to speak aloud. Given the opportunity to "speak" at a keyboard, many found a "voice." A series of messages posted on a single day illustrates how students were able to achieve a sense of community.

The class met on Tuesdays and Thursdays. The discussion list often served to bridge the long separation the students experienced from one week to the next. The particular day I've chosen for this illustration was a Thursday, and it was filled with unexpected electronic "events." On the

Wednesday night before, when I was posting some comments to the class journal from home, I received a notice that the mainframe disk on which the listserv was maintained was full and that my note had been "suspended." I notified the appropriate people at the computing office but suspected nothing would be done until morning. At my office, before class, I once more tried to access the list and encountered a message from a student who had had the same experience. When I arrived in class at 10:15, several students were already aware that something was wrong with the list. As the discussion ensued, there were many signs of stress; and some students commented that having "bonded," if not with each other, then with the "list," they felt bereft. On this day, students were eager to discuss economics and age in regard to the gender-related issues of prostitution and marriage. There were some hurt feelings that none of us was fully aware of in class.

The discussion continued long after the class ended at 11:30. At about 2:30 in the afternoon, one student contributed to the ongoing online discussion of prostitution. Next came a message that had been sent the night before, with some strong language directed against the software for having "suspended" the note. About 10:30 in the evening, another student expressed her rage at some comments made in class:

> I would like to know where the hell we get off telling other people what is right or wrong to do in a relationship concerning age. I can understand maybe if someone was being wronged somehow, especially if it is a friend. But how can we just globally say "couples should be within four or five year age difference" or "the man should be older than the woman" just because we think that's the way it should be and everyone should abide by our rules? Not wanting to get involved in such a relationship is one thing. Declaring it WRONG is quite another. (Pardon my defensiveness—my fiancé is twelve years my senior and we have the best relationship I've ever had or known about.)

A short while later, another student, usually a peacemaker in class, responded rather obliquely to this student's distress:

> I can't type, hate computers, and never find many electronic things to be very user-friendly in my case. However, I like email. It has been a great way to communicate for a classroom setting. I have learned more because this opens up the class in a less limited and more open environment. The trouble I have encountered with email and using the computer has been worth it.

Finally, at nearly midnight, another student took the time to analyze his experience with e-mail and the electronic list:

> Funny how the words fly when we get on email. We have not been taught in class to speak our minds. We listen, we nod, we shake our head, we zone out. In this format we feel liberated to say what we want, edited text which we can shape and refine (or not) before we release it for mass consumption. No one interrupts us while we talk. We can't see other people grimace in pain at our words. I have often stopped mid-sentence to address an expression on someone's face, only to lose my original train of thought afterwards. This medium allows me to precisely spit out my half-baked ideas and to be certain that everyone gets a chance to read my thoughts, and a chance for me to read others.

The majority of the students in this class did what was required; they posted something to the list at least twice a week. Many did much more. There also were some interesting surprises in this electronic space. In early April, when the students were beginning to panic about completing their capstone projects, and were manifesting symptoms of "senioritis," which became a topic on the list, something quite wonderful happened. I received a notice that someone in Poland wanted to subscribe to the list. It is not at all unusual to receive such requests to join a list. My response always has been to write to the would-be subscriber to see whether I might determine his or her motive. In this case, when I asked the students if they would like to have someone from Poland on the list, they all were very enthusiastic. I asked our respondent to post a brief autobiography to the list as his first entry, exactly as the students had done at the start of the semester. His reply was quite charming. It turned out he was a physician and a philosopher living in central Poland and had a number of interdisciplinary interests. He ended up contributing to the students' learning in the course. In response to a discussion of individual and group identity, for example, he commented that the narcissism of personal identity was not such a serious problem in his country.

With a little planning (e.g., giving prior notice of the use of the listserv and providing time at the start of the semester for instruction in the use of the technology) and assigning 15 percent of the final grade to this online activity, the electronic journal was a great success in the seminar. Over the 114–day semester, the fifteen students submitted a total of 470 messages, an average of four messages per day. This period included a week of spring vacation, weekends, exam periods, and other "down" time for the students. I did not count the number of lines they wrote in this writing-intensive course, but, as one student said, "I never thought I'd write so much in a single course."

Clearly, at this point, my use of technology had shifted from Entry and Adoption toward Adaptation; with the listserv, I was able for the first time to create a truly student-centered, journal-writing experience. The occasional unreliability or unavailability of the network was in many ways a useful "real-life" experience for the students, something they had to learn to accept. In terms of interdisciplinary goals, students not only gained perspectives other than their own, but they achieved sensitivity to a number of controversial issues and a greater tolerance of ambiguity. Contact with the visitor from Poland clearly enlarged their perspectives, and there is no question most of the students in the class gained a sense of humility, which, I believe, helped them to survive their last semester in college and to integrate the differing experiences embedded in their interdisciplinary majors. Many of them gained the "cognitive decentering," defined as "the intellectual capacity to move beyond a single center or focus (especially the innate tendencies toward egocentrism and ethnocentrism)," necessary to understand and appreciate varying perspectives (Hursh, Haas, and Moore 37).

Electronic Submission and Peer Reviewing

After using a listserv in a number of courses, I came to understand that computer-mediated communication has the power to transform the way students write, to help them understand the ways in which writing relates to learning, and to engage them in integrative ways of thinking. In the Preface to *The Electronic Word*, Richard Lanham comments:

> Electronic text creates not only a new writing space but a new educational space as well. Not only the humanities curriculum, but school and university structures, administrative and physical, are affected at every point, as of course is the whole cultural repository and information system we call a library. In the university world, it is disciplinarity and its departmental shadow that will be most transformed. (xii)

In a sense, writing with computers frees students from textuality, which has been defined in terms of specific disciplines. Lanham's argument is that changing the "writing space" inevitably leads to other systemic changes. His later observations on the nature of "print" invite us to look at books, and learning, in a very different way:

> We have come to regard print as so inevitable that we have ceased to notice its extraordinary stylization. Print, after all, is a trickery too, not a historical inevitability. Print represents a decision of severe abstraction and subtraction. All non-linear signals are filtered out; color is banned for serious texts; typographical constants are rigorously enforced; sound is proscribed; even the tactility of visual elaboration is outlawed. Print is an act of perpetual self-denial, and electronic text

makes us aware of that self-denial at every point and in all the ways
print is at pains to conceal. (73–74)

Electronic text, thus, is more integrative than traditional print because it
involves more of the senses (sound, color) and can foster nonlinear and linear forms of thinking. It also has the capacity to make the "reader" an active
participant in the text by setting up deliberate forms of interaction. The
modern drama course in which I first used a listserv as well as the senior
seminar were writing-intensive courses in which students were required to
engage in peer reviews of early drafts of each other's work. Given my successes with electronic discussion and journal writing, it occurred to me the
next step might be to try electronic submission, having students submit
their writing online instead of on paper. Where better to attempt this than
in a lower division course with newly arrived students who I assumed might
have had greater computer contact than seasoned juniors and seniors?

For many years, I taught large Shakespeare lecture classes with great success. Part of my success depended on the use of multimedia, slides and
tapes, and, later, clips from video productions of the plays. I also allowed
students to do a variety of multimedia projects as well as more traditional
essays. In fall 1994, I proposed teaching a large Shakespeare lecture course
for up to 350 students, in which a select number, no more than sixty, would
be able to enroll in sections designated as writing-intensive. Students in
the writing-intensive sections would do their writing online. Teaching two
different sets of students would provide a good basis for documenting my
experiments with electronic technologies because it would offer me the opportunity for a controlled comparison between those students who worked
electronically and those who participated in the "traditional" way.

With the help of graduate teaching assistants, we planned to pay special
attention to the students enrolled in the electronically based sections, offering voluntary sessions in a computer lab where we would help them
learn how to submit their work. I and the TAs also planned to return their
papers to them electronically. The Campus Writing Board provided reluctant approval for this experiment, and we had no idea how many students
might enroll. Throughout the spring and summer registration periods, we
watched enrollment with interest and disappointment. At no point had
more than sixty-five students signed up for the course, and no more than a
handful for what we assumed were the writing-intensive sections. Eventually, the Director of Undergraduate Studies in the English Department
noticed that not just the computer sections but the entire course had been
designated writing-intensive (no doubt the result of a mistaken keystroke
when the course was entered on the computer for registration), and that
helped to explain the low enrollment.

At the start of the semester, we were faced with a difficult situation. All the students who enrolled in the course assumed it carried writing-intensive credit, and many were taking the course primarily to fulfill that requirement. Only a dozen students had enrolled in the computer sections. We explained the situation, telling all the students that those specifically enrolled in the computer sections would be expected to submit their work electronically; the others could avail themselves of this option at their own discretion. During the course of the semester, some twenty students, at various times, engaged in online submission.

To handle online submission, those of us involved with the Writing with Computers project convinced Campus Computing to obtain a site license for Eudora so that students could easily submit their essays as attachments to an e-mail message. For the most part, this system worked quite well, except that we had some difficulty "translating" essays when students used an alternative word processor. We would return the successfully transmitted essays with our comments, usually in bold or italic type, bracketed into the students' text. One advantage of electronic submission was that we were able to return those essays more quickly than those submitted on paper because we didn't have to wait until the next class period. This facilitated the revision process considerably. Some students even engaged in a bit of invention in their editorial comments and introduced colored type into their essays. Neither I nor my assistants in the course had realized that most word processors allowed for this feature. We quickly learned that making comments on their essays in color was better than using bold or italic type. Students who engaged in electronic submission did a great deal more revision than the other students. Typically, "revision" for many students means responding to an instructor's comments on spelling, punctuation, and grammar. The students in the special section, by contrast, seemed more concerned with honing their argument or reorganizing the structure of an essay. Ultimately, however, there were too few students in this class on whom to base any conclusions of the differences between traditional and online submission.

Having found electronic submission a relatively easy matter, I asked students in my next course to engage in an online peer-review process by having them send the original drafts and return the reviewed drafts as attachments. Prior to this course, I had asked students to engage in peer reviews, but the exchange of writing was always done on paper, in a two-part process—actually making comments on another student's draft as well as responding on a separate sheet to a number of review questions. Unlike the previous Shakespeare lecture, this class, once more on modern drama, was conducted in a computer classroom. Working side by side in front of their computers, students could easily manage this procedure and were delighted to be able to make—and receive—comments in color, boldface, or italic type. Still, this process remained rather cumbersome, and not all students would complete their reviews quickly enough to allow sufficient time for revision.

In this class, I continued to use a listserv to extend and enhance discussion beyond the classroom. The technology was very simple: essentially I was asking student to use e-mail to fulfill various assignments in a course. Online discussion continued to provide opportunities for students to comment outside class. Many students found this asynchronous approach to discussion useful in giving them a "space" to participate. They learned "role negotiation" and the way in which learning is achieved by means of teamwork (Klein, *Interdisciplinarity* 189). My own discovery was that, whereas some of the students had moved into appropriation and invention, I had not fully relinquished my role as the "leader" in class. In terms of interdisciplinary goals, I may have led some of them to creative, original, even unconventional thinking by encouraging them to use the technology to work together, but I myself had not moved very far in these directions. Much as I was able to create some student interactivity, I still was very much involved with the "delivery of instruction," and not with fully de-centering the classroom. I was still "suffering" from coverage anxiety.

The Web-Based, Paperless Classroom and Lecture Hall

In the fall of 1995, I offered my first Web-based course, "Survey of British Literature: Beginnings to 1784." One of the most problematic courses in any English curriculum, the typical survey, usually conducted over two semesters, attempts to "cover" the tradition of British literature from the earliest beginnings to the present. In traditional survey courses, students are asked to read a dismaying amount of material, from complete texts to "snippets" culled from lesser works. Instructors do most of the talking, while students remain passive listeners. Through a Web-based, paperless classroom, I discovered how to make students and their learning the central focus. The Website provided an interactive environment where students could engage in peer group work and in-depth discussion of particular texts. Asynchronous discussion—fostered by an electronic "space" for anytime, anywhere interaction—can be integrated easily with assignments and classroom activities to create a greater focus on the issues of literary theory and canon formation. A Website also facilitated easy access to online sources of information related, for example, to the art and history of the period, allowing for a good deal of interdisciplinary discussion and synthesis on the part of the students. Providing links at the Website to other sites prompted the discovery of information from a variety of disciplines; working with some of those sites in class encouraged many students to synthesize this information.

Most significantly, the Website created space for an archive of student work (discussion comments, drafts, reviews, and revisions) where issues could be revisited. The archives offered insight into the very "purpose" of the humanities to maintain an historical continuum of human learning and discourse. These students were not all English majors. Indeed, many took the course to fulfill the requirement for a second writing-intensive course as well as to meet the distribution requirement for humanities. Their messages to the discussion list as well as their essays revealed distinctly different disciplinary perspectives. I found it much easier to engage students in online discussion, peer reviews, and electronic submission of their polished work precisely because the Website remained available throughout the course. This archiving involved them with course material and with each other in ways that enhanced their learning. It also became clear that computer-mediated writing and discussion were preparing them for a world in which the electronic transmission of information is now routine. Students returned again and again to past discussions on the electronic list as well as to their submitted essays, all of which were available for them as archives. One of the techniques I developed to make sure they looked at one another's work was to ask that they include comments from fellow students in their longer essays. They were required to deal with their peer's writing as they would with any other source, evaluating and incorporating their words and ideas into their own writing. In this way, students learned to evaluate each other's ideas as if they were "the testimony of experts."

Putting students in touch with one another's writing proved to be an invigorating process. For many years, I have asked students in survey courses to write their own Elizabethan sonnet and ten lines of heroic couplets as a way of gaining appreciation for the poetry of earlier periods. Having them write this verse with the knowledge that all their classmates would see their work made them take these no-credit assignments more seriously. Their verse archives also provided them with a good deal of entertainment. Students, in my experience, came to understand their own writing and thinking processes much better in this setting. They also learned to value their work in a new way; they literally became producers of text as well as consumers. A student in one of my survey courses reported to me several years later that when she began studying Library Science in graduate school, one of the first exercises she had to complete was a simple search of the Web. When she typed her name into one of the standard search engines, she was delighted to find that an essay she had written for my class had been reviewed at another university as an example of good writing.

I had moved into the invention phase with this kind of course, and students were more able to place themselves within the historical context of the tradition of British literature. This does not mean they all developed a great "love" for the tradition, but they were able to think critically about it and to move into a more creative, critical, and original understanding of their study of literature and its relation to other disciplines. As interdisciplinarians, we are concerned that students have this kind of integrative experience that provides a "framework flexible enough to allow for shifting groupings of information and knowledge" (Klein and Newell 15).

In the fall of 1997, I returned to the Shakespeare lecture course for a somewhat different experiment. The assigned lecture hall seats about 120, including space for students with special access requirements. It is equipped with an Ethernet connection, an overhead data/video projector, and the more conventional audio/visual features of today's lecture halls. To maintain security, however, instructors are required to provide their own computers and VCRs. This creates a need for set-up time, which is easily accommodated if there are assistants for the course, as there were with this one. The need to set things up created an interesting sense of process, a new way of beginning a class. Many students, in fact, arrived early and said they rather liked watching the desktop image emerge on the screen, and the trials to determine whether the videotapes were properly cued. Indeed, the use of videotape is a great boon to teaching Shakespeare, even where there are no other "technologies" used. The beginning of each class session was signaled by the appearance of the Turbobard Homepage, a name consistent with other courses in the Writing with Computers Project I had helped establish in the fall of 1994. It was almost as if a trumpeter announced the beginning of a play.

At the homepage, students had instant access to the course schedule, the writing assignments, the class roster (from which students could access other students in the course through email links), and the archives (again the most important interactive site for the course, where students could access comments sent to the discussion list, essay proposals, and final drafts of all the work in the course). As in other Web-based courses I have taught, the course schedule contained a daily calendar with links to lecture notes. In these notes, I used a TV icon to indicate points at which a video would be shown in class. The use of the computer in this way, along with the easy switching to video projections, proved useful in focusing student attention. (Teaching in a computer lab where each student sits before a computer, by contrast, is sometimes problematic; students often have to be reminded to pay attention and not surf off somewhere else.) Many students said they were better able to follow the lecture when the notes were present on their screen. Many commented that they preferred these "notes" to PowerPoint presentations they encountered in other classes, where they felt instruction was still being "delivered." Through the Website, students had easy access to what would have been polished notes for a more formal lecture. These notes provided students with more than the schematic outline of "points" that presentation programs like PowerPoint facilitate.

Online student discussion in a class of this size was more limited than in smaller courses. Still, there were well over one thousand messages posted during the semester, with a significant number of students writing two to three messages each week. As in other classes, the discussion list allowed students to bring their own knowledge to bear on the study of Shakespeare. For example, Dr. Kevorkian was in the news a great deal that fall, and there was an extended discussion on Shakespeare as a doctor of death, a rather natural response to a reading of the tragedies.

I also found that my writing-intensive procedures for this course worked much better than in other large, non-electronic classes. Students were asked to write three preliminary essays, 250 to 500 words in length, involving the analysis of dramatic conventions, individual speeches, and scenes. From the start, they were told that these short essays could be incorporated into their longer essays on character construction, dramatic construction, and interpretation. For these longer essays, they would be required to make appropriate use of materials from the work of another student. As in the survey course, they were told that such material could be gathered from the discussion list archives or the archives of the preliminary essays. This requirement provided an effective means, even in a relatively large class, of encouraging students to work collaboratively with one another. It also improved the peer review process and facilitated their finding other students working on the same kinds of problem. The titles of some of the student essays provide a sense of the range of work they were encouraged to do in this course, not at all the usual literary essays: On *Antony and Cleopatra*—"Shakespeare's Take On Women," "To The Movies with Antony & Cleopatra," and "Power and Politics and Love"; on Caliban in *The Tempest*—"Will you just quit trying to teach me . . . ," "Caliban, the Civilized Gentleman," and "Shakespeare's State of Nature"; on Shakespeare as he is reflected in the plays—"The Final Curtain," and "I Am Outta Here!" In one way or another, each of these essays benefited from insights gained from other disciplines, insights students encountered in the asynchronous discussion, from intensive Web-based searches, and through their attention to one another's work.

As with other computer-supported courses I have taught, I resisted using specialized software. Students were encouraged, but not required, to use

Eudora for e-mail as well as for the submission of essays. Given Eudora's options for text editing, it provides an easy medium for exchange of peer evaluations and final drafts. Students access the course Website with whatever browser they have on their own machines or with the browsers they find on machines in the campus or residence hall labs. Although there were no required laboratory sessions for the course, I did schedule four afternoons a week throughout the semester in two computer-equipped rooms to help students complete their work. During the first two weeks of the course, my assistants and I met with students on a voluntary basis to familiarize them with the software they would be using. At the start of the semester, the success rate was astonishing. Of the 117 students enrolled in the course, more than 100 were able to engage in an initial peer review and submit a final draft of an essay. Within the ten-day drop/add period, however, enrollment fell to ninety-one. Those students who volunteered a reason for dropping the course indicated that it was not so much discomfort with the technology as a lack of time. All but a handful of those who remained in the course consistently submitted their work on time.

No doubt part of the success of this course was due to increased access to computers, as well as familiarity with the new media. When we started the Writing with Computers project in fall 1994, responses to surveys indicated that about 10 percent of the students had access to their own computers, and some 30 percent had made prior use of email. By fall 1997, the same surveys revealed that nearly 50 percent had access to a dedicated machine, and e-mail use was almost universal. A great many also had experience with chat rooms, bulletin boards, and electronic discussion lists.

Problems with the Web-based Lecture Hall

With the Shakespeare course, it became clear that technology could be too much of a good thing. A great many students, as we soon discovered, had two or three courses that involved some degree of computer support. Many students were experiencing severe e-mail overload. They also were being asked to master a variety of software that their individual instructors could not master. For example, some of them had courses for which they were expected to use different paint and spreadsheet programs. Those of us who wish software manufacturers would maintain a version of their product without "upgrades" for at least six months can hardly begin to envision the problems students encounter having to use several programs.

This experiment in attempting to engage a relatively large number of students in the study of Shakespeare with a major computer-mediated writing component provided a number of insights into my experience with smaller classes. In the smaller classes, nearly all the students in the class appear to develop closer working relations. They learn to write collaboratively; in many cases, they begin to cherish those opportunities to work closely with others. In the large course, fewer students appear to have this experience. The use of a discussion list for expanding student responses does not work as well; to put this a bit differently, it does not inspire all students equally, perhaps some not at all! But this is a problem with all lecture courses, whether there is computer support or not. What surprised my assistants and me was the number of students who said they found the experience of learning to write in an electronic environment of great value. One student, only half in jest, as it appeared from later discussion, included these comments with his proposal for the essay on dramatic construction,

> I intend to show how this class is dramatically killing me slowly . . .
> how Shakespeare is turning my brain into mush . . . and how writing
> these essays is warping my sense of humanity . . . all in five pages or less.

This comment provoked a good deal of discussion. An older student, quick to respond with more positive comments, provided an opportunity for other students to reflect on their experiences in the course:

> Mush? You've got to be kidding! This class is like eating prime rib. Yea,
> sometimes I find myself thinking in Shakespearean English and that
> can be a scary thing but if delving deep into these plays is taking your
> humanity away then, well, don't let it. Take hold of yourself, man! I'm
> not sure who I'm replying to . . . please forgive, I'm not your run of the
> mill undergrad. But one advantage I have is that, after several adventures in life, I know . . . what I want to do with my life, for the next 10
> years anyway, and studying Shakespeare is like opening a door. I didn't
> realize how many lines out of his plays are a part of today's expressions.
> Doesn't that mean something?

Many students responded positively to this comment; but then the originator of this discussion thread, allowing that perhaps he had learned something of use from studying Shakespeare, noted he had learned something much more useful professionally in having to do so much online writing. He claimed these skills had landed him a management position with the company he had been working with for two years.

Course Management Software

In the past several years, a number of companies have formed to produce "course management software" to facilitate large-scale implementation of computer support for instruction. No doubt, there will be a shakeout among these software providers, and it is much too soon to say exactly how the software will revolutionize teaching. Many of these providers claim goals that correspond to those of the interdisciplinary community. WebCT.com, for example, has established a great many "e-Learning Communities" for both faculty and students designed to facilitate discussion across a wide range of institutions. In fall 1998, the University of Missouri–Columbia began offering training for implementation of a course management pilot program, using WebCT. We chose their software precisely because of their plans to create online learning communities to support individual disciplines as well as to carry out cross-disciplinary work.

Our pilot, which began in January 1999 with relatively few courses, moved to an installed base of over 100 courses with over 11,000 enrollments in the fall 1999 and winter 2000 semesters. Our primary goal was to use WebCT to enhance student learning across the entire curriculum and, at the same time, reduce the administrative burden of teaching, in both on-campus and distance courses from lower-division, large lecture courses to graduate seminars across a variety of disciplines. My own teaching in this current revolution with course management software, which strikes fear in many academic hearts, has enabled me to find ways into students' minds, and hearts, that I thought, for all my success, were still years away.

WebCT's integration of the necessary technology into one seamless package has further transformed my classes; they are more truly student-centered than I imagined possible. E-mail, a bulletin board, collaborative workspaces are all internal to WebCT. This means that students may access a WebCT course using any computer platform and may upload work from a Mac or PC. There is no need for students to send their work to each other; instead, they can work collaboratively within the same space for peer reviews and revision. Because the communication software is internal to WebCT, e-mail does not so easily get lost, nor are students tempted to forward all those virus warnings and jokes they receive through regular e-mail.

As noted earlier, my initial use of technology taught me that students needed an orientation session early in the course. When I first used WebCT in the winter of 1999 for the Senior Interdisciplinary Seminar, this "online class meeting" went so quickly that I was ready to dismiss the students, when one of them remarked, "We still have twenty minutes." She then looked about and said, "I can't believe I said that." The other students agreed they wanted to stay and discuss their capstone projects, and one even remarked, "I wish I had classes before this where I wanted them to last longer." Student work in this course was far more integrative than it had been in past semesters, precisely because students found collaborative work easier. Three students, for example, decided *together* to create an interactive Website for their capstone projects. One decided to include photo-

graphs with her final essay, which was a revisiting of her initial autobiographical statement from the vantage point of the end of her last semester. Using technology thus enabled the form of student work to become
more integrative. This process also engaged them in different kinds of
learning and encouraged them to think and express themselves in writing
as well as in other media.

WebCT's integrated environment similarly enabled me to take the first
half of the British Literature Survey further than I had before. It was an easy
matter to set up workspace for peer reviews so that a draft essay along with
its reviews could be archived along with the revised essays. Given the func-
tionality of the WebCT Bulletin Board, it was far easier to focus discussion
on selected questions. At the end of the semester, students simply were
amazed how much more they were able to learn through the collaboration
afforded by WebCT.

CONCLUSIONS

The use of technology in teaching is forging new partnerships in the educational enterprise. We all managed to teach for decades without giving
much credit to the people who typed our syllabi, but we can't avoid the
"techies" who provide the IT support for our courses. Previously, we ordered textbooks or assembled course packs; today, we are having to deal
with "content providers," a name publishers have assumed in attempting to
market their materials in new ways. Faculty members in all disciplines are
being asked to develop some level of computer proficiency. The real evidence of change is that the Internet is now under attack for a long list of
reasons—making privacy impossible, corrupting our children, spawning
impersonal education, putting teachers out of business. More than anything else, what interdisciplinarity has taught me over the years is to avoid
easy either/or constructions. I do not believe we will be able to make a simple choice, either to avoid technology or embrace it wholeheartedly. As I
observed at the beginning of this chapter, the future of education is very
much involved with technology. At the same time, as long as we continue
to provide instruction in more or less "traditional" campus settings, the
"new" technologies are not going to replace face-to-face instruction. The
potential of technology to enhance what we do is enormous, but technology alone will not produce good teaching. The problems we encounter remain pedagogical, not technical.

As I observed at the beginning of this chapter, the use of technology
alone will not enhance learning. I am confident that no software program
ever will provide for "ideal" instruction. The use of instructional technol-

ogy quickly leads to the insight that information and knowledge are quite different "things." Information is a collection of raw data; knowledge occurs when we are able to use information to make inferences, draw conclusions, and come to a useful understanding that informs the way we live and act. We have long assumed that students want an education to further their careers or perhaps to benefit them personally. In *The Social Life of Information*, John Seely Brown and Paul Duguid set learning in a compelling context:

> Learning is usually treated as a supply-side matter, thought to follow teaching, training, or information delivery. But learning is much more demand-driven. People learn in response to need. When people cannot see the need for what's being taught, they ignore it, reject it, fail to assimilate it in any meaningful way. Conversely, when they have a need, then, if the resources for learning are available, people learn effectively and quickly. (136)

Information technology can provide these resources in abundance.

Children, it seems to me, start out without discipline in every sense of the word. The process of American education strives to tame children, to instill a sense of discipline, and to lead them into "disciplines." Progressively, indoctrination into the language of particular disciplines is the main business of schools. Often these disciplinary ways of thinking are opposed to each other, not complementary, in their approach to knowledge and in their approach to "the human condition." The impact of technology in K–12 education is already beginning to have an impact on expectations in college on disciplinary boundaries. As Don Tapscott put it in *Growing Up Digital*,

> For the first time in history, children are more comfortable, knowledgeable, and literate than their parents about an innovation central to society. And it is through the use of the digital media that the N-Generation will develop and superimpose its culture on the rest of society. Boomers stand back. Already these kids are learning, playing, communicating, working, and creating communities differently than their parents. They are a force for social transformation. (1–2)

My own experience is that first-year students arrive at colleges and universities as intuitive, seasoned interdisciplinarians, ready for active learning, not for the passive "reception" of knowledge. Unfortunately, many of us still are "teaching" them the error of their ways. Even in "true" interdisciplinary classes, the focus more often is on the nature of the instruction than on what the student receives. With the widespread use of computers in schools and at home, students are beginning to arrive on college campuses with a new set of expectations. Many have already integrated technology into their ways of knowing. We must learn to value these experiences and use them to further our integrative goals.

Although we often complain that technology takes up too much of our time, computers and information technology can reinstate a useful sense of time for learning. Having time to compose one's thoughts outside of class—to work asynchronously—provides more time for thinking. The repetitive drills required in language acquisition and some scientific inquiry, for example, can be done in much more productive ways with computers, allowing more time in class for discussion of issues that engage students in integrating that information with their own thinking. This is particularly crucial in the area of writing.

Many of us recognize that teaching literature is and always has been an interdisciplinary endeavor. Julie Thompson Klein's penetrating account of literary practices in "Interdisciplinary Genealogy in Literary Studies" amply demonstrates the "multiple interdisciplinarities [that] have emerged from the interplay of mainstream and alternative practices" (*Crossing* 133). The use of technology in the classroom facilitates and enhances working with other media in relation to the study of literature and drama. Those of us who have practiced our professions in higher education for a while have learned to work with students who grew up with expectations and learning patterns engendered by *Sesame Street* and MTV. As Tapscott's research demonstrates, more and more students are coming to us with computer skills and "browser savvy" that surpass our own skills. They have been doing e-mail with one of the free Web-based services. They expect to do more of that in college. It has been suggested by a great many of us engaged in this endeavor—those of us who are eager to see where the technology will lead us, those who are skeptical, those who see it as the devil's work—that the term "distance education" is undergoing radical change; and as time progresses, we will be at some distance from the consumers of our "product."

It is likely that we will be living with these changes for some time to come. As interdisciplinarians, we are used to moving and working at the boundaries of our disciplines. Klein once more comments,

> Every interdisciplinary course, like every problem-focused research project and every attempt to deliver interdisciplinary care, begins anew, because each attempt at synthesis involves special characteristics and techniques of the fields being examined. (*Interdisciplinarity* 181)

This also is true with technology. No sooner do we find a particular solution to a complex problem than we find new ways of addressing other problems with technology. Change, it would appear, is going to be with us for some time to come.

Finally, the use of information technology to de-center the classroom and emphasize student-centered learning is not so much creating as exacerbating other problems in higher education. The student-centered classroom does not reduce the time faculty must spend preparing for and thinking about their classes. Nor does technology. What we often overlook is that the move to make students the focus of the process is creating enormous stress in a culture that already has developed many means for increasing the stress we all feel. Student performance often increases in computer-mediated courses, but the burden of work for students and for faculty also increases.

In her 1972 essay, "Teaching Language in Open Admissions," Adrienne Rich reports that she and her colleagues "felt that students learn to write by discovering the validity and variety of their own experience" (57). Rich was working with student populations—mostly African American—just beginning to gain a foothold in higher education. Our present educational enterprise is bringing to us "traditional" age students who nonetheless are very different from their predecessors. For one thing, there are many more of them now than ever before. We are having to address more diverse educational needs. And we are having to do this in the "information age," which means students must be prepared for the use of technology in their working lives. As interdisciplinarians, we are more challenged than ever to find a place for multiplicity, for teaching with technology that provides both knowledge and skills. The question, finally, is not only how well are we succeeding in teaching literature—or any other "body of knowledge"—but how well are we meeting the needs of our students. Surely teaching to the needs of the great variety of our students is at the heart of the interdisciplinary project.

LOOKING FURTHER

The courses for which I have used a Website are being maintained on the Web as archives. In the spring of 1999, the University of Missouri legal department suggested that I restrict access to student writing unless I had student release forms. Since then, I have asked students to sign a release for the courses in winter and fall 1999. Over time, the addresses for these courses as well as the passwords may change. Up-to-date information is maintained at my personal Website: http://web.missouri.edu/~engbob. Interested readers are welcome to view any of these sites. Note that for the first three listed, you will be required to use a userid and password.

Fall 2000 . . . English 370—Genres: European and American Drama, 1890 to the Present (https://courses.missouri.edu/SCRIPT/english_370/scripts/serve_home), you will need to log in as a guest (with the userid *demoguest* and the password *guest*).

Fall 1999 . . . English 370—Genres: European and American Drama, 1890 to the Present (https://courses.missouri.edu/SCRIPT/english_370/scripts/serve_home), you will need to log in in as a guest (with the userid *webctguest* and the password *guest*).

Fall 1999 . . . British Literature: Beginnings to 1784 (https://courses.missouri.edu/SCRIPT/english_215/scripts/serve_home), you will need to log in in as a guest (with the userid *demoguest* and the password *guest*).

Winter 1999 . . . Interdisciplinary Studies 290—Senior Seminar (https://courses.missouri.edu/SCRIPT/intdsc_290/scripts/serve_home), you will need to log in as a guest (with the userid *demoguest* and the password *guest*).

Fall 1998 . . . English 370—Genres: European and American Drama, 1890 to the Present (http://web.missouri.edu/~engbob/courses/370-98/)

Fall 1997 . . . English 135—Major Authors—Shakespeare (http://web.missouri.edu/~engbob/courses/135/)

Winter 1997 . . . English 215—Survey of British Literature: Beginnings to 1784 (http://web.missouri.edu/~engbob/courses/215-97/)

Fall 1996 . . . English 370—Genres: European and American Drama, 1890 to the Present. (http://web.missouri.edu/~engbob/courses/370/)

Winter 1996 . . . Interdisciplinary Studies 290: Senior Seminar (http://web.missouri.edu/~sdpwww/courses/290/)

Fall 1995 . . . English 215—Survey of British Literature: Beginnings to 1784 (http://web.missouri.edu/~engbob/courses/215/)

WORKS CITED

Bender, Bob. "Creating Communities on the Internet: Electronic Discussion Lists in the Classroom." *Computers in Libraries* 15, no. 5 (May 1995): 38–43.

Brown, John Seely, and Paul Duguid. *The Social Life of Information.* Boston: Harvard Business School Press, 2000.

Hursh, Barbara, Paul Haas, and Michael Moore. "An Interdisciplinary Model to Implement General Education." Newell, *Interdisciplinarity* 35–50.

Katz, Richard N. et al. *Dancing with the Devil: Information Technology and the New Competition in Higher Education.* San Francisco: Jossey-Bass, 1999.

Klein, Julie Thompson. *Interdisciplinarity: History, Theory, Practice.* Detroit: Wayne State University Press, 1990.

———. "Women." Newell, *Interdisciplinarity* 453–61.

————. *Crossing Boundaries: Knowledge, Disciplinarities and Interdisciplinarities.* Charlottesville: University of Virginia Press, 1996.

Lanham, Richard A. *The Electronic Word: Democracy, Technology, and the Arts.* Chicago: University of Chicago Press, 1993.

Lebow, Richard Ned. "Interdisciplinary Research and the Future of Peace and Security Studies." Newell, *Interdisciplinarity* 463–79.

Munitz, Barry. "Changing Landscape: From Cottage Monopoly to Competitive." *EDUCAUSE Review* (January–February 2000): 4 pp. 18 February 2001. http://www.educause.edu/pub/er/erm00/erm001.html

Newell, William H. "Designing Interdisciplinary Courses." *Interdisciplinary Studies Today.* Eds. Julie Thompson Klein and William G. Doty. New Directions for Teaching and Learning, No 58. San Francisco: Jossey Bass, Summer 1994. 35–52.

————, ed. *Interdisciplinarity: Essays from the Literature.* New York: College Entrance Examination Board, 1998.

————. "Professionalizing Interdisciplinarity: Literature Review and Research." Newell, *Interdisciplinarity* 529–63.

Newell, William H., and Julie Thompson Klein. "Advancing Interdisciplinary Studies." Newell, *Interdisciplinarity* 3–22.

Noble, David. F. "Digital Diploma Mills: The Automation of Higher Education." *First Monday* 3, no. 1 (1998): 31 par. http://www.firstmonday.dk/issues/issue3_1/noble/index.html.

Rich, Adrienne. *On Lies, Secrets and Silence: Selected Prose, 1966–1978.* New York: W. W. Norton, 1979.

Shakespeare, William. "All's Well That Ends Well." *The Riverside Shakespeare.* Ed. G. Blakemore Evans. 2nd ed. Boston: Houghton Mifflin, 1997.

Tapscott, Don. *Growing Up Digital: The Rise of the Net Generation.* New York: McGraw-Hill, 1998.

"Teacher-Centered Staff Development." Apple Classrooms of Tomorrow Project. Cupertino, CA: Apple Computer, Inc. 34 par. http://www.apple.com/education/professionaldevelopment/tchcenterstaff/html.

"Teaching at an Internet Distance: The Pedagogy of Online Teaching and Learning." The Report of a 1998–99 University of Illinois Faculty Seminar. University of Illinois, Office of Vice President for Academic Affairs. December 1999. http://www.vpaa.uillinois.edu/tid/report.

CHAPTER 6

Interdisciplinarity, Diversity, and the Future of Liberal Education

Debra Humphreys

"Language Differences a Challenge for Courts," "Census to Define Multiracial in Myriad Ways," "Discrimination's Lingering Sting—Minorities Tell of Profiling, Other Bias," "Taking a Hard Look at Discrimination and Stereotypes in Medicine," "Census Shows Big Increase in Gay Households." These recent newspaper headlines testify to the many ways in which diversity pervades our lives. Clearly, diversity will also continue to shape the challenges the nation will face in the coming decades. Although originally seen by many as a politicized effort to satisfy the demands of special interests, the necessity of teaching college students about issues of diversity is now widely recognized as essential to their capacity to succeed in the future. Indeed, many believe that the future of our diverse democracy depends on an informed citizenry well educated in the complexities of diversity today and the role that issues of race, class, culture, gender, sexuality, and other forms of classification and difference have played in shaping our nation's institutions over its history (*Drama*; Humphreys, "Diversity").

The issues raised in these newspaper articles also vividly demonstrate how interdisciplinary our nation's diversity challenges are—how much future leaders will need interdisciplinary knowledge and the capacity to see complex interconnections. From environmental racism to medical research priorities to immigration and welfare policies and the reform of the nation's school systems, understanding diversity in all its interdisciplinary complexity is more essential than ever.

While efforts to diversify the college curriculum still cause controversy, it is now widely accepted in higher education, but also in business and industry, that college graduates need to be educated about issues of diversity. As Anthony Carnevale puts it in an article entitled "Diversity in Higher Education: Why Corporate America Cares,"

> Improving diversity on campus and in the workforce is not just a 'nice' social or political goal. It is a necessity—for both social and economic reasons. . . . In the 21st century, the United States is well positioned to continue as the world's preeminent economy, with diversity giving us a unique advantage. To maintain our competitive edge, corporate America needs employees that are increasingly creative and agile. To meet that need, we require a pool of diverse workers with college educations to match. (Carnevale 6)

This acceptance of the necessity of diversity as a value essential to educational quality today is demonstrated in a recent survey conducted by the Association of American Colleges and Universities (AAC&U), where I have worked for the past eight years. In its survey conducted in spring 2000, AAC&U found that 63 percent of 543 responding colleges and universities either have in place a diversity requirement for all students or are in the process of developing one. Of the 434 responding four-year campuses, 60 percent report that they already have requirements in place (Humphreys, "National Survey" 1).

This trend toward requiring all students to study issues of diversity is also consistent with public opinion on the subject. A national opinion poll of registered voters sponsored by the Ford Foundation found that 68 percent of those polled support "requiring students to take at least one cultural and ethnic diversity course in order to graduate." An even larger majority (94 percent) agreed that, "America's growing diversity makes it more important than ever for all of us to understand people who are different than ourselves" ("National Poll" 1).

How is the academy doing in meeting this challenge? What are students learning in these courses? What is the nature of the requirements that colleges and universities are developing? What is educational research telling us about the impact of diversity on student learning? How have efforts to diversify the college curriculum changed over the past decade? What are the most innovative models being developed? The AAC&U has worked with hundreds of colleges and universities each of which is diversifying its curricula through a national initiative called "American Commitments: Diversity, Democracy, and Liberal Learning." Drawing on the work AAC&U has done in this project and scores of other campuses whose innovative courses and programs are featured on the Website, DiversityWeb (www.diversityweb.org), developed by AAC&U and the University of Maryland, I will sketch out some of the trends and innovations we have found in the ways in which higher education is responding to the challenge of diversifying the curriculum and the ways these responses relate to interdisciplinarity.

In the early days of what has come to be a widespread campus diversity movement, efforts to diversify the curriculum concentrated on remedying inaccuracies or omissions in the core curricula and disciplinary programs of many colleges and universities. Frequently at the urging of previously underserved students who had only recently gained widespread access to higher education, African-American studies, ethnic studies, and women's studies programs were developed to teach about issues that were ignored in traditional disciplines. Whereas these programs were conceived of as interdisciplinary from the beginning, in practice, many of the courses developed for them remained primarily focused on one discipline. In fact, many courses in these programs were designed to remedy inadequacies in the curricula of traditional departments. As a result, incredibly valuable scholarship and corresponding courses emerged in areas such as African-American literature or the history of immigrants or working people in America. Although the early founders of these programs recognized the need to develop truly interdisciplinary curricula, all too often institutional structures held in place the disciplinary silos that too often prevent cross-disciplinary cooperation and integration. The subsequent interdisciplinary curriculum development I will discuss next, however, would have been impossible without these early efforts.

During this initial stage, these programs also tended to serve only a minority of students. As more and more faculty and college leaders came to realize—often again at the urging of students—that issues of diversity were essential for all students, the effort to diversify the curriculum became increasingly widespread, touching more and more departments and on many campuses reaching every student. As these efforts matured and expanded, diversity courses also became more and more interdisciplinary. It has become clear when studying issues of diversity that multiple disciplinary perspectives are essential in both scholarship and teaching.

Given that diversity education works best when it is interdisciplinary, then how do we ensure that diversity programs are interdisciplinary? In this chapter, I will argue that the creation of interdisciplinary diversity curricula is a developmental process that often entails distinct stages that move increasingly toward more sophisticated forms of integration. Interestingly, some of the most prominent researchers in both interdisciplinary and multicultural education have articulated separate theories on the developmental quality of curricular reform that bear some striking similarities with one another. Yet rarely do thinkers within the two camps of interdisciplinarity and multiculturalism directly recognize one another. By creating greater dialogue between these two approaches toward education, both forms of teaching can gain insight and be further enhanced.

LEVELS OF INTEGRATION IN DIVERSITY AND INTERDISCIPLINARY EDUCATION

For the past decade, James A. Banks has been developing a theory of multicultural curriculum reform that includes a four-step typology of content integration. According to him, four approaches to the integration of multicultural content have evolved since the 1960s: contributions approach, additive approach, transformation approach, and social action approach. He notes that many instructors and programs evolve from the simplest (the contributions approach) to the most complex (the social action approach) over time. Others simultaneously mix and blend two or more of the four approaches, depending on their needs and opportunities at the time (Banks 195–214). Level one, the *contributions approach*, is characterized by the insertion of discrete cultural artifacts and information into the curriculum, using criteria similar to those used to select mainstream elements. The *additive approach*, or level two, is characterized by the addition of content, concepts, themes, and perspectives to the curriculum without changing its basic structure, purposes, and characteristics. In other words, content, materials, and issues are added to the curriculum as appendages rather than as integral parts of a unit of instruction.

The next level, the *transformation approach*, however, does entail a fundamental alteration of the curriculum's goals, structure, perspectives, and assumptions. It enables students to view concepts, issues, themes, and problems from several ethnic and cultural perspectives and points of view. In this approach, the emphasis should not be on the ways various cultural and ethnic groups have contributed to mainstream culture and society, but rather on "how the common U.S. culture and society emerged from a complex synthesis and interaction of the diverse cultural elements that originated within the various cultural, racial, ethnic, and religious groups that make up U.S. society" (204). Finally, the *social action approach* includes all of the traits of the transformation approach but adds components that require students to make decisions and take actions related to the concept, issue, or problem studied in the unit. Important in this approach is the goal of helping students become reflective social critics and eventual agents of change.

Like Banks, William H. Newell also generated a four-step scale for curricular integration in an interdisciplinary course (55). *Multidisciplinary* courses present various disciplinary perspectives serially with no integration attempted. *Pluridisciplinary* courses compare and contrast disciplinary insights into the course topic, but there is no attempt to synthesize these insights—that is, to combine them into a new whole. In the third integrative approach—the *cross-disciplinary* course—one discipline is applied to the characteristic subject matter of another, yielding new insights but not an integration of the insights of both disciplines, and providing a new but not a larger, holistic perspective. The final, and most sophisticated approach is the *interdisciplinary* course in which the insights of the disciplines are synthesized to offer a richer, more complex perspective.

Both Newell and Banks underscore the idea that a fully integrated curriculum is a developmental, complex process that works best when it is reinforced by other dimensions, such as a supportive campus culture, an innovative faculty, and a critical attention (on the part of the instructor and students) to the way knowledge gets constructed. Yet, whereas Banks's model focuses on the level of integration of *cultural* frameworks, Newell's model focuses on the level of integration of *disciplinary* frameworks. I argue that an interdisciplinary, multicultural curriculum should do both. In other words, interdisciplinary, multicultural courses should prompt students to investigate disciplines and cultures in both celebratory and critical ways, analyzing the epistemological and ideological assumptions that undergird them, and dismantling the notion of universal forms of truth and knowledge. Moreover, multicultural and interdisciplinary ways of thinking can provide a corrective on the other, causing us to see cultural biases in disciplinary frameworks and disciplinary biases in cultural frameworks. As will be discussed later, what is exciting is that considerable evidence exists that this process of integrating these two curricular and pedagogical approaches is already under way in a variety of settings—in general education programs, interdisciplinary programs, service learning, and residence life.

THE NATURE OF DIVERSITY REQUIREMENTS

The development of requirements that all undergraduate students study diversity has been a core part of the continuing examination of general education learning outcomes by colleges around the country. In another recent survey of its member campuses, AAC&U found that 57 percent of responding institutions reported that they were currently conducting formal reviews of their general education programs. More than 67 percent of respondents reported working on cultural diversity as one of their curricular goals for general education (Ratcliff).

What is the nature of the diversity requirements colleges and universities are currently implementing? AAC&U's survey on diversity requirements previously mentioned found that there is a wide array of curricular models. Confirming that indeed many campuses are relying heavily on existing interdisciplinary programs like those already mentioned, by far the most common model among respondents was one in which students are required to take one course among a list of different approved courses. This model was chosen by 68 percent of respondents. Although many of the courses that students can take to satisfy these requirements may be quite interdisciplinary, this model does allow institutions to rely on courses that focus only on one discipline rather than developing more interdisciplinary courses that would provide students with a learning experience that better captures the complexity of diversity issues. In the AAC&U survey, 17 percent of respondents require all students to take a single course with a shared syllabus and another 12 percent report having a diversity requirement within one or more major.

While the most common model of diversity requirements entails one or in some cases two courses chosen from an existing list of discipline-based and interdisciplinary courses, many colleges and universities are reexamining these requirements to see if they are designed well enough to enable students to learn what they need to know. Many campus leaders now believe, in fact, that diversity needs to be addressed in more sophisticated and increasingly interdisciplinary ways and in more places throughout a student's college career. The national panel guiding AAC&U's American Commitments initiative, in fact, made recommendations about what students today should be able to expect from their college experience in the area of U.S. diversity. In their report, *American Pluralism and the College Curriculum*, they recommend "that preparation for meaningful citizenship in the United States today be addressed through multiple forms of learning, and, in a variety of educational contexts, across the college experience." (25) Although different campuses will reach these goals in distinct ways, they recommended that every student's education should include explorations of the following four things:

> *Experience, identity, and aspiration*: The study of one's own particular inherited and constructed traditions, identity communities, and significant questions, in their complexity.

U.S. pluralism and the pursuits of justice: An extended and comparative exploration of diverse peoples in this society, with significant attention to their differing experiences of U.S. democracy and the pursuits—sometimes successful, sometimes frustrated—of equal opportunity.

Experiences in justice seeking: Encounters with systemic constraints on the development of human potential in the United States and experiences in community-based efforts to articulate principles of justice, expand opportunity, and redress inequities.

Multiplicity and relational pluralism in majors, concentrations, and programs: Extensive participation in forms of learning that foster sustained exploration of and deliberation about contested issues important in particular communities of inquiry and practice. (25)

Although this vision probably does not reflect the scope of the experiences most college students are currently having in their courses about diversity, it is intriguing because it fosters sophisticated levels of interdisciplinary and multidisciplinary integration. Not only does it underscore the importance of synthesizing personal, disciplinary, and cultural frameworks into a larger understanding of self and society, but with its emphasis on social justice and its call for an empathic grasp of the ways that diversity and issues of social justice affect real people, it also pushes the student toward what Banks refers to as the fourth or highest level of integration, the social action approach.

DIVERSITY AND INTERDISCIPLINARY PROGRAMS OF STUDY

In addition to interdisciplinary, multicultural general education courses, complex, diversity-oriented interdisciplinary programs continue to grow. Whereas many remain underresourced, many others are institutionalized enough to be able to offer full-fledged, interdisciplinary majors. According to the National Women's Studies Association's most recent database, there are currently 734 women's studies programs in the country. Philip Q. Yang reports in his recent book, *Ethnic Studies*, on a 1996 study that recorded almost 700 ethnic studies programs or departments emphasizing American minority groups. As Yang puts it, these "included 587 ethnic-specific programs or departments (including 359 programs on African Americans, 41 on Asian Americans, 127 on Chicano/Latinos, and 144 on Native Americans). There were also ninety-four multiethnic studies programs or departments, and six ethnic studies programs within traditional departments" (273).

Many of these programs—whether new or established—are also transforming their curricula in exciting and more integrative ways. Interdisciplinary programs that have existed for well over a decade are expanding the scope of disciplinary and intellectual perspectives offered within their programs. Women's studies programs, for instance, were traditionally founded by faculty members in the humanities or social sciences. Some programs, however, are now developing courses that teach students scientific knowledge and skills. They are drawing on an expanding new field of scholarship called feminist science studies (*Frequently Asked Questions*). Courses being developed cover such issues as "The Laboratory and Social Life of Genes" or "Cultures of Biology, Medicine, Gender and Race," two courses offered at the University of Arizona.

In addition to broadening their disciplinary perspectives, many interdisciplinary programs are joining an overall trend toward internationalizing the undergraduate curricula. As part of this effort, they are developing important links with other interdisciplinary programs enriching the integrative nature of their students' learning. For example, women's studies programs are collaborating with area studies programs to bring comparative perspectives about gender and women's status to women's studies programs and to bring scholarship on gender into area studies programs. New courses are being developed that teach about women's lives and the social construction of gender and sexuality in regions and cultures around the world. Students are learning about the challenges women face not only in the United States, but also in nations without developed feminist movements or in nations where feminist political agendas differ markedly from those in the United States.

Some of the women's studies programs working to internationalize their curricula were involved in a curriculum transformation project funded by the Ford Foundation in 1995. As part of that grant program, working groups of faculty members from both feminist and international studies programs at the University of Minnesota, for example, worked to revise and develop new courses that comparatively examine issues such as women in combat, population politics, and the gender-differentiated effects of global economics. At Spelman College, faculty members brought together elements from African studies courses and women's studies courses. The African studies program had traditionally focused more on issues of race, class, and region than on gender. Spelman's new "Women and African Diaspora Studies Program" offers a compelling new perspective on women around the world and on feminist thought outside of the United States and Western Europe.

These programs clearly continue to serve as essential sources of new scholarship and are now providing thousands of students who major in these fields with rich educational experiences and essential and marketable skills. And it appears that colleges and universities depend on these programs to provide courses on diversity to all their students. The fact that some universities are expanding the types of disciplines addressed in their courses and self-consciously integrating differing interdisciplinary fields underlines the complex integrative curricular approaches of current interdisciplinary courses.

DIVERSITY AT HOME AND ABROAD: NEW CURRICULAR AND INTELLECTUAL FRAMEWORKS

Although many interdisciplinary programs are moving toward a greater internationalization of their curricula, others realize that studying issues of culture anywhere in the world is not the same as studying about diversity challenges in the United States. As the AAC&U report referenced earlier puts it, "Education for United States democratic and cultural pluralism is not the same task . . . as the education for global knowledge and interconnection. . . . Students require both global knowledge and domestic knowledge" (*American Pluralism* xx). Although certainly still in the minority, increasingly, some campuses are requiring students to take one course that deals with issues of diversity in the United States. and another that exposes them to diversity issues abroad.

In one of the most innovative and interdisciplinary diversity programs in the country, St. Lawrence University has developed a major in Global Studies. Although not required of all students, this program provides a groundbreaking model for curricular development bringing together issues of diversity here in the United States with those around the world and incorporating experiential and study-abroad learning opportunities within it. As two faculty members involved in the founding of the program describe it, "Global Studies is not only interdisciplinary in the minimal sense, but draws on all the major divisions of knowledge, including the arts, humanities, social sciences, and natural sciences. The depth of the major lies in area studies concentrations (including one on the United States). The program teaches theory and methods drawn from both cultural studies and political economy." They describe the goals of the program this way: "to teach students to analyze comparatively the impact of global processes on specific phenomena connected with, across, and between geographical areas. Students examine how similarities and differences in these larger contexts affect human actions and beliefs in two or more geographic areas" (Stoddard and Cornwell 1).

In addition to its extraordinary interdisciplinary nature, the program is also distinctive in that it positions the United States as one of a series of studies that includes African Studies, Asian Studies, Canadian Studies, Caribbean and Latin American Studies, European Studies, Native American Studies, and U.S. Studies. In this way, it fundamentally undermines a traditional intellectual framework that assumes the United States as a norm against which other areas of the world are compared. The program also involves all students in experiential learning opportunities in minority communities in the United States or in regions around the world; study abroad options are available in Kenya, India, Costa Rica, Trinidad, Australia, Japan, Russia, Denmark, England, Austria, France, Spain, and Canada.

Another approach to teaching students about the challenges of diversity both in the United States and abroad can be found at St. Edward's University in Austin, Texas. Since 1991, St. Edward's has had a core curriculum required of all students that addresses both U.S. and global diversity issues. Within their required fifty-seven-credit core program, eighteen hours are devoted to "Cultural Foundations." Students take six courses, each of which is interdisciplinary; two of the courses focus on gender, race, ethnicity, and social class in American society. Other courses in the core focus on Western Civilization and explore non-Western societies and related global issues. One of the advantages of this model is that students are able to develop their skills and knowledge in a progressive way over the course of their four years.

Given their innovative structure, goals, and content, both the St. Edward's and the St. Lawrence's approaches constitute what Banks terms transformative and Newell deems interdisciplinary teaching. Students are encouraged to view concepts, themes, problems, and issues from diverse perspectives, and they are given multiple disciplinary methods and insights to form a holistic, comparative and global view of U.S. society.

DIVERSITY, COMMUNITY-BASED LEARNING, AND JUSTICE SEEKING

Whereas the programs described thus far demonstrate a broadening of disciplinary and global perspectives, other diversity programs are expanding teaching and learning outside the traditional classroom walls in another way—through experiential learning opportunities. At Wagner College in Staten Island, for instance, new, required learning communities include interdisciplinary courses on diversity topics and involve students in reflective tutorials drawing on the interdisciplinary knowledge gained in these classes and helping students to understand the complexity of diversity issues in the sites where they are engaged in community-based learning. This merging of experiential and diversity learning is part of an entirely new curricular plan at Wagner called "The Practical Liberal Arts." As two participants in the program at Wagner put it, "The centerpiece of the new curriculum design is our reinterpretation of the concept of learning communities. The entire plan is grounded in an understanding of the need to prepare today's graduates to live and work in diverse communities" (Coia and Barchitta 2).

Building these dynamic connections among a campus, its neighboring communities, and its classrooms is an important new frontier for diversity learning, and much progress is occurring. Recent research by the Higher Education Research Institute (HERI) at the University of California, Los Angeles, reveals the enormous growth of service learning. They found that 30 percent of more than 22,000 students surveyed nationwide had participated in course-based community service during college, and an additional 46 percent participate in some other form of community service. Too few students, however, are getting the most educational benefit from their service experiences. The HERI report underscores the importance of connecting service back to classroom-based learning. In the best tradition of interdisciplinarity, there is clearly a reciprocal influence of "academics" and "service." Students need to experience diverse communities and their many challenges first hand, but they also need to reflect on these experiences in a curricular-based setting (Service Learning 14).

Yet connecting service to classroom learning does not necessarily ensure that students are reaching those higher levels of integration that Banks and Newell have endorsed. As a result, in addition to providing students with more diversity-related experiential learning opportunities, some schools foreground in their diversity courses and requirements the role discrimination, prejudice, and justice seeking have played in America's history. Reflecting the nature of early diversity requirements around the country, Haverford College instituted a requirement in 1984 that allowed students to complete one course on either (1) the history, perspective, or cultures of non-Western peoples, U.S. minorities, or women; or (2) the nature, history, and workings of prejudice. When a committee reviewed the requirement a decade later, two significant facts emerged. More than 150 courses had been developed for the first option. By contrast, very few courses on prejudice had been created. The first type of course did not require a truly interdisciplinary approach, nor did it necessarily demand that the course structure, goals, or assumptions be transformative in Banks's sense of the term. Various ethnic groups, women, or non-Western peoples could still be studied in isolation or without explicit attention to differing experiences of American democracy and justice.

As a result of this finding, in 1990, Haverford faculty members adopted a new "Social Justice Requirement" that focuses not on a particular culture or group, but on the critical analysis of prejudice and discrimination. This is one example of a larger trend to supplement curricular developments focused on previously neglected cultural or racial/ethnic groups with more comprehensive, comparative, and interdisciplinary courses that address systematically the pursuit of justice in America and around the world. Instead of presenting cultural or minority groups in isolation, more and more diversity courses are looking at the ways in which the history of diversity needs to be mapped onto a history of discrimination and unequal treatment across groups as well.

DIVERSITY IN THE CLASSROOM AND BEYOND

In addition to an increasing expansion of the cultural and disciplinary perspectives as well as academic and nonacademic experiences, another feature of the current diversity movement in higher education is a new conception of diversity as a means rather than an end—a vital element to the building of strong communities. Diversity as an element of a college education is about more than just previously neglected knowledge. It needs to engage students in the larger national project of creating ways to live together productively in communities that value difference. This new conception of diversity's value in education has led to the development of many more thoughtful connections between what students are learning both inside and outside of the classroom.

In this way as well, diversity is a project demanding integration. Working on the challenge of teaching students about issues of diversity has surfaced for many campuses the fissures between divisions of student life and those of academic affairs. As one begins to teach about such topics as racial profiling or reproductive rights or the sociopolitical dimensions of HIV and AIDS, one cannot help but confront how students are coping with these sorts of issues in a direct way in their dorms, their workplaces, or their home communities. Campus leaders have also begun to realize the crucial connection between classroom learning and their own efforts to foster healthy intergroup relations on increasingly more diverse campuses.

The University of Michigan has probably gone further than any other institution in bringing together student life and academic programs in an effort to build a strong campus community that values difference, but acknowledges that with difference often comes conflict. The Program on Intergroup Relations, Conflict, and Community (IGRCC) was founded in 1988 as a pilot project, but now links formal academic coursework in a variety of disciplines to the living and social experiences of students outside the classroom. In IGRCC classes, people from various social and racial/ethnic backgrounds are brought together to discuss commonalties and differences, address issues of conflict, and learn how to deal with these issues constructively. The courses in the program teach students not only content about the history and contemporary status of the groups represented, but also valuable skills in conflict mediation and group process.

Dozens of courses have been developed, each of which is team taught; coursework in the program includes both general introductions to intergroup relations and conflict and specialized mini-courses addressing the particular experiences of different racial, ethnic, and cultural groups nationwide. Many campuses are developing similar programs or other creative ways to help students connect what they are learning in their diversity courses with what they are experiencing in their day-to-day lives on campus and beyond. Such an ambitious holistic approach enables students not only to study multiculturalism and interdisciplinarity, but also to live them. Because they are immersed in these issues in their daily lives, they necessarily must "learn to identify social problems and issues, gather pertinent data, clarify their values on the issues, make decisions, and take reflective actions to help resolve the issue or problem" (Banks 209). Both Newell and Banks describe these skills as characteristic of the most sophisticated levels of interdisciplinary and multicultural integration.

ARE THESE COURSES MAKING A DIFFERENCE?

While many campuses across the country are still at the beginning of their efforts to diversify their curricula, some institutions have had requirements and diversity programs in place for several decades. They are reexamining these programs and redesigning them to incorporate new, more sophisticated elements such as those previously discussed. Some of them are also now in a position to evaluate the impact their programs are having. National education researchers are also now looking carefully at the impact diversity in the curriculum and in the campus and classroom environment is having on student learning.

Some of the findings from this new research confirm what many diversity practitioners would suspect. Diversity courses are increasing students' understanding and appreciation of diversity in our society, reducing prejudicial attitudes, and creating more openness to difference. Research is also uncovering, however, some interesting unexpected benefits of diversity for college learning outcomes. One comprehensive study has found that faculty emphasis on diversity in courses has positive effects on openness to racial understanding *and* overall satisfaction with college (Astin). Another study has found that cognitive development improves among students participating in diversity courses (Adams et al.). A 1996 study examining the impact of diversity courses on white students' sense of community, cultural awareness, interest in promoting racial understanding, and satisfaction with college also reported positive results in each of these areas (Tanaka).

A few studies have examined diversity requirements in particular and found very positive outcomes. A study completed in 1999 found that completing a diversity courses requirement significantly reduced students' level of racial prejudice. This study examined one of the most common diversity requirement models—that which requires students to take one course chosen from a wide array of courses from many departments. The results of this study indicate that "diversity course requirements are good vehicles for shaping students' racial views and assumptions toward improved race relations even though the actual topics and the way they are addressed in courses may be broad and varied" (Chang).

The current backlash against affirmative action in higher education has also spurred some new research on the impact not only of diversity in the curriculum, but also learning in a diverse environment. The University of Michigan has generated some of this new research as part of its defense in two affirmative action lawsuits. They have found that not only is coursework dealing with diversity effective in reducing prejudicial attitudes, but that learning in a diverse environment can have a significant impact on students' intellectual development. In fact, they found that students with the most diversity experiences during college had the most cross-racial interactions five years after leaving college (Gurin 5).

Although we are undoubtedly a long way from providing students with all the learning experiences and knowledge they need to function effectively in our increasingly diverse society, the research certainly suggests that some of these interdisciplinary teaching innovations are having a significant positive impact on important student learning outcomes.

CONCLUDING REMARKS

Diversity is but one area of learning where interdisciplinarity is increasingly the norm. From sciences to humanities to social sciences, educators are reinventing college curricula breaking down traditional disciplinary barriers to provide today's students with much more integrative learning experiences. Innovations like those discussed earlier and in the other chapters in this anthology are, in fact, helping to shape a new academy. Yet they are not easy to effect. Developing courses that are integrated in sophisticated ways requires substantial faculty development, curriculum revision, and institutional support. Such innovative approaches may be longer in duration than traditional approaches, but they are well worth the effort. Carol Geary Schneider, president of AAC&U, has suggested that this powerful educational transformation is involving "students directly with the multiple cultures, communities, struggles and aspirations that collectively frame the history of United States democracy." (43) She argues that this educational transformation can be seen as a successor curriculum to the traditional staple of general education—the course sequence in Western civilization. As she puts it, "This successor curriculum is intensely and creatively engaged with the most central challenges confronting American society at the turn of the twenty-first century" (Schneider 43).

In this way, we can see this new frontier of curricular development as providing the framework for a contemporary liberal education that provides students with exactly the set of skills and capacities they need for the coming age. As Schneider and her co-author Robert Shoenberg put it in their influential paper, "Contemporary Understandings of Liberal Education,"

> Fifty years ago the Harvard "Red Book" posited a curriculum focused on a unified national culture based in Western thought. By contrast, the emerging curriculum assumes a world society characterized by a multitude of life experiences and informed by complex intersections among historical experiences, gender, race, ethnicity, socioeconomic status, sexual orientation, religious values, political assumptions, cultural styles, and so on. The liberally educated person, many now argue, needs not only substantial knowledge but also the skills and awareness to negotiate what philosopher Maxine Greene has called "a world lived in common with others." (Schneider and Shoenberg 12)

I fervently believe that the innovative interdisciplinary models I've only been able to describe briefly represent a promising new framework that can guide the academy toward this vision of a new liberal education.

WORKS CITED

Adams, Maurianne, et al. "The Sociomoral Development of Undergraduates in a 'Social Diversity' Course," paper presented at the annual meeting of the American Educational Research Association, April 1994, New Orleans, Louisiana.

American Pluralism and the College Curriculum: Higher Education in a Diverse Democracy. Washington, DC: Association of American Colleges and Universities, 1995.

Astin, Alexander. *What Matters in College?: Four Critical Years Revisited.* San Francisco: Jossey-Bass, 1993.

Banks, James A. "Approaches to Multicultural Curriculum Reform." *Multicultural Education: Issues and Perspectives.* 2nd ed. Eds. James A. Banks and Cherry A. McGee Banks. Boston: Allyn and Bacon, 1993. 195–214.

Carnevale, Anthony. "Diversity in Higher Education: Why Corporate America Cares." *Diversity Digest* 3, no. 3 (1999): 1, 6.

Chang, Mitchell. "Measuring the Impact of a Diversity Requirement on Students' Level of Racial Prejudice. *Diversity Digest* 4, no. 2 (2000): 6–7.

Coia, Lesley and Julia Barchitta. "Engaging with the World: Diversity in the Practical Liberal Arts at Wagner College." *Diversity Digest* 4, no. 2 (2000): 2–3.

The Drama of Diversity and Democracy. Washington, DC: Association of American Colleges and Universities, 1995. Referred to in text as *Drama.*

Frequently Asked Questions About Feminist Science Studies. Washington, DC: Association of American Colleges and Universities, 1999.

Gurin, Patricia. "New Research on the Benefits of Diversity in College and Beyond: An Empirical Analysis." *Diversity Digest* 3, no. 3 (1999): 5, 15.

Humphreys, Debra. "Diversity, Democracy, and Civic Engagement: Higher Education and Its Unique Opportunity." *Higher Education Exchange.* Washington, DC: Kettering Foundation, 2000.

———. "National Survey Finds Diversity Requirements Common Around the Country." *Diversity Digest* 5, no. 1 (2000): 1–2.

"National Poll Reveals Strong Public Support for Diversity in Higher Education." *Diversity Digest* 3, no. 1 (1998): 1, 4–5.

Newell, William H. "Interdisciplinary Curriculum Development." *Interdisciplinarity: Essays from the Literature.* Ed. William H. Newell. New York: College Entrance Examination Board, 1998. 51–65.

Ratcliff, James, et al. *The Status of General Education in the Year 2000: Summary of a National Survey.* Washington, DC: Association of American Colleges and Universities, 2000.

Schneider, Carol Geary. "Education for Cultural and Democratic Pluralism," in *General Education and American Commitments: A National Report on Diversity Courses and Requirements.* By Debra Humphreys. Washington, DC: Association of American Colleges and Universities, 1997.

Schneider, Carol Geary, and Robert Shoenberg. *Contemporary Understandings of Liberal Education.* Washington, DC: Association of American Colleges and Universities, 1998.

"Service Learning Has Positive Impact on Key Student Learning and Diversity Outcomes." *Diversity Digest* 4, no. 3 (2000): 14, 21.

Stoddard, Eve, and Grant Cornwell. "Pathbreaking Global Studies Major Offers New Framework for Diversity and Learning." *Diversity Digest* 4, no. 2 (2000): 1, 12–13.

Tanaka, Gregory. "The Impact of Multiculturalism on White Students." Ph.D. Dissertation, University of California, Los Angeles (1996).

Yang, Philip Q. *Ethnic Studies: Issues and Approaches*. Albany: State University of New York Press, 2000.

PART III

Applying One Disciplinary-Based Pedagogy to Interdisciplinary Teaching

CHAPTER 7

Being There

Performance as Interdisciplinary Teaching Tool

Jeff Abell

My favorite metaphor for interdisciplinary teaching is the pie. Discipline-specific education will teach you everything you need to know about the slice. You'll learn how to sharpen knives, how to apply tools (like spatulas) to extract data, and how to use a discrete vocabulary to discuss these matters. But interdisciplinary instructors are not interested in slices: they are interested in the pie as a totality. How was the crust made? What spices will be needed? Deep analysis of the "filling" will be called for, as well as study of cross-cultural traditions of pie-making and of the pie as symbol in American culture. (I know a lesbian scholar who'd love to teach that class!)

Most important, in this program of the pie, we would eat pie whenever possible. Every faculty meeting, every student colloquium, on any occasion we could think of, we would devour pie of every description, form, and kind. Of course, in order to consume pie, we would have to make it; and we would spend a great deal of time teaching our students how to concoct one for themselves. In this way, our attention would be focused not only on concepts, but also on both the creation and the shared experience of that creation (i.e., our discussions and activities would engage both artist and audience). But the deepest reason for all this pie-eating would be that *you are what you eat*; and by eating all this pie, we would become one with our object of study. We would embody it.

These are educational goals that French philosopher Henri Bergson (1859–1941) would applaud, as they are consistent with his concept of knowledge. Bergson, in his 1903 essay, "An Introduction to Metaphysics," characterizes knowledge as being "relative" or "absolute." According to Bergson, "Description, history, and analysis leave me in the relative" (22). He then goes on to note that only through "intuition" can one arrive at absolute knowledge. "By intuition is meant the kind of intellectual sympathy by which one places oneself within an object in order to coincide with what is unique in it and consequently inexpressible" (23–24). No amount of analysis, discussion, and labor will replace the moment when that one specific pie before us first makes contact with our tongues, and object and subject become one.

If I have belabored this little metaphor, it is in part because as a teacher and interdisciplinary scholar, I am surprised at how easily even those supposedly dedicated to interdisciplinary studies are willing to stop at what Bergson calls the relative. In other words, we are willing to look at the analysis of a subject, but not engage its actual creation or experience it on a physical level. This problem is most pronounced in the arts. At Duke University, for example, one can matriculate in music history or music theory, but not in music performance or composition. And more can be added to the list: art history, but not painting; kinesthesiology, but not dance. It's okay to read a Shakespeare play as literature, but the instructor who attempts to perform scenes from one of his plays in class will probably be charged with "wasting valuable classroom time." While a history professor might valorize Walt Whitman's poetry for the vivid picture it offers of Civil War era America, she and her colleagues might find it difficult to graduate a student who wanted to study history by creating poetry. Apparently, poet Wallace Stevens got it backwards when he titled a work "Not Ideas About The Thing But The Thing Itself," at least as far as university curricula are concerned.

A number of years ago, the Getty Foundation invested a large amount of money to "improve" and "standardize" arts education in public schools (*Improving*). This was an admirable initiative because in far too many schools around the country, "art" classes consisted of little more than the drawing-a-turkey-by-tracing-your-hand or gluing-macaroni-to-a-box projects many of us remember from childhood. Yet, while the Getty Foundation's efforts may have helped to raise awareness of the value of rigor and concepts in art classes, their conclusions caused national controversy because their recommendations would have resulted in replacing hands-on art classes with courses in analysis and "appreciation." The Getty agenda simply reaffirmed the traditional educational paradigm for the arts: it's fine to talk about them, but you better not send my child home with paint on her clothes.

The reasoning underlying the Getty agenda is that most people will have an involvement with the arts as consumers rather than as practitioners. Using this reasoning, the Getty goals of art appreciation and analysis are both economical and helpful. Not only will schools save all that money they would have "wasted" on art supplies, but they will help to increase connoisseurship in students (Pie-slicing 101, if you will) and, at the same time, resolve all the messy issues about how one can quantify "creativity" as a learning outcome. Much of the appeal of the Getty agenda is that it allows easy, unequivocal testing. Certainly, it simplifies things. After all, the question "Who painted 'Bedroom at Arles'?" has a correct answer. The teacher is spared the difficulty of grading papers on more ambiguous matters such as *why* Van Gogh might have created the work or *how* our fantasies of perfection spill over into our environments. Unfortunately, their form of art education leaves us with the standard academic problem: observation and cognition as the only forms of engagement with a subject leaves out both the students' bodies and all their embodied emotions.

Howard Gardner's studies of differently-abled learning patterns (first put forth in the 1983 *Frames of Mind: The Theory of Multiple Intelligences*) has begun to change this viewpoint. Gardner's work on what he calls the different "intelligences" has demonstrated not only that the mind is not divorced from the body, but also that different individuals show marked preferences for certain forms of sensory information. Hence, there are kinesthetic learners, who understand through movement and the body, and aural learners, who will comprehend a spoken text more quickly than a text viewed silently from the page. Many teachers at the elementary, junior high, and high school levels have begun to incorporate Gardner's concepts with great success. The student who seems to be struggling with reading, for example, may simply need to hear the text read aloud to increase comprehension. Someone who is bored with a lecture on the water cycle might come to life if asked to act it out.

Another way to think of Gardner's different intelligences is that the various senses (especially sight, hearing, and touch) provide sensory "windows" to the human mind. For whatever quirk of genetics or enculturation, different students prefer certain windows to others, and a good teacher will attempt to throw open as many of these windows as possible when approaching a particular subject. This also helps to explain why interdisciplinary approaches to learning can be so effective, as they encourage the student to view the subject through several different vantage points, either simultaneously or sequentially. As Klein and Newell note, "there is no unique interdisciplinary pedagogy. [Interdisciplinary studies] typically draws on innovative pedagogies that promote dialogue and community, problem-posing and problem-solving capacities, and an integrative habit of mind" (15). Despite these interdisciplinary scholars' emphasis on the need for a variety of pedagogical approaches, the examples that they offer stress cognitive, rather than affective or bodily, forms of learning.[1] I argue that rather than focus solely on left-brain analysis, using numbers and language as the sole forms of access, interdisciplinary teaching ideally should encourage a more broadly experiential approach to learning and acknowledge the unity of mind and body in the learning process.

As academics, we tend to sell the body short, relying on the brain to the exclusion of the rest of the body, which often has its own surprising wisdom. When I played in Balinese gamelan ensembles, I had to learn melodies that interlocked with neighboring melodies. These rapid little patterns require that each note be damped as the next note is played. One hand strikes, the other damps, with the damping hand one note behind the striking hand, in a perpetual canon. I found that if I tried to perform this act by *thinking* about it, I stumbled every time. When I trusted my body to remember the phrase, I had no problem: my body knew the pattern, not my mind. Even now, I suspect that my conscious mind no longer remembers all those tunes; but if placed in front of a *gangsa*, my hands would still know the patterns.

Being forced into an acknowledgment that my body is not merely the vehicle my mind rides to work in each day, but rather something that holds its own intelligence, apart from what my "mind" tells it to do, was both enlightening and humbling. It taught me that if one can instill a concept into the physical body as well as into the cognitive mind, one reaches a different, richer understanding of that concept, a literal "embodying" of the idea. This realization now guides my work as an interdisciplinary instructor and has led to my development of a performative pedagogy that encourages students to think not only with their brains, but with their skin, their tongues, and their noses.

As a teacher, I have been fortunate to teach almost exclusively in interdisciplinary programs. In my twenty years with the Interdisciplinary Arts Department at Columbia College in Chicago, and in nine years with the First-Year Program at the School of the Art Institute of Chicago, and in three years with the Illinois Summer School for the Arts, and even in the summer spent teaching in Duke University's prestigious Talent Identification Program (TIP) for gifted junior high school students, I have always taught either interdisciplinary courses or discipline-specific courses that focused on a topic in an interdisciplinary context. I have been privileged to work with other instructors who have taught me a great deal about myself and about teaching in the process.

One of the outcomes of my teaching and of my own interdisciplinary work as a "performance artist" has been learning how to engage students' bodies as well as their minds with a particular subject matter. Of course, if I were teaching "dance," that would be a given. But over the past decade or so, I have used performance as a way of teaching literary analysis, humanities, and art history—subjects typically taught exclusively through linguistic analysis. This approach raises the questions: What is to be gained through "performing" these traditionally academic subjects? Can performance be utilized in a way that transcends the social studies "skits" many of us endured in grammar school?

My initial impetus to use a performance-based approach first emerged in a class I taught at Duke University in the summer of 1989. Students in Duke's TIP program are classified as "verbally and mathematically gifted," and the class of twelve- to fifteen-year-old students I was teaching (in collaboration with Nana Shineflug, my colleague from Columbia College) were easily the intellectual match of any college undergraduate I had encountered in a classroom. At one point in our course, we wanted students both to write and interpret poetry. The students were already adept at traditional forms of literary analysis, so the question became how to push them to new insights into how a poem creates meaning.

We decided to have students perform poems. Students were to read and present poems that they selected from an array of poems provided by me and my co-teacher. We first coached them on how to read the text effectively, and they quickly discovered that the inflections of their readings mirrored what they thought the poem meant. In other words, simply reading the poem aloud involved interpreting and analyzing the poem. Next, we encouraged them to set their reading within a performative environment. This new process of contextualizing their reading in a particular space also quickly revealed new insights into what a given poem was trying to say (or trying *not* to).

Some of their performances were remarkable. Two immediately come to mind. One young woman gave a reading of the W. B. Yeats's poem, "The Second Coming," in which she was enclosed in a closet and lit from behind. With her long hair streaming from an electrical fan behind her, she almost had to shout to be heard over the drone of the fan. Not only did the pouring of her hair seem to personify Yeats's words about "turning in a widening gyre," the overall effect was frightening and vivid. Here was an angry angel with a warning for humanity. To this day, whenever I read Yeats's poem, I envision her standing in that tiny closet.

Two other students, working collaboratively, attacked Wallace Stevens's poem, "The House Was Quiet and the World Was Calm." As one student recited the poem in a nervous, apprehensive manner, his partner slunk around the edges of the room, a shadowy, sneaky presence that we in the audience were never sure whether we were supposed to be aware of or not. In the discussion that followed the performance, we pondered issues of subtext and deconstruction. On the one hand, by filling us with a nameless anxiety, the performance had undermined everything the poem was saying about the nocturnal calm of a house on a summer night. On the other hand, most people know that staying alone in an empty house is rarely a completely calm experience; its very silence sensitizes us to small noises and things, real or imagined, that we can't see. Indeed, the performance had found a way of examining an unstated emotional subtext of the poem, one that might not have been revealed when silently reading or talking about the text.[2]

The following year, I began teaching a class on the History of Interdisciplinary Arts in the Masters Program in Interdisciplinary Arts at Columbia College. In approaching this class—the only required art history course in the program—I was struck by two conflicting concerns. On the one hand, to examine the interdisciplinary impetus in art-making would require an extremely broad survey approach, drawing information as much from the social sciences (especially cultural anthropology) as from art history. On the other hand, a graduate-level art history course seemed to me to cry out for a seminar approach in which students could focus their attention on a very specific period in art history. Rather than try to choose only one of these approaches for my class, I decided to teach both kinds of class at once and to use performance as a central aspect of the class.

Luckily for me, there is no set curriculum on the history of interdisciplinary art, as it has typically existed at the peripheries of art historical discussion. As a result, I was able to invent a curriculum focused on the role that the arts play in culture and on the way the forms of art, which are influenced by culture, change over time. I drew on sources as diverse as anthropologists Victor Turner and William Irwin Thompson, historian David Fromkin, and art historians Lisa Jardine and Steven Watson.[3] Because I am concerned with the interdisciplinary aspects of the arts, I tend not to talk about works created during times of "specialization" in the arts. That is, I move in fast leaps from cave paintings to the Renaissance; but in considering the arts from the seventeenth through the nineteenth centuries, I focus on opera, the only truly "interdisciplinary" form happening during these times of specialization.

Fully half of the semester is spent on twentieth-century movements and events that were interdisciplinary in nature. Movements such as Futurism and Surrealism, for example, manifest themselves in visual art, music, literature, and performance; thus, they make useful material for research on interdisciplinary art. I also spend time on collaborative projects such as the ballet *Parade*, which featured Cubist sets by Picasso, a libretto by Jean Cocteau, and a score by Erik Satie. Often such collaborative projects appear on the margins of art history, things mentioned in passing, but not discussed in detail. I invert the normal order and focus on collaborations, rather than on individually produced paintings or other artistic phenomena. By the end of the semester, I have provided a long-term, broad-based perspective that many students in the class find empowering: it is what they had always wanted to know about the history of the arts, but had never found in discipline-specific classes.

My past experience has led me to believe that most of my students are not prepared to do the extensive research I did to organize these lectures. Thus, the "seminar" portion of the class takes a different tactic, in which performance plays a crucial part. Students select a time period and location on which to focus (I suggest many possibilities, and they vote for their choice). I encourage them to select a time and place when artists from different backgrounds would have been working together and influencing each other. (Some examples include Paris in 1909, Paris in 1935, Berlin in 1925, New York in 1967, or San Francisco in 1969.) Then each student selects an artist, writer, composer, dancer, and so on who would have been active during the time period in question and preferably would have worked primarily in the place suggested. (An artist who worked mostly in Paris might have conceivably visited New York, so we can sometimes stretch the point.) No anachronisms are allowed, however: Isadora Duncan cannot return from the grave, for example.

Each student then writes a research paper in the first person about the life of the artist and from the vantage point of the artist that he or she has selected; and this paper constitutes the student's midterm examination in the class. The paper is written in first person to encourage students to subjectify their topics. How would this artist have described his or her own life? Writing from the viewpoint of the author also prompts the student to make a variety of disciplinary connections—that is, to synthesize the artist's diverse social, cultural, and political experiences and influences and to see the connections between the artist's context and his or her artistic creations. Students are engaged in this first level of research even as I am lecturing on patterns of conspicuous consumption in the Renaissance or discussing the importance of religious belief to the art of the Middle Ages. The students' midterm presentations of summaries of their papers occur just as my own lectures are entering the twentieth century, and just as performance begins to enter the class.[4]

Having now created a personal identification with a particular artist in a particular location, students, for the second half of the semester, prepare for the final exam. The general time and place selected at the beginning of the semester are now narrowed to a particular day and specific site. (For example, instead of San Francisco in the 1960s, the focus tightens to City Lights Bookstore, July 20, 1969. Or, instead of Paris in the early 1900s, it becomes Gertrude Stein's atelier at 27 Rue de Fleurus on January 3, 1909.) Often, the date is selected on the basis of a particular historical event (the opening night of a ballet, the moon landing of Apollo 12, a birthday party, etc.) or because it is an occasion when people might have a party (New Year's Eve seems to figure prominently). After selecting this highly focused time and place, the students then prepare to attend an evening event *as their chosen artist*. This performance requires that they know not only *who* they are (i.e., they must have a clear grasp of the minutiae of the artist's biography and a solid recollection of what their artist did when, where, and why), but also *how* they would interact with all the other people in the room that evening. Who would they snub? Who would they embrace? With whom would they have slept? Who would they cross the room to avoid? And to all these questions, one must add the important question: Why?

I myself arrive as a reporter, out to interview everyone in the room. Typically, I am accompanied by our department chairperson, who likes to play the role of "gossip columnist" and grill everyone about the embarrassing details of their personal lives. I also warn students that they had better be cognizant of what is happening in the world on the particular date in question, including knowing such mundane facts as what the weather was like that day or what was on the front page of the newspaper. (I also advise them that in some cases, the most appropriate response for their person will be "Oh, who reads the newspapers?")

To facilitate the fairly intense planning and preparation needed to pull off this "historical recreation," I abbreviate my lectures during the second half of the term so that students can use part of each week's class as planning time for the final. On the week before the final exam, I am presented with an "invitation" to whatever the occasion is that prompts the gathering. These invitations have ranged from carefully engraved invitations to an "at home" with Gertrude Stein and Alice B. Toklas to directions scribbled on the back of a napkin about a party being held at City Lights Bookstore in San Francisco. In nine years of teaching this class, only once has this final exam taken place in a college classroom. In all other circumstances, students have carefully arranged and prepared a unique location for the exam. Most memorable among these events was the time the students converted one of their apartments into Gertrude Stein's flat with the most telling object being a recreation of Picasso's portrait of Stein carefully hung on the wall. The portrait had even been "tweaked," so that the Gertrude in the portrait resembled the person playing Gertrude that evening.

Although this event may sound like (and usually is) a "fun" evening, I hasten to point out the sheer effort involved in it, both for myself and the students. In essence, I give a series of oral exams that evening, with each student receiving a different set of questions. To succeed, students must memorize a wealth of factual information ranging from birth dates to significant others to gallery representatives to publications. They need to be ready, in their persona, to answer any question posed about their life and work. In recent years, I have moved away from picky factual questions toward discursive "essay questions": What do you think of contemporary art these days? What's the best book you've read recently? Which artist was most influential on your work, and why? These kinds of questions can be tricky enough to answer for oneself, but to answer it for an historical figure requires extensive research and preparation as well as the ability to remain calm under pressure. Many students report that what makes the exam most daunting is having to know what it might have been like to live—with all of the attendant ephemeral knowledge that implies—during another period of time.

Along those lines, it is often the simplest, most benign conversational question that catches students off guard. A favorite question of mine is the seemingly innocent "So, what about this weather, huh?" Having a clear knowledge of what the weather was like on a given date, such as the 1925 New Year's Eve in Berlin, is sometimes not simply a matter of academic trivia. As it happens, in this case, the city was flooded after several days of torrential rain, something much reported in the news and an event of some consequence. A party of influential people gathered at that time would certainly have been talking about such a phenomenon, and, indeed, everybody at our fictional party was.

Another example occurred when the exam was set in San Francisco in 1969 and I launched each interview by asking the person, "What's your sign?," a question included in many party conversations in the late 1960s. In several instances, I watched the student's eyes widen, as he or she mentally tried to recall their date of birth and to calculate under which sign of the zodiac that date fell. Again, my question was not intended simply to stump them, but to help them realize that if one is supposed to "be" another person, you would know certain kinds of information without thinking; and you would need to organize and synthesize those diverse bits of information using a historical and personal perspective that is not your own. This ability to shift and act out different perspectives and to integrate multiple sources of information deepens students' learning by prompting them not only to think about interdisciplinarity but also to literally *embody* it.

Because students are engaging in activities that are not the traditional fare in college classrooms and are absorbing the material in their bodies as well as in their minds, they are actually learning the course content more deeply and are more motivated to pursue the course material more fully. Indeed, their motivation and deep learning is evident in the depth of their research. For example, after asking a student (who was "being" artist Judy Chicago for the evening) where she studied art, she proceeded to go back to her grade school art teacher and then outline every important teacher she'd had since then. On the other hand, a student portraying Robert Motherwell, who had the artist's exhibition record and theoretical concerns down cold, was completely stumped when I casually asked, "So, Bob, are you married right now?"

Performance has turned out to be such a valuable way of increasing student insight and learning in my art history course that I have also applied it in a humanities course called "Humanities for the Performing Artist." In this course, I used a performative final exam of another kind. After reading works from a range of time periods (including Sophocles' *Oedipus Rex*, Shakespeare's *The Tempest*, Ovid's *Metamorphoses*, and Friedrich Dürrenmatt's *The Visit*), students selected a character from one of these works to impersonate in the final. Working collaboratively in groups of four or five, students created "talk shows" in which one of them acted as "host" and the others appeared as "guests," to discuss a selected topic.

The results of these collaborations were wonderfully strange and deliciously funny. Try to imagine *The Jove Show* with a blusteringly confident Jupiter as host, and all of the guests being women he had raped or seduced. Needless to say, things got ugly in a hurry. Or try to picture a retake on *Judge Judy* as "Judge Juno," who really got flustered when she found herself trying to deal with complaints from mortals about her own dear husband. Other situations mixed time and place willy-nilly, as Joan of Arc debated Icarus about "who got burned worse."

These presentations, which are hands-down students' favorite aspect of my humanities class, provide students with insights that connect works of literature with the present. It is impossible to read the story of Daphne and Apollo the same way once you have heard Daphne nervously hold forth about this guy claiming to be a god who's been "stalking" her. Performance also brings to life the interconnected concepts that run from one literary work to another. Rather than take notes as I lecture on the related themes of various works of literature, students discover them for themselves as they place temporally diverse literary figures on the same couch in an imaginary TV studio.

In his commentaries on the ancient Chinese book, the *I Ching*, Richard Wilhelm notes the following: "The way to study the past is not to confine oneself to mere knowledge of history, but through the *application* of this knowledge *to give actuality to the past*" (105). This is the driving concept behind my use of performance in my classes. In completing their performances, students learn how to conduct research, work in seminar formats, and acquire intellectual information, but the goal is never simply the acquisition of data for its own sake. Rather, the most important learning objective of performance-based pedagogy is to teach students—both in their bodies and in their minds—how diverse disciplinary data can be integrated and applied to render the past as living present.

NOTES

1. The same emphasis on cognitive forms of learning exists in Newell and Green's article in which they underscore the need for interdisciplinary teaching to promote the higher order thinking skills in Bloom's taxonomy (32). See also Hursh, Haas, and Moore who prioritize cognitive development in interdisciplinary general education courses. Even Carlisle who focuses on the importance of the arts in interdisciplinary teaching and who wisely criticizes disciplinary teaching for teaching "the results of the discipline but not the nature of the discipline itself" (390), ends up focusing on logocentric, rather than embodied, forms of teaching (by stressing the need for dialogue with people from other disciplines and the importance of metaphors and language of form for understanding cross-disciplinary connections).

2. The curriculum we developed for this course at Duke was carefully documented at the time, but remains unpublished.

3. Turner's essay, "Acting in Everyday Life and Everyday Life in Acting," is required reading. Thompson's *The Time Falling Bodies Take to Light* is worth seeking out. Fromkin's *The Way of the World* is a very useful overview of human history. Jardine's *Worldly Goods: A New History of the Renaissance* affirmed my sense of the Renaissance as an era of multiculturalism and disposable income. Watson's *Strange Bedfellows: The First American Avant-Garde* and *Prepare for Saints: Gertrude Stein, Virgil Thomson, and the Mainstreaming of American Modernism* are models of interdisciplinary art history. Steven Watson has twice been a guest lecturer in my class.

4. Over the years, students have periodically gone to great lengths to make these research projects memorable. One student, investigating the work of Juan Gris, created a faux journal/sketchbook of the artist, with extensive comments and observations, all in Spanish, despite the fact that the student himself did not speak Spanish. He therefore had to write the entire text out first in English, have it translated, and then write it all out in longhand into the sketchbook. (The original English paper was turned in as a "translation" of the sketchbook.) In another case, a student investigating Käthe Kollwitz created a "letter" from Kollwitz to her son, on the eve of being presented a major award. This letter so beautifully captured the artist's concerns about human rights, her perspective as a parent who had lost one child to war, and her own integrity as a human being, that many in the class were in tears after hearing the letter read in class. Another student created a whole series of faux-historical letters and telegrams to describe key elements in the life and work of the German film director George W. Pabst.

WORKS CITED

Bergson, Henri. "An Introduction to Metaphysics." 1903. Indianapolis: Bobbs-Merrill Co., 1955.

Carlisle, Barbara. "Music and Life." Newell, *Interdisciplinarity* 389–98.

Dürrenmatt, Friedrich. *The Visit.* New York: Grove Press, 1962.

Fromkin, David. *The Way of the World.* New York: Alfred A. Knopf, 1999.

Gardner, Howard. *Frames of Mind: The Theory of Multiple Intelligences.* New York: Basic Books, Inc., 1983.

Hursh, Barbara, Paul Haas, and Michael Moore. "An Interdisciplinary Model to Implement General Education." Newell, *Interdisciplinarity* 35–50.

Improving Visual Arts Education: Final Report on the Los Angeles Getty Institute for Educators on the Visual Arts (1982–1989). Santa Monica, CA: J. Paul Getty Trust, 1993.

Jardine, Lisa. *Worldly Goods: A New History of the Renaissance.* New York: Doubleday, 1996.

Klein, Julie Thompson, and William H. Newell. "Advancing Interdisciplinary Studies." Newell, *Interdisciplinarity* 3–22.

Newell, William H., ed. *Interdisciplinarity: Essays from the Literature.* New York: College Entrance Examination Board, 1998.

Newell, William H., and William J. Green. "Defining and Teaching Interdisciplinary Studies." Newell, *Interdisciplinarity* 23–34.

Ovid. *Metamorphoses.* Trans. David R. Slavitt. Baltimore: John Hopkins University Press, 1994.

Shakespeare, William. *The Tempest.* New York, Washington Square Press, 1961.

Sophocles. *Oedipus Rex.* New York: Players Press, 1993.

Stevens, Wallace. "Not Ideas About The Thing But The Thing Itself" and "The House Was Quiet and the World Was Calm" *Collected Poems.* New York: Vintage Books, 1982. 358; 534.

Thompson, William Irwin. *The Time Falling Bodies Take to Light: Mythology, Sexuality and the Origins of Culture*. New York: St. Martin's Press, 1981.

Turner, Victor. "Acting in Everyday Life and Everyday Life in Acting." *From Ritual to Theatre: The Human Seriousness of Play*. New York: Performing Arts Journal Publications, 1982. 102–123.

Watson, Steven. *Prepare for Saints: Gertrude Stein, Virgil Thomson, and the Mainstreaming of American Modernism*. New York: Random House, 1998.

———. *Strange Bedfellows: The First American Avant-Garde*. New York: Abbeville Press, 1991.

Wilhelm, Richard, ed. *The I Ching or Book of Changes*. 3rd. ed. Trans. C. F. Baynes. Princeton NJ: Princeton University Press, 1967. 105.

Yeats, W. B. "The Second Coming," *Selected Poems and Two Plays*. New York: Collier Books, 1962. 91.

CHAPTER 8

Margaret Sanger, Marie Curie, Maya Angelou, Marcel Duchamp, and Mary Belenky Teach a Women's Studies Course

A Discussion of Innovative Interdisciplinary Approaches to Feminist Pedagogy

Nancy M. Grace

LET'S PRETEND

Picture, if you will, a comfortable seminar room. Two walls, the north and the east, feature large floor-to-ceiling windows facing an expansive green rimmed with large conifers and oak trees. Figures in white can be seen in the distance chasing a ball back and forth across the field, the faint "ahh" of their voices and the "pauck-pauck-pauck" of their bats barely audible through the glass. A third wall is lined with wooden bookcases holding dozens of leather-bound volumes. The center of the room embraces a large oak table, round and golden. Arcing it from all four poles are plushly upholstered chairs, enough to comfortably accommodate twenty people. Fifteen young men and women, three of the former and twelve of the latter, have already found places at the table. They chat quietly among themselves, shuffle papers occasionally, sip coffee and bottled water, and squirm ever so slightly in their chairs. Their eyes stray to the five empty seats, all contiguous along the northern crescent of the table. They're waiting for class to begin. Waiting to see how an undergraduate introduction to women's studies course can be taught by such luminaries as Margaret Sanger, Marie Curie, Maya Angelou, Marcel Duchamp, and Mary Belenky. All seated there know that Margaret Sanger pioneered the reproductive rights movement in the United States; that Marcel Duchamp revolutionized the visual arts into what we now call the postmodern; that Maya Angelou dared to make art of her life story as a black woman and victim of sexual abuse; that Marie Curie won two Nobel Prizes, one in physics and one in chemistry; and that Mary Belenky, with several colleagues, transformed our thinking about women's understanding their text, *Women's Ways of Knowing*.

Ten minutes later, all five have entered and taken their seats. The atmosphere is electric, tiny dust motes dancing spasmodically in thin bands of light that braid the air. If you're anything like the students, you're hoping that one or more of the instructors will explain what the course is all about. You've read the college catalog; you think you know. It's called "Introduction to Women's Studies," and if it functions at all like a more conventional disciplinary introductory course, it should identify basic concepts and principles in the field and require that students read and discuss seminal texts.

Good. A syllabus is being distributed. This should help clarify. All heads dip down to note the text that now lies in front of them. It informs us that the course will examine the diversity of women's lives and the complex intersections of race, class, and gender in culture and society; explore varieties of women's experience, the ways in which that experience has been socially constructed and the ways women have developed their own understandings of their lives; and introduce some of the tools for both evaluating and generating knowledge about women and gender. It also states that the course will be interdisciplinary, critically drawing on multiple disciplines, as well as alternative perspectives—particularly the lived experience of self and others—in order to lead the class toward an integration of insights.[1]

The syllabi are quickly discarded, however, and attention redirected as Marie Curie stands to speak. The renowned scientist dressed in black reads softly from a small slip of paper: *I was one of only two hundred and ten women among nine thousand men when I came to study at the Sorbonne. All my mind was centered on my studies, and all that I saw and learned that was new delighted me. It was all very complicated because the men did not think of me as a thinker, and they did not think of me as a woman either. But I was a part of a movement in Poland, my home country, called Polish positivism, which believed that through science we could overcome oppression. I still hold that belief* (Bragg 248–50).

As she retakes her seat, the class sits in appreciative silence. The stillness of the room is quickly broken, however, by Margaret Sanger, an elegant woman who strikes a pose of defiant heroism. In her clenched fist, she holds a pamphlet titled "The Woman Rebel," and her words, emanating from a Madonna-like face framed with soft brown hair, are intended to jolt the students from complacency: *No Gods, No Masters! Look the world in the face with a go-to-hell look in the eye—have an idea—speak and act in defiance of con-*

vention! No woman can call herself free who does not own and control her own body. To that end, we'll proceed so that you, the younger generation, can push the cause over the top (Chesler 154, 192, 395; Douglass 50).

It is Marcel Duchamp who then extends his lanky frame toward the students: *I want to change my identity. Wait! I have an idea—why not change sex? It's so much simpler than changing my name. Please, allow me to introduce myself: I am Rose Selavy,* and he tilts his head provocatively, pursing deeply rouged, red lips under coal-smudged, dark, oval eyes. With pinky fingers extended, he snuggles his fur collar up against his chin. *We will pay close attention to my piece called "To Be Looked At (From the Other Side of the Glass) with One Eye, Close to, for Almost an Hour" done in 1918. It is a glass work, an anti-retinal, conceptual object. Here is a photograph of it* (Cabanne 144).

Maya Angelou, with a slight nod to her colleagues, stands and begins to speak, her deep, rich voice filling the chamber: *People have read that I was*

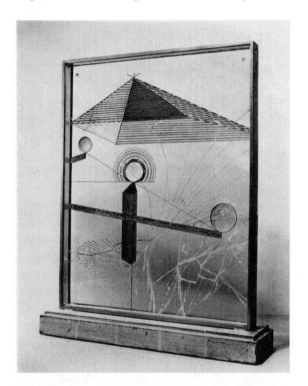

Marcel Duchamp, "To Be Looked At (From the Other Side of the Glass) with One Eye, Close to, for Almost an Hour" (Buenos Aires, 1918). Reprinted with permission of the Museum of Modern Art, New York. Katherine S. Dreier Bequest. Photograph © 2001 The Museum of Modern Art, New York.

raped at seven-and-a-half, that I went through traumatic experiences, that I was an unmarried mother. Now they want to know, how did I make it over? That's a question with almost one million answers. My life is my message, and my message to all aspiring Black women is the reconstruction of my experiential "self." My multi-volume autobiography is the text of my life and the text of this class (Williams 32, 47, 48).

Mary Belenky assumes the role of concluding the presentations: *Much of what we now know and want to communicate to you came to us as fresh knowledge, even though we realize that this knowledge is not new but has been underground, unarticulated, intuited, or ignored. As we worked, we were aware of the gradual shifts in our perspectives on the nature of scientific inquiry, feminist theory, and the nature of human adaptation and potential. Ideally, we would wish for you the satisfaction of discovery and the pleasure of insight that we have experienced during the months of collecting, reading, and planning for this course* (Belenky et al. 20). *And now we'd like to hear what you have to say. Let's open this up for discussion.*

Silence falls for a few short moments. Then papers rustle and chairs squeak. Several hands are slowly pushed up into the air, and with them voices, tentative at first but soon vibrant and excited, collectively congregate. For the next hour, class is under way.

FICTION IS REALITY

This case is, of course, imaginary but nonetheless grounded in truth. We've all most likely fantasized about what it might be like to take a class with the heroes of our reading histories. All five are products of my imagination, functioning to portray the ongoing struggle among women's studies scholars and teachers to define the field, to maintain its shape, and to advance feminist political goals. In this chapter, I will use them to provide an understanding of the intersection of women's studies, feminist pedagogy, and interdisciplinary teaching. In particular, they will show us that women's studies strives through interdisciplinary thinking to create innovative pedagogy that (1) addresses and incorporates difference meaningfully (e.g., sex, race, class, ethnicity, culture); (2) values experience, both of the students in the course and those who are studied in the course; (3) honors and inquires about the notion of identity through voice, including coping with resistance to feminism; (4) questions assumptions and authority; (5) teaches process as well as product, using conflict productively; and (6) fosters learning in multiple contexts and in multiple ways (e.g., field experience, service learning, understanding the privilege and limitations of traditional academic approaches). In totality, our five instructors illustrate that interdisciplinary feminist pedagogy must be mutable, relational, and dynamic, and it must work toward the conscious integration of disciplinary insights.

At first glance, the five may seem incompatible and inappropriate companions for such a purpose, and indeed there was a certain arbitrariness in the way that I chose them, a "chanciness" about the whole project, just as there is about so much of the real learning that we do. On the one hand, I simply liked the fact that their first names started with "m." But, at the same time, the selection was highly plotted and contrived—all to move me, and ultimately my readers, toward an articulation of a difficult topic. My goal is to bring together what appear to be disparate pieces and forge them into something larger, an argument that will illuminate the nature of thinking about women's studies and interdisciplinary teaching. These two fields, just like my five luminaries, at times seem distinct and unique; at other times transmogrified into a terrible unity. Their boundaries blur as they swim toward and into each other; and at still other times, they seem charged with properties of both particles and waves. The tension that the reader might feel upon being introduced to such disparate figures mirrors what often happens in interdisciplinary courses. Students are given what seem to be very different viewpoints, texts, and methods, and asked somehow to synthesize them. Their appearance in this context replicates that cognitive dissonance and illustrates strategies for easing students toward integration.

Achieving integration for women's studies students is no mean feat—especially when we consider the ambitious scope of feminism itself. Feminism is "the political theory and practice that struggles to free all women: women of color, working-class women, poor women, disabled women, lesbians, old women—as well as white, economically privileged, heterosexual women. Anything less than this vision of total freedom," according to Barbara Smith, "is not feminism, but merely female self-aggrandizement" (Cohee et al. 11). There are many different kinds of feminism, including liberal, Marxist, essentialist, African-American, and existential; however, the fundamental goal of all feminisms is a radical restructuring of the social order, including the academy, to affect equality between women and men. Feminist thought, when introduced into the classroom, becomes feminist pedagogy, a theory about teaching and learning processes that affects our classroom practices by providing criteria to evaluate strategies and techniques in the context of the course goals.[2] In light of these pronouncements, our five panelists fall considerably short of the feminist ideal: Duchamp was not overly concerned about furthering the equality of women. Angelou speaks from a narrowly defined racial standpoint. Sanger dabbled with the eugenics movement to maintain her own political agenda. Curie never rallied to lead a feminist movement, and Belenky has produced a theory that appears to privilege the thinking of educated women.

The five-star panel also suggests something other than what it claims to be: While the instructors have created a syllabus that names its course as interdisciplinary, their presentations reflect more accurately multidisciplinarity that marshals many disciplines without synthesizing these perspectives. Early women's studies courses were typically organized in this way, perhaps to illustrate that feminism was relevant to all. Often, these courses focused not so much on issues essential to women's lives but rather on the disciplines compartmentalized within the academy (see Tavris and Offir's *The Longest War: Sex Differences in Perspective* as an example of this approach). In fact, our teaching team seems readymade (no Duchamp pun intended) for such a course: Angelou = Literary Studies; Duchamp = the Fine Arts; Sanger = Political Science/Social Activism; Belenky = Psychology; and Curie = the Natural Sciences. As a pentad, they create a whole with distinct and autonomous parts, mirroring the early stages of feminist pedagogy and, to some extent, the current state of many women's studies courses: taught within disciplines from a feminist perspective.

Yet, to achieve interdisciplinarity, these five teachers must teach as a coherent unit throughout the duration of the course and help students grasp "the diversity of women's lives," by explaining this specific phenomenon in its totality. They will have to be willing to engage other disciplines and to adopt temporarily their assumptions and worldviews (Newell and Green 31–32), thereby connecting their different perspectives with one another "to establish a unity of thought through the intermeshing of the questions of various lines of inquiry" (Hübenthal 429). With this in mind, it is not difficult to conclude that no single discipline can adequately address issues of identity, self, and other, and no single discipline can effectively destroy itself in order to transform both the academy and the larger social context in which it exists. It is rather the interdisciplinary world that promises greater potential for those who aim to achieve gender justice and to overcome oppression, for those who, as Stanley Fish argues, distrust the barriers between the academy and the outside and seek to "subvert the larger social articulation within which the academy" constructs its voice—to effect "revolution tout court" (103).

In this respect, Marcel Duchamp's object focus of the course becomes a critical metaphor enabling us to articulate features grounding interdisciplinary feminist pedagogy. *To Be Looked At (from the Other Side of the Glass) with One Eye, Close to, for Almost an Hour*, also known as the *Small Glass*, is a construction of lead wire, oil paint, rusty metal, magnifying lens, and silver leaf on glass. The work, which Duchamp finished in 1918, was later cracked by Katherine Dreier, Duchamp's lover and patron, and he left the cracks intact. The piece is approximately 2×1.5 feet and is part of the permanent collection of the Museum of Modern Art in New York City. What makes it so fascinating and appropriate for our purposes is both its name and its physical construction. The piece speaks to the process of human identity, the mechanization/transformation of such identity through the process of seeing and being seen. A viewer of the *Small Glass* can walk around the work, peering through it from any position around a circumference of 360°; and as he or she does so, the thing(s) seen shifts in form. For example, if viewed straight on, the images of the magnifying lens, the striated pyramid, and the suspended girders dominate the work, but the viewer can also see the cracks in the glass and can peer through the glass to the white, slightly cracked wall, which the glass foregrounds.

As one moves around the piece, other features float in and out of the work, including transitory, kinetic forms of art patrons and museum guards passing by or stopping to look at the work. The viewer can also see his or her *own* reflection in the glass, a virtual hologram that morphs as the viewer shifts position from cracked to uncracked spaces. If one were, for instance, to look at the piece for "almost an hour," the work would be in perpetual dynamism, despite its illusion of static form. As the name of the work suggests, self is "to be looked at . . . from the other side." In other words, what we know as self is constructed by others, from a subjective stance distanced from the object of construction; but paradoxically, that act of being seen is also a self-reflexive act—the viewer views herself, thereby making the viewer and the viewed one and the same. The piece then powerfully suggests that identity, the self as we commonly know it, is a reality of fluidity and plasticity, a composite of selves, parts consciously arranged but reconstructed through both intentionality and chance, a collaborative and constantly changing phenomenon.

As a metaphor of self, the *Small Glass* suggests that any pedagogy directed at the exploration of self, which women's studies certainly does, must acknowledge and work from the realization that self is neither universal nor individual. It is, in fact, relational. This means that no single standpoint has epistemological supremacy. The self that Duchamp's work opens up for us integrates distinct perspectives and encourages the manipulation and transformation of these perspectives. In the context of women's studies, the *Small Glass* signifies that if we are to speak of issues of identity and empowerment, we can no longer speak in simplistic terms (as we did in the 1960s and 1970s) and advance a universal, stable notion of woman who stands in direct opposition to the supreme and normalized "Man." Rather, we must understand that both concepts are dependent on their cultural and historical context as well as on their relationship to one another. As the context changes, so too do our conceptions of gender; and as the notion of *woman* changes, so too does our view of *man*.

Just as the *Small Glass* perpetually opens up the possibility of new relationships and perspectives on the self, the study of women opens up new networks of disciplinary relationships. Women's studies, then, must also be a study of men, a study of race, a study of class, a study of the divine, a study of self-representation, and the list goes on. It must, ultimately, engage the learner in a dynamic space where the concept of fixed identity is obliterated. In this place, the learner begins to understand positional methods of constructing identity, methods that ground different forms of identity in their respective material contexts and bring them into relation to each other (Goldberger et al. 162). Here, we are more likely to encounter and create new theory, new language, and new knowledge through integration and synthesis. And we are likely to see students view disciplines not as static entities, but as positional ones, ones that stand in relation to one another and to one's context.

Addressing and Incorporating Difference Meaningfully

In the "Let's Pretend" section, Duchamp's introduction of the *Small Glass* leads to Maya Angelou's declaration that her story is the text of the class. At this point, the class must shift its focus, must look at the "other" for an extended period of time, must enter into Angelou's world, her struggles with poverty, racism, and sexual abuse; and in the process, while watching her, they must take on her identity, merge with her, and assume her voice and body. All members of the class become the "to be looked at," at least for a short while. Many may find that the transformation demands Amazonian strength, challenging them to shift perspectives and see themselves in a shape heretofore unimagined. Even those who have had experiences analogous to Angelou's may resist the invitation to acknowledge commonality, which can in itself be a form of epistemological challenge, an experience that a student may or may not desire.

But no matter how difficult, the move is important and replicates a major challenge for women's studies and feminism during the twentieth century and into the twenty-first. We need to acknowledge that white, middle-class feminism is not the universal model, that black women and other women of color communicate important human realities that can be affected by the goals of feminism, and that women's studies as a phenomenon of the white-dominated academy must be willing to reposition itself to include all women. Consequently, the very "discipline" of women's studies, configured predominantly by white, middle-class women to reflect their respective political needs and concerns, is forced to rethink its own boundaries, its own hegemonic practices, the ways in which it has often executed the same invidious methods that it has accused patriarchy of practicing. In other words, the women's studies classroom, following the lead symbolized by Duchamp's *Small Glass* and Angelou's daring move to place herself in front of it, demands that feminists implement a pedagogy that compels us to look at ourselves as the other, and in so doing expands the vision of what we know as "woman."

To its credit, the field is attempting to meet the challenge. We are seeing more and more courses in women's studies, particularly the introductory course, dedicated to exploring issues of race and gender. In many cases, the course will emphasize women from the United States, so the syllabus might explore Caucasian representations through more "canonical" women's studies texts such as Betty Friedan's *The Feminist Mystique*, Kate Millet's *Sexual Politics*, and Charlotte Perkins Gilman's *The Yellow Wallpaper*. African-American perspectives are then introduced in nonfiction works such as Angela Davis' *Women, Race, and Class* or bell hooks' *Ain't I a Woman*. It is not uncommon to place these beside literary texts such as Zora Neale Hurston's *Their Eyes Were Watching God* or Toni Morrison's *Beloved*. The range of African-American experiences is often expanded through critiques of more current events such as the Clarence Thomas/Anita Hill hearing and through the visual arts, including films such as the Steven Spielberg adaptation of Alice Walker's *The Color Purple* and the photographs of the African-American conceptual and performance artist Adrian Piper. Some introductory courses may even push the national, and thus conceptual, boundaries even farther, addressing the black diaspora, concentrating on the interdisciplinary investigation and integration of the languages, histories, economies, and cultures of women from the Caribbean or Africa.

This focus on race, first seen from the perspective of African-American women, has also sensitized women's studies to the need to address all women of color, and thus introductory courses often strive to pay some attention to Native-American, Latina and Asian-American women. We have also become much more aware of white as a category of race, and it too becomes part of the discussion of how women's lives are determined within the framework of skin color.

No introductory course can do justice to all of these issues, and no student new to women's studies can make sense of this kaleidoscope of information in a mere quarter or semester. Consequently, what is now developing in women's studies programs across the United States is a body of upper-level courses, often taught from the interdisciplinary and global perspective, on the lives of women from India, China, Brazil, Chile, Japan, Russia, and other countries. As these courses have matured, they have also given rise to courses that merge these perspectives and resist balkanization according to race, ethnicity, and nationality.[3] These discussions are appropriate in the context of women's studies not only because these issues are being raised in the women's movement generally, but also because women's studies is a context in which women of all colors from around the globe actually come together.

Whether introductory or upper level, courses that engage students in the discussion of the dynamics of race and gender need to take heed of bell hooks's warning that we must not simply tack on "the black perspective," or any other perspective, at the end of course (see *Teaching*). This "add-on" approach does little to help synthesize a more complex vision of women's lives and, more often than not, merely perpetuates the belief in the marginalization of these perspectives. If we are to engage students in dynamic interdisciplinary thinking, we must develop course content that integrates multiple perspectives much like Watson and Cricks's double helix. Such content fosters kinetic thinking, the kind of thinking that spins like a dreidel, propelling one to circle, step back from, move toward, in effect dance with, Duchamp's *Small Glass*. This approach encourages us to see and be seen from many perspectives in order to discover that the one is actually a palimpsest revealing the many.

A course that does so, as our imaginary introductory class purports to do, will take the class full circle to Duchamp's provocative declaration in the "Let's Pretend" section that it's easier to change sex than a name. His statement wittingly plays with the paradoxes of gender. What emerges is a further complication: difference includes not only race, ethnicity, and nationality, but also sexuality. His remark implies that we have misunderstood the public markers of "woman" and "man." Sex, often considered a clear dualism of biological determinism, may be fairly plastic and open to morphing. A name, so seemingly arbitrary and superficial, may be rather recalcitrant. Duchamp himself changed sex by changing both name and the overt signs that signal sex and gender (makeup, clothes, posture), the result being that he highlighted the fact that gender is culturally coded. His adoption of the female persona of Rrose Selavy symbolically opens the door to issues of sexuality, gender studies, men's studies, masculinities, and queer theory, some of which, while related to women's studies and the goals of feminist pedagogy, can redirect the discussion away from women and back toward men. For example, one can ask the following: To what extent does the Duchampian enterprise of expanding male possibilities via the female/feminine truly empower the female; or is she diminished when her "territory," no matter how routinized and prescribed, is subsumed into that of the male? How do we talk about realities such as female and male eroticism, transsexuality, or homosexuality? How does the pursuit of men's studies generate from, rely on, and affect women's studies?

As with the concept of race, these lines of thinking ultimately encourage, if not demand, women's studies practitioners to think in interdisciplinary ways about their teaching practices. They must locate new discourses and methods—such as those provided by the synthesis of the visual arts, sociology, psychology, biology, and literary studies. At the introductory level, a women's studies course can introduce these issues quite effectively by using texts such as *Men's Lives* edited by Michael Kimmel and Michael Messner or *The Gendered Knot: Unraveling Our Patriarchal Legacy* by Allan Johnson to illustrate that man or woman *cannot exist without* woman or man and that both men and women *are and must be* involved in the praxis of social transformation. Upper-level courses can focus more specifically on topics such as queer theory, motherhood, fatherhood, or the erotic life, blending insights from disciplines such as biology, legal studies, cognitive neuroscience, and history.

Exploring Identity Through Voice

Both Duchamp's daring reconstruction of a gendered self as well as Angelou's brave narration of her life story reposition feminist pedagogy in that they nudge us, quite forcefully really, to reinvent an understanding of how knowledge is constructed and communicated. Knowledge does not come solely through textbooks or theoretical treatises—rather it comes through the language of women (and men) who find ways to tell their own stories. Virginia Woolf was keenly aware of this in 1929 when she wrote *A Room of One's Own*, still one of the fundamental feminist stories about female autonomy, power, and epistemology and a staple in many introductory courses. Following her lead, women's studies practitioners have long sought to enable students to speak from experience and to generate knowledge through narration, in the process systematically breaking down debilitating myths of gender. These stories can be of actual events in our lives or of what we would imagine our life narratives to be. Angelou represents the former, her life told in a series of memoirs; Duchamp the latter, his story told through photographs of Rrose Selavy and her signature on works of art. Both signal to us the need to develop women's studies pedagogy that focuses on individual and group voices, finding innovative ways to tell stories and work through ideas.

For many women's studies practitioners, this focus on stories means engaging students in the telling of their life stories by creating autobiography and memoir, forms that while historically undervalued and demeaned as inferior women's texts, have achieved a recent status as powerful vehicles of self-creation and revolution. As literary critic Suzette Henke claims, autobiography

> has the potential to be, a revolutionary form of writing. As such, it lends itself particularly well to the evolution of an enabling feminist discourse rooted in a diversity of ethnic backgrounds. As a genre, autobiography has always encouraged the author/narrator to reassess his or her past and to reinterpret a plethora of racial, sexual, and cultural codes inscribed on personal consciousness. It is no wonder, then, that minority women authors have reacted to the impetus of the second wave of feminism in the 1960s: they have appropriated the autobiographical act as a potential tool for liberation. Women's life-writing, cast in the form of memoir or confessional narrative, promises mastery over a fluid, shapeless, episodic history. (100)

There exist, however, distinct disciplinary biases against self-writing, characterizing a pedagogy that employs it as "soft"—not academically rigorous. While effective narration is by no means easy and flabby, the telling of life stories can be engaged more emphatically in an interdisciplinary setting where students are helped to see that storytelling is not merely a form of entertainment arising from a subjective standpoint but rather a central epistemological paradigm underpinning all disciplines. On some level, every disciplinarian tells stories. Moreover, when one engages in narration of life experiences, one is involved in critical and creative analysis of the culture that generated those experiences.

In this endeavor, it behooves us to think about how Angelou and Duchamp's projects can be augmented with the insights of Mary Belenky and her colleagues in psychology. Belenky's innovative work of recording and analyzing women's voices and ways of knowing reveals that, to know "woman," we must combine forms of discourse that reveal the complexities of women's speech and thought as contextually formed, admittedly an often shifting and amorphous phenomenon. Just as Belenky et al. were able to construct a new theory of female cognitive development by listening to women talk about their experiences and their dreams, feminist pedagogy can build interdisciplinary analytical frameworks to (re)position the student to examine self/other. We can create such frameworks by studying social science and historical texts as well as the texts of women outside the academy to explore issues such as agency, systemic oppression, auto/genocide, ethnic and gender identity. In the process, we effectively reconstruct the worldview of the autobiographer(s) as well as de- and reconstruct the worldview of the student. Students at any course level can be asked to keep journals to record their experiences, write memoirs of their childhood, create narrative fiction, poetry, or visual art that speaks to what they most fear or most want in life. These texts can be compared to the assigned readings. Because the students have become writers like those they are studying, the students' own work can exist as core material for the course.[4]

In addition, this practice directs us to reconsider the very language we use in the class, the way we define and understand voice, and the processes by which both teachers and students use their voices in the classroom to achieve the goals of feminist pedagogy. For anyone who has taught in an interdisciplinary context, these matters are already quite evident, as they are for practitioners of women's studies. In fact, the issue of language—the question of who is speaking and what is being spoken—arises quickly. This is because the very material by which disciplines build their barriers initially assumes an oppositional relationship to other disciplines and then evolves (ideally) into dialogic reciprocity as synthesis takes place. In this respect, the research of feminists Frances Maher and Mary Kay Tetreault has been extremely important. Their study of feminist classroom practices in six college and university settings reveals that instead of considering voice to be the marker of a unique perspective (i.e., the "true" or authentic voice of an individual as we have defined it over the last several hundred years), it is more appropriate to consider voice as an interpretive device "for looking at the construction of the classroom discourses" (Goldberger et al. 159).

Thus, voice is no longer a monolithic phenomenon but becomes a method that when combined with other methods functions as a tool to create knowledge: students in such an interdisciplinary context learn to navigate *among* and *with* diverse voices. For example, in our imaginary classroom, the students will have to deal with the aggressive and challenging voice of Margaret Sanger, which speaks from a set of values grounded in action and self-reliance; the more accommodating and self-effacing voice of Marie Curie, which emerges from a multicultural context of guardedness and self-protection; and the voice of Mary Belenky, which resonates with those of her collaborators as well as the pantheon of cognitive psychologists within and against which their research on women's ways of knowing emerged. These voices, as well as the students' own, become vehicles to create a more expansive framework within which to interpret gender and women's lives.

Questioning Authority and Assumptions

Interdisciplinary feminist pedagogy also leads us to reconceptualize the definition and function of "authority." As Maher and Tetreault point out, "Traditionally professorial authority arises from superior knowledge of a field; it is lodged in the hierarchical relationship of expert to teacher to student and is enforced institutionally by the power and duty to assign grades" (Goldberger et al. 159). Authority is also grounded in larger social beliefs regarding the value and thus the status of certain disciplines or areas of study. Such value is derived from the cultural receptivity to the fundamental assumptions of the disciplines. In Western culture, those that posit more pragmatic, rational, empirical assumptions are likely to be more highly respected. Thus, one derives authority from an inextricable link to often invisible but always autocratic belief systems. Maher and Tetreault, however, found that feminist pedagogy produced a new understanding of authority: "For us, authority . . . became an evolving factor within the framework of each classroom, reflecting professors' and students' varying relationships with each other as well as the material. In fact, we learned that . . . authority, like voice, is situational and constructed" (Goldberger et al. 159–60).

It is an interdisciplinary context that can enable classroom instructors to come to this very understanding, especially if the situation requires or allows a course to be taught by more than one person from across disciplines. In our imaginary scenario, we find it likely that all five instructors can learn from each other, and, in fact, will have to, since we cannot assume that, for example, Curie's knowledge of chemistry and physics is shared by the others, or that Duchamp's more mechanistic approach to art is grounded in the kind of knowledge that Curie herself has of physical processes. Knowledge of women's lives will vary considerably among the five, and sharing of perspectives will be necessary as each contributes to our understanding and, in the process, redefines the term "authority."

In cases where a team-teaching arrangement is not possible, the course instructor is wise to call on colleagues who are authorities or on students in the class who have special knowledge of specific fields of study. At the introductory level, instructors are most likely to be the ones who will take authority positions, but first-year students can be called on as well, particularly to speak as authorities on popular culture, work, family, and other broad-based cultural issues. In upper-level women's studies courses, students often bring a more solid body of conventional disciplinary knowledge and can act as reliable communicators of this knowledge. At any level, then, authority becomes a collaborative process, rather than a goal, a system of seeking knowledge, of moving in and out of positions as student and teacher. Doing so realigns the curriculum so that feminist pedagogy becomes more process-oriented than content-oriented and thus relevant to gender-resistant fields such as chemistry, mathematics, and physics.[5]

Whenever authority in an academic setting is reconstructed, participants encounter the very epistemological assumptions on which the disciplinary methods they use to generate knowledge are based: the questions they ask, the evidence they seek, the processes they employ. We certainly can't expect that all the instructors in our imaginary introductory course would agree with Curie's belief in the scientific method as a rational, gender-neutral pathway to the truth. Belenky might, but *Women's Ways of Knowing* intimates that good feminist science must consider the possibility that women exhibit patterns of cognitive development that differ from men's; therefore the science that we employ to understand gender will have to become more flexible and acknowledge the importance of social context—the interplay of nature and nurture—to a greater extent than the laboratory now allows. This feminist position might also seem plausible to Margaret Sanger, who developed her political vision as a result of dealing daily with poor women who had no choice but to become human incubators. Maya Angelou may argue vehemently against positivism of any kind as a tool for eliminating oppression, citing hundreds of years of so-called "good" scientific research which has been used to denigrate African Americans and women.[6] Angelou and Duchamp will likely seek and design pedagogical situations in which the imagination reveals truths, whereas Curie and Belenky may question the presumed unreliability of untested theory. Duchamp may declare that art is not responsible for speaking for anything other than itself, a position that might well anger Angelou and Sanger, whose worldviews advocate an existential imperative to act for the greater good.

For all, the intellectual encounter can reveal the strengths and weaknesses of these discrete positions. Each will come to realize that the theories with which they are accustomed to working cease to generate acceptable answers to complicated questions about women's lives. Each may eventually find, as did literary critic Carla Peterson when she wrote about African-American women activists, that their discourse at times "is disrupted by unanswered questions that mark the loss of a professional authority" (113). As the group continues the dialogue, however, they will find themselves engaged in the building of a new architecture, the buttressing of old beliefs with new epistemological technologies. As a result, not only are individual authority and supremacy critiqued, but so too is our belief in the authority and supremacy of specific disciplinary perspectives. They may even decide, as did Peterson, that the unanswered question, or speculation, is itself a methodology that encourages the thinker to push aside disciplinary authority and "claim the personal 'I' as its own authority" (115). This process is probably the most effective way to reconstruct the academy, to achieve the most radical of feminist goals; and for those of us who believe in the mission itself, the interdisciplinary work can be extremely exhilarating and exciting.

For students, however, the process of living with, learning from, and challenging individual or disciplinary authority may not be so exhilarating or liberating. In fact, first-year students in introductory women's studies courses may be more enervated than energized by such inquiry. After all, they have little sense of what constitutes a discipline, let alone the intellectual equipment with which to critique the foundational assumptions of multiple disciplines and to integrate knowledge through the process. They will likely struggle to see the import of the exercise when asked, for example, to contemplate the interdisciplinary significance of books such as Adrienne Rich's *Of Woman Born*, which blends the history of obstetrics, personal confession, and literary criticism, or Susan Bordo's *Unbearable Weight: Feminism, Western Culture and the Body*, which unifies traditional philosophical perspectives with sociology and media studies. When they next find themselves reading Angela Davis's *Women, Race, and Class*, Anne Fausto-Sterling's *Myths of Gender*, or Wendy Chapkis's *Beauty Secrets*, the intellectual leaps will be quite demanding. Most of them will not be familiar with the Marxist theory that underpins Davis's work or the empiricism of observation and experimentation in which Fausto-Sterling believes or the sociological theory with which Chapkis critiques the construction of beauty. They may well like or dislike the texts, but the act of questioning the texts may be more than they can do at other than a minimal level.

This does not mean, however, that interdisciplinary teaching of women's studies should not address this issue of textual authority. It most definitely should, but we need to be cognizant of how much we can ask of our students. First-years will need to be shown how to ferret out the assumptions of a text and look for evidence supporting the assumptions. They will need classroom activities such as journal writing and discussion (in class, in conventional print form, or online) that will consistently allow them to compare texts, to identify points of conflation and divergence as they encounter new and varied arguments about gender and women's lives. For students at this developmental stage, it may be most helpful to focus on asking questions, keeping in the forefront the goal of exploring women's lives by moving back and forth among a number of disciplines, returning to previously covered material as often as possible to build a comparative base.

More advanced students will be more adept identifiers and critics of disciplinary assumptions, but they too, like the first-year student, can benefit greatly from a pedagogy that places them in the positions of the authors they study. By doing this, they can become that kind of thinker, *that kind of authority*, at least for a short while, and thus develop the strategies to identify and critique different perspectives in order to take more measured footsteps toward synthesis.

Whatever the level of student, the interdisciplinary women's studies classroom can ask that students write their own poetry, design a scientific experiment, conduct qualitative or quantitative data through surveys, deliver a political speech, or create a visual representation of the material or metaphysical world. As they do so, the students should question what they hope to learn from the process, how the process compares with and differs from others, who benefits from the exercise, where such methods are appropriate, and how they can be combined. In effect, they will be immersed in a dialectic whereby they experience the power of authority as the personal "I" authority and as an expert (albeit neophyte) in a discipline(s).

Teaching Process and Product

Negotiating such processes is not easy, and feminist perspectives in an interdisciplinary context must take this into account. As I have intimated several times in our discussion thus far, the traditional linear, top-down method of imparting knowledge just doesn't work, and finding a pedagogy that follows a different method can be difficult for all learners (students and teachers). For example, again imagine Maya Angelou and Marcel Duchamp tackling issues of expression; each bristles at the perspective of the other, Angelou believing strongly in the redemptive power of language expressed in art and autobiography and Duchamp believing that art is not autobiography, nor even self-expression.[7] Dealing effectively with these two representations of apparently antithetical views of self and expressive material requires that the class as a whole must first struggle to understand each viewpoint, giving up (at least temporarily) one's own position. Then, they must ask critical questions to reveal ways in which each perspective either promotes or diminishes gender bias, and finally they must work to synthesize the two into a larger and new set of beliefs, values, and assumptions. In this scenario, the class should consider not only theories of both language and art but also the definition of gender itself, investigating the extent to which language and art are connected with the categories of masculine and feminine, the ways in which men can enter into discussions of women's oppression, and the ways in which gender has oppressed men as well. These inquiries build on and reveal the relational quality of gender—that we cannot know the feminine except in relation to the masculine and vice versa.

Feminist process, or the use of various strategies to stimulate learning and construct new epistemological frameworks, is not something that comes naturally to most of us; it is not central to the structure of Western education, and we don't pick it up easily through osmosis (Schniedewind 15). Therefore, learning how to listen to and work with opposing (or different or new) viewpoints must be stressed in women's studies courses, to the same degree as in more conventional content areas. Feminist process, then, automatically requires that we be willing to engage in ways of processing information that draw on strategies from disciplines other than our own and are more often an integration of various approaches. The process necessitates what Uma Narayan, an Indian feminist, calls "methodological humility," or the outsider's ability to "sincerely conduct herself under the assumption that, as an outsider, she may be missing something, and that what appears to her to be a 'mistake' on the part of the insider may make more sense if she had a fuller understanding of the context." Narayan advocates that such humility be coupled with "methodological caution," the outsider's careful attempt to criticize an insider position without denigrating or dismissing that position (38).

Feminist Nancy Schniedewind identifies several features of feminist process that instructors can integrate into their interdisciplinary courses to promote this kind of thinking. She recommends that at the introductory level, where the sharing of feelings is important to a student's ability to learn the course material, students need to be taught how to give and accept feedback. From a feminist perspective, feedback must be constructive, and students can be taught to create such feedback by describing rather than evaluating, being specific rather than general, focusing on behavior rather than a person, and taking into account the needs of both the receiver and giver of the commentary (18–19).

These techniques are particularly important at the introductory level where we find one of the great ironies of teaching women's studies at the beginning of the twenty-first century: the reluctance of young women (and of the few young men who take these classes) to call themselves feminist, even when their own behaviors, stands, and choices identify them as such. Connected with this reluctance is a belief pervasive among the traditional college-aged population that historically feminist problems no longer exist for most women—that the Margaret Sangers, Marie Curies, and Maya Angelous have already fought the hard fight and won the battles for us. Margaret Sanger's words of anger and confrontation, in particular, may sound odd and outdated to today's eighteen-year-old woman who has the class background that allows her the freedom to choose whether to work, has had as her role models numerous female lawyers, doctors, and professors, has enjoyed reproductive freedom options, and sees her world of possibilities as unlimited. If that student is middle class and Caucasian, she may listen to and admire Angelou's words, but find little connection between herself and a black woman; she may actually find more commonality with Marie Curie who at times appeared oblivious to the gender barriers confronting her. The zones of convergence between academic configurations of women's lives and the experiences of many of our students are invisible to them, the course as a powerful tool for social change eluding them because the voices of women's studies seem old, the problems "solved" or invisible.

Feminists Ardeth Dea and Judith Stitzel address this situation not only by teaching the feminist process but also by reconstructing the introductory course to make it more interdisciplinary, grounding investigation in what they call field exercises: reading, discussing, and writing about sets of public discourse that sustain traditional binary gender dynamics, such as marriage contracts, advertising, letters from family members, religious documents, popular films, and textbooks. Their intent is to challenge the students' preconceived notions of individual success and utopian reality by teaching them how to be responsible investigators, moving among different fields of inquiry, to build a new vision of the interrelationships of one's own experiences, the experiences of others of different races and classes, and the patriarchal institutions that shape all experience (90).

Once this groundwork has been laid, resistance to the term "feminist" begins to subside as does the myth that women have achieved equality. At this point, in more advanced women's studies courses, instructors can focus feminist process instruction on how to function in groups, particularly strategies for conflict resolution, such as role reversal, mirroring (paraphrasing positions before rebutting them), and role playing (Schniedewind 21–22). These strategies are particularly effective in an interdisciplinary class where both students and teachers are learning new languages, new paradigms, and new worldviews, all activities that can easily produce conflict, one-up-manship, confusion, and resistance.

Fostering Learning in Multiple Contexts

Feminist pedagogy inevitably takes us out of the classroom, to consider the very spaces in which we do its work. Of course, feminism did not begin in the classroom. It began in the sitting rooms, bedrooms, kitchens, workhouses, hospitals, and churches of women who struggled to live to their fullest potential. Most were unable to do so—the struggle to live was more than enough for them—but a few were able slowly to make their voices heard, to leave a mark heretofore unseen. Here again, feminist pedagogy reveals a shift in positionality: the axis of Angelou meets the axis of Belenky; the new axis on which they reside meets the axes of Sanger and Curie, two women who teach us that feminists must acknowledge those places where women spend most of their lives. In Curie's case, the classroom was where she taught physics, but it was also the shed in the back of her home where she and her husband Pierre Curie slavishly stirred vats of pitchblend to produce pure radium. This shed was conjoined with their home where she raised two daughters as well as with the French Academy of Sciences, which refused her membership by one vote. While Curie's personal writings indicate that she wished she could have stayed in the haven of the laboratory, her life pulled her in many different directions. She did not have the luxury of remaining in that one place, but instead had to traverse multiple paths and multiple identities throughout her illustrious life.

Sanger represents even more radical settings. Her "classroom" was the tenement room where as a nurse she witnessed poor women die in childbirth, their reproductive capacities held hostage by institutions that considered reproductive rights violations of both divine and human law. It was the women's clinic that she founded in Brooklyn where poor Polish, Italian, and Jewish women dared the wrath of the law to gain knowledge about their own bodies. It was the cell where she was jailed for disseminating birth control information. And it was the home she shared with her own three children and a husband whom she later divorced. We can speculate that for both Curie and Sanger, as for many other women, physical space came to denote social and personal identities that were continually negotiated. Feminist Aido Hurtado calls this shifting consciousness, the ability of women to "shift from one group's perspective of social reality to another, and, at times, to be able simultaneously to perceive multiple social realities without losing their sense of self-coherence" (Goldberger et al. 385). This kind of consciousness often becomes visible and palpable through interdisciplinary processes, that is, those experiences that demand that a problem be solved with whatever means possible, through the mixing and creating of new forms of knowledge.[8]

What we have revealed are the interstices created when the academy is forced to extend itself into other public spaces, or when other spaces extend themselves into the academy—which both women's studies and interdisciplinary studies have done. What we are discussing here is fundamentally how the early call to action to transform women's lives results in new ways of thinking about the classroom as a physical space and about course content. Women's studies and feminist pedagogy, devoted to transforming for the better the lives of all women, has to consider as its center of activity venues other than the academic classroom. Here is where our teaching team symbolizes representative places where transformational pedagogy can take place. Their very presence in our imagination compels us to reconfigure the setting of the "Let's Pretend" scene that opens this discussion, to rethink the lyric and romantic image of the classroom.

As we reimagine the scene, we come to see it not only as a privileged place for those advantaged by race, class, and gender, but also as a place where a kind of learning has been elevated, where the life of the mind has been severed from the body and daily life. We must be willing to see that the "pauk-pauk" of ball against stick gives way to the cries of babies, the laughter of children, the shouts of angry adults. The book-lined room is replaced by cluttered offices, tiny kitchens, courtrooms, and hospital wards. The eighteen-year-old students become single mothers with three children, retirees on fixed incomes, and forty-something bank managers. In this respect, the world of interdisciplinary feminist pedagogy not only begins to draw on conventional disciplines, but also breaks these barriers to extend the classroom into places that have little historical authority as sites of legitimate learning.

One way that women's studies programs do this is to require or offer as an elective a practicum course or, in the current parlance, a service-learning experience. Such courses, integrative by nature, couple the academic setting with other environments in which feminists work to affect change. Students are sent to work as secretaries, research assistants, home health care givers, teachers in settings as diverse as inner-city elementary schools, upscale law offices, shelters for victims of domestic violence, and psychological counseling centers. They may be required to read theory relevant to the setting, but, more importantly, they interact on a daily or weekly basis with the people who are actually doing the work (both service providers and those who use the services), dialoguing with them about the challenges and rewards that confront them.

In such a space, students can encounter productive critical thinking. They are encouraged to confront new experiences and people directly rather than adopt stereotypes and secondhand viewpoints (Novak and Goodman 65). This kind of nontraditional classroom experience opens up for students the opportunity, as compositionist Bruce Herzberg argues, to develop a social imagination that makes it possible "not only to question and analyze the world but also to imagine transforming it" (317). The opportunities for transformation can appear more explicit here than in a classroom. When a women's studies student teaches an underprivileged child to read, constructs a set of resource materials to educate women on "the date rape drug" (Rohypnol), or assists a legal aid attorney to prepare a young wife to testify in court against her abusive husband, that student is brought immediately into contact with the power of individuals and systems to affect change, assessing the strengths and weaknesses of the network of relationships that forms what we call self and other.

It is also at this point that students often become much more comfortable calling themselves feminists.

CONCLUDING REMARKS

It's highly unlikely that an introductory women's studies course would be taught by five people—and by five such august individuals as the ones I have gathered together for this discursive experiment. Such an arrangement in reality is fraught with all sorts of political difficulties. But it's fun, and productively so, to imagine the possibilities. In a fictional world, our characters act as we want them to—or so we'd like to think. In mine, they have voice but little mimetic form. For the most part, they seem more like pieces on a chessboard that I move at will to make my points. Even their language is not entirely their own: I've manufactured it as a pastiche of words that they have written and that others have written about them. Yet they do serve an important purpose—to illustrate the complex, vexed, positional, and playful nature of interdisciplinary feminist pedagogy.

The teaching of women's studies in an interdisciplinary context is inherently complex; and with such sweeping goals as those espoused by feminist pedagogy, it is no wonder that women's studies courses have struggled with the concept of interdisciplinarity, claiming it and simultaneously rejecting it for disciplinary status. The development of the field suggests that there is space for both kinds of teaching, that one can move back and forth as the situation demands. However, that same development also strongly argues for the efficacy of interdisciplinarity, that as we come to acknowledge the relational nature of the very categories we use for critical analysis, we must be willing and able to engage in thinking that forms odd alliances. Through these pairs, triads, quads, and, yes, even pentads, we open the way for the creation of new forms of thought. We come to see ourselves through the other side of the glass. And if we are patient enough to look for what Duchamp calls "almost an hour," we may very well discern the matrix from which we can affect change on a global scale.

NOTES

1. This text is a pastiche of the course description for "Introduction to Women's Studies," The College of Wooster catalog 1999–2000 as well as text from Newell and Green.

2. For a discussion of this process, see Shrewsbury 6–14.

3. See, for example, the *Women's Studies Quarterly* 3–4 (1998) for an impressive overview of these kinds of courses.

4. See James for a discussion of a course on autobiography, race, and activism.

5. Karen J. Warren makes this important claim in Cohee et al., 45–60.

6. See Fausto-Sterling for an excellent overview of how science has been used to oppress women.

7. Duchamp was referring to his most famous work, the *Large Glass*, or *The Bride Stripped Bare by her Bachelors, Even*; see Tomkins 57.

8. Hurtado developed this term out of her study of women of color and epistemology. She argues convincingly that shifting consciousness characterizes many women of color. I have extended her argument to include women such as Curie and Sanger who may also have experienced a similar reality finding themselves in multiple positions of subordination.

WORKS CITED

Belenky, Mary Field, Blythe McVicker Clinchy, Nancy Rule Goldberger, and Jill Mattuck Tarule. *Women's Ways of Knowing*. New York: Basic Books, Inc., 1986.

Bordo, Susan. *Unbearable Weight: Feminism, Western Culture, and the Body*. Berkeley and London: The University of California Press, 1993.

Bragg, Melvyn. *On Giants' Shoulders: Great Scientists and Their Discoveries from Archimedes to DNA*. New York: John Wiley & Sons., Inc., 1998.

Cabanne, Pierre. *Dialogues with Marcel Duchamp*. Trans. Ron Padgett. New York: Da Capo Press, 1987.

Chapkis, Wendy. *Beauty Secrets: Women and the Politics of Appearance*. Boston: South End Press, 1986.

Chesler, Ellen. *Woman of Valor: Margaret Sanger and the Birth Control Movement in America*. New York: Simon and Schuster, 1992.

Cohee, Gail E., Elisabeth Daumer, Theresa D. Kemp, Paule M. Krebs, Sue A. Lafky, and Sandra Runzo. *The Feminist Teacher Anthology: Pedagogies and Classroom Strategies*. New York: Teachers College Press, 1998.

Conway-Turner, Kate, Suzanne Cherrin, Jessica Schiffman, and Kathleen Doherty Turkey. *Women's Studies in Transition: The Pursuit of Interdisciplinarity*. Newark: University of Delaware Press, 1998.

Curie, Eve. *Madame Curie*. Trans. Vincent Sheean. New York: Doubleday and Co., 1937.

Davis, Angela. *Women, Race, and Class*. New York: Random House, 1981.

Deay, Ardeth, and Judith Stitzel. "Reshaping the Introductory Women's Studies Course: Dealing Up Front with Anger, Resistance, and Reality." Cohee et al. 87–97.

Douglass, Emily Taft. *Margaret Sanger: Pioneer of the Future*. Garrett Park, MD: Garrett Park Press, 1975.

Fausto-Sterling, Anne. *Myths of Gender: Biological Theories About Women and Men.* 2nd ed. New York: Basic Books, 1992.

Fish, Stanley. "Being Interdisciplinary Is So Very Hard To Do." *Profession* 89 (1989): 15–22. Rpt. in *Issues in Integrative Studies* 9 (1991): 97–125.

Friedan, Betty. *The Feminine Mystique.* New York: Norton, 1963.

Gilman, Charlotte Perkins Gilman. *The Yellow Wallpaper.* Boston: Small, Maynard, 1899.

Goldberger, Nancy Rule, Jill Mattuck Tarule, Blythe McVicker Clinchy, and Mary Field Belenky. Eds. *Knowledge Difference, and Power: Essays Inspired by Women's Ways of Knowing.* New York: Basic Books, 1996.

Heilbrun, Carolyn G. *Writing a Woman's Life.* New York: Ballantine Books. 1988.

Henke, Suzette A. "Autobiography as Revolutionary Writing in *I Know Why the Caged Bird Sings*" Williams. 99–104.

Herzberg, Bruce. "Community Service and Critical Thinking," *Journal of College Composition and Communication* 45, no. 3 (October 1994): 307–19.

hooks, bell. *Ain't I a Woman? Black Women and Feminism.* Boston: South End Press, 1981.

———. *Teaching to Transgress: Education as the Practice of Freedom.* New York: Routledge, 1994.

Hübenthal, Ursula. "Interdisciplinary Thought," Newell, *Interdisciplinarity* 417–44.

Hurston, Zora Neale. *Their Eyes Were Watching God.* Philadelphia: J.B. Lippincott, Co., 1937.

Hurtado, Aido "Strategic Suspension: Feminists of Color Theorize the Production of Knowledge." Goldberger et al. 372–92.

James, Joy. "Reflections on Teaching: 'Gender, Race, and Class'" Cohee et al. 75–86.

Johnson, Allan. *The Gender Knot: Unraveling Our Patriarchal Legacy.* Philadelphia: Temple University Press, 1997.

Kimmel, Michael, ed. *Changing Men: New Directions in Research on Man and Masculinity.* Newbury Park, CA: Sage Publications, 1987.

———, and Michael A. Messner, eds. *Men's Lives.* 4th ed. Needham Heights, MA: Allyn & Bacon. 1998.

Kuenzli, Rudolf E., and Francis M. Naumann, eds. *Marcel Duchamp: Artist of the Century.* Cambridge, MA: The MIT Press, 1990.

Lupton, Mary Jane. *Maya Angelou: A Critical Companion.* Westport, CT: Greenwood Press, 1998.

Maher, Frances. "Classroom Pedagogy and the New Scholarship on Women." *Gendered Subjects: The Dynamics of Feminist Teaching.* Eds. Margo Culley and Catherine Portugea. Boston: Routledge and Kegan Paul Press, 1985.

Maher, Frances A., and Mary Kay Thompson Tetreault. *The Feminist Classroom.* New York: Basic Books. 1994.

————. "Women's Ways of Knowing in Women's Studies, Feminist Pedagogies, and Feminist Theory." Goldberger et al. 148–74.

Millett, Kate. *Sexual Politics*. Garden City, NY: Doubleday, 1970.

Morrison, Toni. *Beloved*. New York: Knopf, 1987.

Narayan, Uma. "Working Together Across Difference: Some Considerations on Emotions and Political Practice." *Hypatia* 3, no. 2 (Summer 1988): 31–48.

Newell, William, ed. *Interdisciplinarity: Essays from the Literature*. New York: College Entrance Examination Board: 1998.

Newell, William, and William Green. "Defining and Teaching Interdisciplinary Studies." Newell, *Interdisciplinarity* 23–34.

Novak, Cynthia Cornell, and Lorie J. Goodman, "Safe/r Contact Zones: The Call for Service Learning." *The Writing Instructor* (Winter 1997): 65–77.

Paz, Octavio. *Marcel Duchamp: Appearance Stripped Bare*. Trans. Rachel Phillips and Donald Gardner. New York: Viking Press, 1978.

Plimpton, George, ed. *The Paris Review Interviews: Women Writers at Work*. New York: Random House, 1998.

Rich, Adrienne. *Of Woman Born: Motherhood as Experience and Institution*. New York: W.W. Norton & Co., 1986.

Schniedewind, Nancy. "Teaching Feminist Process." *Women's Studies Quarterly* XV, nos. 3–4 (Fall/Winter 1987): 15–31.

Shrewsbury, Carolyn M. "What Is Feminist Pedagogy?" *Women's Studies Quarterly* XV, nos. 3–4 (Fall/Winter, 1987): 6–14.

Tavris, Carol, and Carole Offir. *The Longest War: Sex Differences in Perspective*. New York: Harcourt, Brace, Jovanovich, 1977.

Tomkins, Calvin. *The Bride and the Bachelors: The Heretical Courtship in Modern Art*. New York: Viking Press, 1962.

Walker, Alice. *The Color Purple*. New York: Harcourt Brace Jovanovich, 1982.

Warren, Karen J. "Rewriting the Future: The Feminist Challenge to the Malestream Curriculum." Cohee et al. 45–60.

Williams, Mary E., ed. *Readings on Maya Angelou*. San Diego: Greenhaven Press, 1997.

Woolf, Virginia. *A Room of One's Own*. New York: Harcourt, Brace & World, 1957.

CHAPTER 9

Transforming Undergraduate Science Through Interdisciplinary Inquiry

Christopher Myers and Carolyn Haynes

INTRODUCTION

Seven-forty-five A.M. on Monday and Wednesday mornings were the worst for us as first-year undergraduate students. That was the time that we, along with the 300 other sleepy eighteen-year-olds, trudged off to chemistry class on the other side of campus. Squeezed in chilly, molded plastic desk chairs affixed firmly to the floor, we tried diligently to take notes on the usually incomprehensible monotone lecture delivered by a white-haired professor whose head barely cleared the lectern. We wanted nothing more than to crawl back in bed and sink into dreams of lands unknown. Week after week, we suffered through the chemistry lectures, finding that we had reluctantly entered into a rigid contest to memorize material for our exams. We were not asked about our own ideas, or even prompted to test the ideas of others. And when the semester and our obligatory physical science course were completed, we gladly took home mediocre grades, content never to reflect on the course content again. We did not get the sense that our entire world could be investigated in the atoms, compounds, and forces that are at the heart of chemistry. For us, chemistry never left the lecture hall.

According to recent studies, this unfortunate experience still occurs for first-year students today, not only in chemistry but also in a range of introductory science courses. Gogolin and Swartz report that science students with positive attitudes toward science felt less positive about it after taking an introductory botany class. However, even nonscience students were energized by anatomy and physiology courses that stressed relevant, high-interest activities (5). Whereas large, impersonal classes may establish an important, introductory knowledge base, they rarely inspire a life long passion for discovery or instill confidence in students that they can one day be scientists themselves. The problem, which is systemic, can be seen in the mode of instruction, in the lack of student interaction, in the tendency of the scientific disciplines to be studied in isolation, and in the educational materials themselves.

The scope and sequence of many introductory courses are driven by textbooks written in the third person; these textbooks emphasize the material outcomes of important discoveries rather than the human process that led to those discoveries. As George Ladd points out, often these science writers do not show you

> the first 12 proofs attempted, since they were logically invalid or incomplete. They do not tell you about all the mistakes made in developing the valid proof, even after insight suggested the general outline, nor about all the consequences of the assumptions. They do not tell you that [the investigators] knew the truth of the material . . . long before they could prove it. . . . Or they may have stumbled across proof and theorem while searching for something else. (8)

Even some journal articles written by scientists about their own findings are written in third person, as though some outside observer—and not the author—dispassionately recorded all that had happened.

The process of collaboration is also missing from most textbooks. Leonard and Wharton write that "science, which . . . has a history (and mythology) of lone-genius orientation (da Vinci, Galileo, Newton, Einstein, etc.), has, in the face of twentieth-century complexity and the fragile limits of even the most agile minds, inclined more and more toward group undertakings and joint publications" (32). Austin and Baldwin report that while collaboration is not widespread in the humanities, it is almost the norm in the physical and natural sciences (25). It seems that collaborative models of science education would be better suited to prepare students to address today's pressing scientific issues. By excluding the actual practice of researching scientists—including the group work, hopes and aspirations, inevitable haphazard efforts, false starts, fruitless ideas, frustrations, and mistakes—these introductory science courses shortchange students who hope to become professional scientists and incite science-phobia among nonscience students.

Our case for interdisciplinary science education builds on the premise that education should be a transformative process of critical investigation that requires authentic participation, reflection, and communication. We believe that interdisciplinary science inquiry offers teachers a means of motivating students to become actively engaged in the scientific process, to enter into a community of learners, and to reflect critically on the intersections of the physical, natural, and human dimensions of the world. Students' questions easily escape the confines of disciplinary knowledge and provide a natural bridge to diverse fields and interdisciplinary learning. Providing time to develop these questions will allow students to discover the power of investigation to answer questions they care about. By interdisciplinary science inquiry, we have in mind question-driven models of learning that retain the hallmarks of science but also welcome relevant ideas, methods, and practices from other disciplines in the social sciences, humanities, and fine arts. In this chapter, we will discuss ways of promoting interdisciplinary science inquiry in the undergraduate classroom. In particular, we will consider ways of transforming a traditional, lecture-based pedagogy to an interdisciplinary, inquiry-based one by: (1) shifting the focus from teaching to learning, (2) building a co-intentional and dialogical community of learners, (3) supporting student investigations, and (4) incorporating critical and personal reflection.

SHIFTING THE FOCUS FROM TEACHING TO LEARNING

> Learning is not a spectator sport. Students do not learn much just by sitting in class listening to teachers, memorizing prepackaged assignments, and spitting out answers. They must talk about what they are learning, write about it, relate it to past experiences, apply it to their daily lives. They must make what they learn part of themselves. (Chickering and Gamson 3)

Transforming a classroom from one centered on lectures, textbooks, and objective tests to one focused on interdisciplinary inquiry is not an easy process. Fundamentally, it means shifting the focus from the professor as primary information-giver and evaluator to the student as active learner. Huba and Freed have likened this transformation to a paradigm shift in which all of the rules, boundaries, and behaviors within the classroom are altered (3). According to them, a teacher-centered paradigm features knowledge being transferred from an expert professor to passive students and emphasizes the acquisition of knowledge outside the context in which it will be used. In this system, focus is typically on a single discipline; and the classroom culture tends to be competitive and individualistic. In a learner-centered paradigm, by contrast, students construct knowledge through gathering and synthesizing information from a variety of disciplines and integrating that information with the general skills of inquiry, communication, and critical reflection. The emphasis is on using and communicating knowledge effectively to address enduring and emerging issues and problems, and the classroom environment is typically cooperative, collaborative, and supportive (Barr and Tagg; Duffy and Jones; Kleinsasser).

Although movement from a more traditional to an inquiry-based classroom is ambitious, this change need not happen all at once. Faculty members may make changes incrementally as need, interest, and opportunity arise. Making lectures more interactive, for example, is not a large step. Common strategies include pausing in order to allow students to respond and ask questions, establishing opportunities for students to share ideas with one another, incorporating brief writing assignments, and voting on controversies raised. These strategies can naturally lead to more developed group interaction strategies such as having students study and work in groups, including more primary source material in the assigned readings, encouraging students to raise questions and critiques on the course material, and finally assigning instructor-generated and then student-generated labs.

The following are some more specific ideas for cultivating interdisciplinary science inquiries in the classroom. These ideas are meant to be suggestive, rather than prescriptive. The only components of this pedagogy that we think are required concern the role of the student and instructor. Over the past two decades, psychological researchers have documented that the human mind actively creates what it knows. From the very first moments of life, humans begin to interact with and explore the world, actively searching for meaning, constructing and reconstructing mental representations of what it is all about (Copple, Sigel, and Saunders; Gardner, *The Unschooled*). Humans seem insatiable for new information and driven to make sense of it. Simply listening and memorizing—which are the bread-and-butter activities of traditional classrooms—simply are not sufficient to support deeper learning. Ideally, the professor and student should actively seek new knowledge in the classroom, integrating it with what is known, organizing it in a meaningful way, and having the chance to share it with others.

To do this, the professor must focus as much on helping students learn the process and skills of investigation as on gaining mastery over the general course topic. In other words, professors must serve as

> supporters rather than judges, as mentors and coaches rather than lec-
> turers, as partners with students . . . rather than isolated experts in the
> classrooms. Fortunately, the best way to ensure our own growth is by
> helping others to grow; the best way to maximize our own potential is
> by helping others to improve little by little, day by day. (Bonstingl 5).

Students, for their part, must be willing to take an active role in pursuing their own questions and investigations and assume responsibility for their own learning and for that of the other members of the class. Because these roles are not generally the norm in most postsecondary classrooms, it is important that time is spent from the first day of class formulating and discussing these student and instructor expectations together. Grading should also take this into account, with points allocated to key participation activities such as group presentations and critical peer review.

BUILDING A CO-INTENTIONAL AND DIALOGICAL COMMUNITY OF LEARNERS

> A teacher who takes students seriously and treats them as adults shows
> that she can be trusted. A teacher who emphasizes peer learning shows
> that it's important to trust other students. A teacher who encourages
> students to point out to her anything about her actions that is oppres-
> sive and who seeks to change what she does in response to their con-
> cerns is a model of critical reflection. Such a teacher is one who truly is
> trustworthy. (Brookfield 26)

At first glance, an interdisciplinary science inquiry classroom may appear to be a chaotic hubbub of activity. Huddled in small groups that are sprawled across the room, students brainstorm a list of different types of questions about pond water and then categorize the questions according to different disciplinary perspectives. At times, laughter may erupt. Or a student will pop up to hunt for a term in a dictionary, pore through a text, or consult the Web. The instructor observes each group for a few minutes, sometimes making a comment, sometimes just nodding approval. At an appointed time, she signals that the groups should prepare to share their ideas with their other classmates.

While seemingly out of control, this environment of activity and enthusiasm is actually well designed to foster learning and forms the heart of inquiry-based pedagogy. Yet this learning-centered environment does not happen automatically. A certain level of trust and respect between students and professor and among the students must prevail (see Freire for an especially persuasive argument for trust in education). Faculty can foster this sense of trust by validating students as knowers. According to Baxter

Magolda, respecting and providing support for students' ideas and struggles "helps them take the risks required to move to more complex ways of making meaning" ("Teaching" 94). This support and respect can be conveyed by demonstrating genuine interest in their discoveries and feelings, allowing them the opportunity to assist in determining the direction of the course, and providing course material and assignments that are relevant to their interests and knowledge. These steps do not mean that the instructor must follow any and all of the students' whims, or lower expectations to appeal to them. What it means is that instructors seek and use student feedback where appropriate and set up the course to maximize student interest in order to challenge students to their fullest. For example, although we would not ask students whether they want to write a paper or not, we might very well invite them to submit possible paper topics, a select number of which we as instructors would choose to assign. Or we might ask them to assist in determining the criteria on which a lab might be evaluated.

In addition to building trust and respect between faculty and students, trust and respect must be fostered among the students. One of the best ways to ensure this is to encourage students to work together as colleagues to pursue important questions and topics. Yet it is important to realize that collaboration is not something that occurs naturally. Not only is it helpful to offer students differing examples of successful collaborations conducted by actual research teams, it is also important to provide in-class and out-of-class time built around group work, to promote students' active application of course material (not simply the instructor's presentation of it); and to foster students' shared responsibility in learning (Gamson; Smith and MacGregor). Underlying the notion of shared responsibility is the presumption that each member of the group is capable of making, and is expected to make, a valuable contribution to the endeavor. Holding students accountable for their individual contributions to the group is crucial and can be done in numerous ways, including asking each student to create their own "job" description, meeting with groups to discuss their working relationships, inviting students to keep daily logs of their tasks, and requiring self- and group evaluations.

Trust is implicit when you ask students to define their questions, make predictions, design experiments, and present results to a broader community—all standard practice for professional researchers. To further the idea that students' contributions are valuable, we maintain an ongoing student-generated database year to year so future classes may access previously collected data to augment their research interests, providing the basis for progressively more in-depth and sophisticated analyses of data gathered by students. A student with a geographical or business question about the local watershed can, for example, access ecological data previously gathered by another student from the same watershed. A shared, student-generated database can build synergistic interactions within and between classes. (For examples of student findings archived in the database, see http://jrscience.wcp.muohio.edu/courses/ns1fallsyl00.html.)

Finally, we further promote respect among students through a Peer Science Center staffed by upper-class students and directed by one of our colleagues, Dr. Hays Cummins. To be effective, peer tutors should be trained in peer learning techniques so that they help students pursue their own inquiries rather than provide the answers for them. Tutors in the science center attend the first-year science course, receive a three-day orientation training session as well as enroll in an ongoing one-credit-hour seminar and participate in center-sponsored events such as a star-gazing night in order to promote student interest in science. The center: (1) serves as an important resource for students thinking through student-generated labs or pursuing independent investigations; (2) provides a living link between the Natural Science Database and ongoing student investigations; (3) allows upper-class student tutors leadership roles in science education; and (4) serves as a central hub where student investigators can use scientific equipment and supplies under the supervision of trained tutors. Most important, a peer center conveys the message that students are teachers as well as learners, and that education happens best within a community where student voices and ideas are respected.

SUPPORTING STUDENT INVESTIGATIONS

> Students learn what they care about and remember what they understand. (Erickson 51)

How can we alleviate world hunger? What causes global warming? Why does algae form on one side of the pond and not on the other? Questions are the driving force behind inquiry-based education. Generating possible ideas for interdisciplinary questions and investigations that are intriguing to students is easy. Many excellent students look to science for solutions to pressing and complex social, global, and environmental problems. The questions raised in such fields as organic chemistry, botany, and physics may rest comfortably within those disciplines during a classroom discussion or in pure research, but all questions become interdisciplinary when applied to the human condition. A person trained in interdisciplinary thinking can no longer think of sulfur dioxide simply as a chemical having certain properties and molecular structure; she must also be aware of its effects on our forests and lakes. She must be ready to assess the costs and benefits of our habits of production and our habits of pollution.

Yet, despite students' innate curiosity and the many pressing scientific problems of today, most students have trouble honing their questions and planning effective investigations. Some of their questions contain invalid assumptions. Other questions are so literal and text-bound that they elicit only a factual answer, and still others jump way beyond the topic or suggest investigations that are not feasible within the given time and resource constraints. Some student questions are simply too big and need to be broken into simpler, manageable parts. Students—of all abilities and levels—can use guidance to question effectively. To begin, we generally explore with students possible criteria for a good interdisciplinary question (e.g., it is open-ended and too complex to be addressed by one discipline alone, can be answered with the time and resources at hand, and can be verified with a viable research method). We also explain to them the differing types of questions that can be raised, such as speculative statements (e.g., "I wonder what would happen if . . ."); analytical questions that challenge assumptions (your own and those of others); comparative questions that address similarities and dissimilarities; and synthetic questions that express hypothetical relationships among variables (e.g., "Does the process of boiling water rid the water of coliform bacteria?"). As students begin formulating questions, it is important to remind them that a good question can start a search, but a line of questioning deepens it. Sustained dialogue about a topic helps to draw out a logical progression. Students can be taught to deepen their questions with such prompts as: Who might find this question particularly important? What comparisons can we make? What two or three disciplines may have some insight into this question? What are some possible steps to take to ensure that we are testing our ideas fairly? How can answering this question add to our understanding of the topic or improve the world around us?

Discussing what constitutes a good question is time well spent, but the litmus test of a good question is whether it will lead to a productive investigation. Our experience has shown that students have difficulty determining what constitutes a viable inquiry. Because most students have only had experience with "cook-book style" labs using predetermined steps and answers, they are often uncomfortable with generating inquiries of their own. To ease them into conducting their own investigations, we first present them with instructor-generated discovery labs that allow students options, flexibility, and creativity to uncover innovative solutions. In these labs, students address alternative hypotheses, investigate various methodologies, and collect data: mastery of content follows engagement. To help them reflect on their learning, students present reports both in written and oral formats once the inquiry is completed. By stressing the process of scientific inquiry, these labs impart the content of science in a manner that is relevant to students, increasing the probability that students will come to understand science as a way of knowing.

These labs can range from earth-sun and earth-moon relationships, to a study of water chemistry changes in a pond, to a geologic time-scale metaphor project (see Ritger and Cummins; Cummins and Myers). The time-scale project has been a wonderful way to link a science topic to our students' other interests. Beginning with the origin of the Earth and moving through the age of the dinosaurs and the evolution of humans, students plot landmark events using a metaphor of their choosing. We've seen, for example, the creation of exceptional musical compositions timed perfectly to a mathematical scaling of major Earth events. These instructor-generated laboratories provide a strong foundation for students as they prepare their own student-generated discovery labs.

In student-generated labs, student groups develop their own hypotheses, design methods, write their own text, run their own lab, analyze the data, and present the results. Because interdisciplinary investigations involve multiple research methods and literatures, some time should be spent discussing how disciplinary conflicts (e.g., conflicting assumptions, specialized vocabulary, notions about truth and what constitutes proper evidence) can be resolved (see Stember 337–50; Bechtel 420–21). What common vocabulary will be used? What assumptions will we hold? These types of conversations foster higher order thinking skills. As Klein and Newell assert,

> achieving synthesis requires proactive attention to process. That means examining how the elements to be synthesized are obtained and interrelated. The skills involved are familiar ones: differentiating, comparing, and contrasting different disciplinary and professional perspectives; identifying commonalties; and devising a holistic understanding grounded in the commonalties but still responsive to the differences. The worldview and underlying assumptions of each discipline should be made explicit. (15)

These types of discussions help students learn to navigate across disciplines effectively and prompt them to make sense of their process of learning.

We have taken two main approaches to defining the scope of investigations that students may undertake: free choice or free choice within a class-dependent theme. Complete free choice gives students maximum flexibility to pursue topics that interest them most. Freedom within a theme restricts their choices, but still allows substantial flexibility—and provides a common unity of purpose that has distinct advantages. Picking a theme that is locally important (such as research on a local watershed, a source of pollution, a nearby corn field, or a pest species) adds relevance and can also help encourage interdisciplinary inquiry. On average, and especially in the early stages of program development, using themes to channel student investigations is more likely to yield positive outcomes that interrelate in meaningful ways than using free choice.

After the scope of questioning has been defined comes the critical stage of developing predictions (or hypotheses). Often, predictions are treated by students as simple, briefly considered guesses. This should be avoided. Of all the elements in the complex art of investigation, predictions are the most frequently glossed over. Rigorously considered, predictions provide a window into how we think the world works. The patterns, questions, and imagined causal mechanisms that lead up to a testable hypothesis should shape the research methods and provide the motivation for an investigation. Students, as with more experienced researchers, will put more effort into testing a prediction they have carefully considered. When asking for predictions, also ask: "Why do you think so?" Reflective writing assignments or paired interviews can also help reveal hidden assumptions and lead to more useful research.

As students begin to think about possible research methodologies, they should consider not only the nature of their question but the strengths of their group. Many of our strongest and most creative successes in student research have come from teams of science and nonscience students in which the nonscientists added an unexpected strength. Architecture students, for example, introduced new ways of analyzing the structural constraints of tree growth on forest edges. A business student was essential in an investigation of alternative uses for honeysuckle—a local invasive plant species. Groups consisting of students of different backgrounds also tend to gravitate toward a richer variety of research methods, such as engaging in traditional library research, using the Internet, collecting field data, conducting a laboratory experiment, surveying people, studying representative cases, role-playing or simulating an event, using mathematical models, engaging in participant observations, or writing an ethnographic narrative. Strong interdisciplinary research typically involves two or more research methods. Student groups that intentionally develop different research methods inevitably foster synergistic findings that deepen their appreciation for their research. Different methods can also be employed effectively across groups. For example, one of our groups investigating the spatial distribution of black oaks benefited from a group working on soil nutrients and from a group characterizing the topography of the study area, resulting in an extraordinary research project, especially considering that the research was conducted by first-year students.

Trust is important throughout the question and design process as well—avoid providing answers for them. As Bateman notes, "The hardest part for me as a teacher was to keep my mouth shut. . . . No shortcuts. Let the students puzzle and wonder and find for themselves that their old blueprints no longer fit. Let them help each other. Let them persuade each other. The roads on the old map do not follow the design of the roads in the real world" (33). Keeping quiet is especially difficult when you see students making mistakes. One of our groups, for example, spent some time developing an interesting study of ant foraging behavior, but it was the onset of winter; and the students soon discovered all the ants had quit their surface activity altogether. The group effectively changed course, addressing foraging theory in birds instead, but, through their mistake, they received one of those useful lessons in field ecology that never occurs in courses that rely on prescribed learning activities that "always work." Convenience is a common reason for reusing labs that yield easily predicted results year after year, but education does not always follow on convenience. In an interdisciplinary inquiry environment where the problems are often necessarily complex and initially ill defined, it's best to assume that students are going to make errors. Rather than events to avoid, mistakes are opportunities on which to capitalize. As Martinez writes, "Errors are part of the process of problem solving, which implies that both teachers and learners need to be more tolerant of them. If no mistakes are made, then almost certainly no problem solving is taking place" (609).

When students are invested in their own questions through the experimental design and testing phase, it shows in their analysis and presentations. They are far more interested in learning statistical methods when it applies to the information they have gathered. A mix of students and a focus in interdisciplinary inquiry motivate students to explore the strengths and weaknesses of qualitative versus quantitative analysis. For example, students are often surprised that empirical investigation can provide new insights into even such abstract areas as music or human values. We also encourage diverse approaches to the public presentation of their research. We insist that presentations include a fair appraisal of their results, but if they can bring some of their points home to the audience more effectively through art, debate, performance, or audience interaction, so much the better.

In order to validate the work of students further, student-generated labs are given status equal to instructor-generated labs, both in the investment of resources and in grading. Students learn basic principles of research design and analysis through their own questions and those of their classmates. Student-generated labs, linked over time in the students' Natural Science Database, are powerful tools for building an undergraduate science community and for fostering a lifelong love of discovery.

INCORPORATING CRITICAL AND PERSONAL REFLECTION

> We also know, from research on cognition, that students who reflect
> on their learning are better learners than those who do not. (Cross 6)

As this quotation suggests, one way of deepening students' learning in the inquiry process is to build in multiple and frequent opportunities for reflection. Based on a growing body of research, Patricia M. King contends that learning can be enhanced when faculty members help learners to understand the knowing process in more complex and encompassing ways, accept uncertainty without being immobilized by it, and learn to use evidence to reason to conclusions and make sound judgments. She claims that teachers are effective when they are "good guides for students' epistemological and personal learning journeys" (25). As Kroll puts it, "When [students'] responses are dogmatic, I foster all their doubts; when they seem mired in skepticism or paralyzed by complexity, I push them to make judgments; when their tactics are not fully reflective, I encourage their best efforts to use critical, evaluative thinking" (13). Allowing some room in a course for students to investigate their questions with their peers is perhaps the most powerful way to reflect on the process by which they learn. Reflection also occurs when students are asked to evaluate sources of information, demonstrate lines of reasoning from several perspectives, evaluate complex issues, or discuss controversial aspects of science inquiry. Reflection on their habitual ways of learning also follows naturally when students are asked in class to make important choices that may change the direction of the course.

Students that have never been asked to take a very serious role in defining their education will need models, preferably drawn from peers. When we were first developing our program, we sometimes had students create and conduct an exceptional investigation, only to be dissatisfied at the end because they were not sure it was valid "science." Many undergraduates assume that science is not a process to be learned though practice, but an esoteric activity undertaken by a group of people whose minds are inherently different from their own. Because of this, we now make sure to share examples of excellent student investigations. From these examples, students can identify the various traits of effective interdisciplinary inquiries. Regular faculty feedback and especially peer review throughout the semester are especially important in keeping students motivated and on track (see Huba and Freed 151–200). Research has shown that having clear standards of performance—that is, being able to describe the defining features of excellent work—is essential for improvement (Loacker, Cromwell, and O'Brien; Wiggins). However, students have to buy into these standards. This will occur more readily if they have the chance to evaluate prevailing standards, then prioritize the expectations that are the most appropriate for their class. Students may come to realize the difficulty in establishing a single set of standards against which all interdisciplinary research should be evaluated. As a result, it may be better to allow them to work with each other to offer feedback that is congruent with professional standards of success.

Beyond involving students in the evaluation of their own and others' work, reflective thinking can be fostered by putting students in the role of teachers. In our first-year science course, in the ninth week of class, all the formal proposals are collected, bound, and titled the *Student-Generated Lab Manual*. This becomes the main laboratory text used for the last half of the course. We typically have about five student groups per section, and each of these student-authors groups is provided one class period to teach their lab—a task that includes providing data sheets and introductory material, overseeing fellow students, and making adjustments for unexpected events. Students are given a list of available equipment and modest funds for research materials. For some, this may seem like an abdication of faculty responsibility. It is quite the opposite and in fact requires considerable faculty commitment. Once the program is developed, however, the time and resource commitment for guiding successful student-generated laboratories (including helping students learn to teach) can be roughly equivalent to running more traditional instructor-led labs, and it is considerably more interesting.

Because learning is a process of transformation, it is important that reflection opportunities do not focus solely on the cognitive aspects of the inquiry process. For that reason, we include opportunities for students to reflect on their emotional responses to the natural world, on the inquiry process, and on the disciplines being studied. For example, we assign naturalist essays on topics that spring from the local environment on campus. We also ask students to write an autobiographical essay that recounts their experience with science—starting from when they were children picking up grasshoppers or box turtles to the present. Journals are proven tools for supporting more long-term reflection, especially when students are prompted to write on specific questions that increase in sophistication as the semester progresses and that address both academic and personal realms of learning.

CONCLUSION

In *Academic Tribes and Territories*, Tony Becher notes that of all the disciplines, the sciences are the classic example of a tightly knit, convergent academic community with impermeable boundaries (13). A long-standing and similar critique is evident in the work of Thomas Kuhn, who observed:

> there are no other professional communities in which individual creative work is so exclusively addressed to and evaluated by other members of the profession. . . . [The scientist] need not worry about what some other group or school will think and can therefore dispose of one problem and get on to the next more quickly than those who work for a more heterodox group. . . . [And he can] concentrate his attention upon problems that he has good reason to believe he will be able to solve. (Kuhn 132)

While tightly focused science communities promote stability, coherence, efficiency, and a good chance for linear progress, there are good reasons to depart from the beaten path. According to Kuhn, although the scientist is "well-equipped for solving problems that are defined and created by that tradition or paradigm . . . it is harder to find a scientist who will discover a fresh approach" (133). The most famous scientists, by contrast, are often greatly influenced by disciplines and experiences seemingly disconnected from their fields. Einstein reportedly commented that the Russian novelist Dostoevsky "gave me more than any thinker, more than Gauss'" (Kuznetsov 178). Poincaré (391–93) and Hadamard (130–32) referred to their aesthetic emotions as guides in their mathematical inventions, and the statistician R. A. Fisher attributed his development of the factorial block experimental designs to his study of Mendelian genetics (Box 1980). Austin has written how his interest in music, watercolor painting, and hunting greatly influenced his research in neurology.

Crossing boundaries is a hallmark of innovation. Interdisciplinary approaches allow students to reshape the science disciplines and construct new knowledge. They may also deepen learning. William Perry, Jean Piaget, and Marcia Baxter Magolda (*Knowing*) have theorized that the capacity to handle multiple perspectives that is required by interdisciplinary study is a factor differentiating stages of cognitive growth. Inhelder and Piaget have labeled this ability "cognitive decentering," which is "the intellectual capacity to move beyond a single center or focus . . . and consider a variety of other perspectives in a coordinated way to perceive reality more accurately, process information more systematically, and solve problems more effectively" (qtd. in Hursh, Haas, and Moore 37; Inhelder and Piaget 342–45). Some theorists contend that students are more likely to move to more complex ways of thinking if they experience this dissonance (Bateman 30; Meyers 14–15).

Research also suggests that the degree to which something is retainable and usable depends on the ability to form associations and networks of associations among items in the memory (Ladd 53; Tulving and Donaldson). Students are unlikely to retain the knowledge gained, be empowered to solve their own problems, or engage in independent intellectual pursuits, if they do not learn through meaningful action and reflection (Astin; Bereiter and Scardamalia). In addition, educational theorist Howard Gardner has identified seven different forms of intelligence and ways of learning (verbal/linguistic; logical/mathematical; musical/rhythmic; bodily/kinesthetic; naturalist; interpersonal; and intrapersonal) (*Multiple*). By expanding the way scientific problems are investigated, students will have a greater chance of learning and connecting with the scientific field.

Science education is changing, and we believe that—even were educational theorists not so convinced—interdisciplinary and inquiry-driven modes of instruction will inevitably increase due to significant societal forces. Notable among these are: (1) a growing awareness of the complexity of environmental and global issues, and (2) the rise of information technology. Many of our best students come to science for solutions to pressing world issues. Environmental, multicultural, and global studies programs are rising nationally, creating significant restructuring across departments on even the most traditional campuses. Universities are increasingly called on to train scientifically literate students capable of addressing complex global problems. The questions raised in such fields as organic chemistry, botany, and physics may rest comfortably within those disciplines during a classroom discussion or in pure research, but, as noted earlier, all questions become interdisciplinary when applied to the human condition.

As the questions that shape the modern educational landscape change, so too do the tools we use. The rapid advance of emerging information technology not only increases access to diverse areas of information (promoting student-centered, interdisciplinary inquiry), but, as Robert Bender argues in Chapter 5, it alters the very medium of learning. The impact of information technology tranforms the basis of information exchange—expanding learning well beyond the classroom and supporting learning communities based on shared questions and concerns—not solely on location or disciplinary interests. We are seeing just the tip of the iceberg, and predict that information technology will progressively transform the nature of education in favor of interdisciplinary science.

Although moving toward interdisciplinary science inquiry may be challenging, research shows that it is worth the effort. In *What Matters in College?*, Astin found that interdisciplinary education has widespread effects on cognitive and academic development, including disciplinary as well as general knowledge, critical thinking, grade-point average, preparation for graduate and professional schools, degree aspirations, and intellectual self-concept. The National Science Foundation, the National Research Council, and the American Association for the Advancement of Science have all endorsed the inquiry approach. Moreover, substantial evidence exists that interdisciplinary and inquiry-based teaching and scholarship are on the rise across the globe (Klein 19–37; Klein and Newell 3–8) because it prepares students better for life beyond the undergraduate institution and fosters a joy of discovery.

WORKS CITED

American Association for the Advancement of Science (AAAS). *Science for All Americans*. New York: Oxford University Press, 1990.

Astin, A. W. *What Matters in College? Four Critical Years Revisited*. San Francisco: Jossey-Bass, 1992.

Austin, James H. *Chase, Chance, and Creativity: The Lucky Art of Novelty*. New York: Columbia University Press, 1978.

Austin, Ann E., and Roger G. Baldwin. *Faculty Collaboration: Enhancing the Quality of Scholarship and Teaching*. ASHE-ERIC Higher Education Report, no. 7. Washington, DC: School of Education and Human Development, George Washington University, 1991.

Barr. R. B. and J. Tagg. "From Teaching to Learning: A New Paradigm for Undergraduate Education." *Change* (November/December 1995): 13–25.

Bateman, Walter L. *Open to Question: The Art of Teaching and Learning by Inquiry*. San Francisco: Jossey-Bass, 1990.

Baxter Magolda, Marcia B. *Knowing and Reasoning in College: Gender-related Patterns in Students' Intellectual Development*. San Francisco: Jossey-Bass, 1992.

———. "Teaching to Promote Holistic Learning and Development." Baxter Magolda, *Teaching to Promote Intellectual and Personal Maturity* 88–98.

———, ed. *Teaching to Promote Intellectual and Personal Maturity: Incorporating Students' Worldviews and Identities into the Learning Process*. New Directions for Teaching and Learning. No. 82 (Summer 2000).

Becher, Tony. *Academic Tribes and Territories: Intellectual Enquiry and the Cultures of Disciplines*. Milton Keynes: Society for Research into Higher Education and Open University Press, 1989.

Bechtel, William. "The Nature of Scientific Integration." Newell, *Interdisciplinarity* 399–426.

Bereiter, C., and M. Scardamalia. *The Psychology of Written Composition*. Hillsdale, NJ: Erlbaum, 1987.

Bonstingl, J. J. *Schools of Quality*. Alexandria, VA: Association for Supervision and Curriculum Development, 1996.

Box, Joan Fisher. "R. A. Fisher and the Design of Experiments, 1922–1926." *American Statistician* 34 (1980): 1–7.

Brookfield, S. *Becoming a Critically Reflective Teacher*. San Francisco: Jossey-Bass, 1995.

Chickering, A. W., and Z. F. Gamson. "Seven Principles for Good Practice." *AAHE Bulletin* 39 (March 1987): 3–7.

Copple, C., I. E. Sigel, and R. Saunders. *Educating the Younger Thinker: Classroom Strategies for Cognitive Growth*. Hillsdale, NJ: Erlbaum, 1984.

Cross, K. P. "New Lenses on Learning." *About Campus* (March-April 1996): 4–9.

Cummins, R. H., and Myers, C. A. "Using the Moon as a Tool for Discovery Oriented Learning." *Journal of Geological Education* 40 (1992): 142–146.

Duffy, D. K., and J. W. Jones. *Teaching Within the Rhythms of the Semester*. San Francisco: Jossey-Bass, 1995.

Erickson, S. C. *The Essence of Good Teaching*. San Francisco: Jossey-Bass, 1984.

Field, Michael, Russell Lee, and Mary Lee Field. "Assessing Interdisciplinary Learning." *Interdisciplinary Studies Today*. Eds. Julie Thompson Klein and William G. Doty. San Francisco: Jossey-Bass, 1994. 69–84.

Gamson, Zelda F. "Collaborative Learning Comes of Age." *Change* 26 (1994): 44–49.

Gardner, Howard. *Multiple Intelligences: The Theory in Practice*. New York: Basic Books, 1993.

Gardner, Howard. *The Unschooled Mind: How Children Think and How Schools Should Teach*. New York: Basic Books, 1991.

Gogolin, Luane, and Fred Swartz. "A Quantitative and Qualitative Inquiry into the Attitudes Toward Science of Nonscience College Students." *Journal of Research in Science Teaching* 29 (1992): 5.

Hadamard, Jacques. *The Psychology of Invention in Mathematical Field*. New York: Dover, 1954.

Huba, Mary E., and Jann E. Freed. *Learner-Centered Assessment on College Campuses: Shifting the Focus from Teaching to Learning*. Boston: Allyn and Bacon, 2000.

Hursh, Barbara, Paul Haas and Michael Moore. "An Interdisciplinary Model to Implement General Education." Newell, *Interdisciplinarity* 35–50.

Inhelder, B., and Jean Piaget. *The Growth of Logical Thinking from Childhood to Adolescence*. New York: Basic Books, 1958.

King, Patricia M. "Learning How to Make Reflective Judgments." Baxter Magolda, *Teaching to Promote Intellectual and Personal Maturity* 15–26.

Klein, Julie Thompson. *Crossing Boundaries: Knowledge, Disciplinarities, and Interdisciplinarities.* Charlottesville: University Press of Virginia, 1996.

Klein, Julie Thompson, and William H. Newell. "Advancing Interdisciplinary Studies." Newell, *Interdisciplinarity* 3–22.

Kleinsasser, A. M. "Assessment Culture and National Testing." *Clearing House* (March/April 1995): 205–10.

Kroll, B. M. *Teaching Hearts and Minds: College Students Reflect on the Vietnam War in Literature.* Carbondale: Southern Illinois University Press, 1992.

Kuhn, Thomas S. "Profess Through Revolutions." *Conceptions of Inquiry.* Eds. Stuart Brown, John Fauvel, and Ruth Finnegan. New York: Methuen, 1981. 130–38.

Kuznetsov, Boris. "Einstein, Science and Culture." *Einstein: A Centenary Volume.* Ed. A. P. French. London: Heinemann, 1979.

Ladd, George W. *Imagination in Research: An Economist's View.* Ames: Iowa State University Press, 1987.

Leonard, J. C., and C. E. Wharton. *The Fluent Mundo: Wallace Stevens and the Structure of Reality.* Athens: University of Georgia Press, 1988.

Loacker, G., L. Cromwell, and K. O'Brien. "Assessment in Higher Education: To Serve the Learner." *Assessment in American Higher Education.* Ed. C. Adelman. Washington, DC: US Department of Education. Office of Educational Research and Improvement, 1986. 47–62.

Martinez, M. E. "What Is Problem Solving?" *Phi Delta Kappan* 79 (1998): 605–609.

Meyers, Chet. *Teaching Students to Think Critically: A Guide to Faculty in All Disciplines.* San Francisco: Jossey-Bass, 1986.

National Research Council. *National Science Education Standards.* Washington, DC: National Academy Press, 1996.

Newell, William H., ed. *Interdisciplinarity: Essays from the Literature.* New York: College Entrance Examination Board, 1998.

Poincaré, Henri. "Mathematical Creation." *Foundations of Science.* Trans. George Bruce Halsted. New York: Science Press, 1913.

Ritger, S., and H. Cummins. "Using Student-Created Metaphors to Comprehend Geologic Time." *Journal of Geological Education* 39 (1991): 1–3.

Smith, Barbara L. and Jean T. MacGregor. "What Is Collaborative Learning?" *Collaborative Learning: A Sourcebook for Higher Education.* Eds. A. S. Goodsell, M. R. Maher, B. Tinto, B. L. Smith, and J. T. MacGregor. University Park, PA: National Center on Postsecondary Teaching, Learning, and Assessment. ED 357 705, 1992.

Stember, Marilyn. "Advancing the Social Sciences Through the Interdisciplinary Enterprise." Newell, *Interdisciplinarity* 337–52.

Tulving, Endel, and Wayne Donaldson. *Organization of Memory*. New York: Academic Press, 1972.

Wiggins, G. *Assessing Student Performance: Exploring the Limits and Purpose of Testing*. San Francisco: Jossey-Bass, 1993.

PART IV

Interdisciplinary Teaching in
Different Settings or to Different
Students

CHAPTER 10

It Takes More Than a Passport

Interdisciplinarity in Study Abroad

George Klein

Learn Spanish, live with a host family, and discover the culture of Mexico. Intern with a manufacturing company in Karlsruhe and use German in a real working context. Study the natural environment and the economy in Kenya. Experience the presence of religion in everyday life in Nepal. Discuss ancient Roman life in the Roman Forum.[1]

These are just a few of the connections that can occur in study abroad programs. Study abroad is a small segment of international education for American students with intense opportunities for interdisciplinary connections. In the past, international education was a marginal activity that changed in the 1990s as interest in international education, research, and service increased across U.S. institutions of all types (Johnston and Spalding 416). As a result, thousands of programs are now listed in directories such as *Academic Year Abroad, Vacation Study Abroad, Peterson's* study abroad guides and on Websites such as studyabroad.com.

Like interdisciplinarity, international education is not a single entity. Sven Groennings called it a "disorderly development, lacking clear definition, boundaries or framework" (29). In their state-of-the-art account in the *Handbook of the Undergraduate Curriculum*, Johnston and Spalding identified four major categories of international education: language study, study abroad, education of foreign students in the United States, and the internationalization of American higher education. A small number of institutions claim to send at least 10 percent of their students abroad at some point. A few even cite rates up to 90 percent. That is not the norm, however. The number of Americans studying abroad is growing, but remains small (Johnston and Spalding 418–21). In the latest figures released by *Open Doors*, a comprehensive information resource sponsored by the Institute of International Education, 129,770 United States students studied abroad in 1998–99. This represents an increase of 13.9 percent over the previous year. More impressive is the 45 percent increase in study abroad enrollments in the last four years (*Open Doors*). However, even the latest figures constitute less than 2 percent of total college enrollments in the United States.

The most common types of study abroad are exchange programs with foreign universities, programs sponsored by U.S. universities, travel-study, field-study, and direct enrollment in foreign universities. As the name suggests, students in "exchange" programs switch places. An American student attends a foreign university, and vice versa. These programs typically occur during the academic year and last at least one semester. American students can also choose from a variety of semester-, year-long, and summer programs sponsored by U.S. institutions at foreign universities or their own overseas branches. Travel-study programs often occur in the summer and typically have multiple destinations. Faculty members from a sponsoring institution usually lead students through the itinerary and conduct classes. Field-study is an extension of travel-study featuring field research, service learning, or internships at foreign sites. Occasionally students enroll on their own directly in foreign universities.

While study abroad programs come in many forms, their focus has traditionally been Eurocentric. The majority of Americans studying abroad go to the United Kingdom, Spain, Italy, and France. Over the last decade, though, interest in Asia and Africa, along with Latin America, has grown. The model of study abroad has changed as well. Previously, foreign-language majors constituted the majority of students. They tended to spend a junior year in France, Spain, or Germany. Today, study abroad is a more feasible opportunity for a wider range of students with a greater variety of programs. Even so, females still outnumber males, and liberal arts majors (excluding math and sciences) outweigh other fields. Males, minorities, science majors, working adults, and professional students (with the exception of business majors) are also underrepresented (Cornwell and Stoddard 2, 4; Johnston and Spalding 418–20).

Although information about the models and types of programs and students in study abroad education has increased, less has been explored about the relationship between interdisciplinarity and international education.

INTERDISCIPLINARY PATTERNS OF PRACTICE

International education has several interdisciplinary dimensions. Among the most popular interdisciplinary approaches to international education is area studies that focus on a specific geographical region. Despite the prominence of area studies, a range of other interdisciplinary opportunities exists in international education. Programs in global perspectives, majors in international relations, and some civilizational and intercultural approaches also have an interdisciplinary orientation. Greater comparative perspectives are evident in certain disciplines. Over time, economics has broadened from self-contained local units to national communities and now the global economy. Journalism increasingly reflects global information and connectedness. Political science has evolved from an American focus to interest in developing countries and the subfield of comparative political economy. Likewise, the discipline of history has broadened beyond Western civilization, and world history is a growing subfield. Cross-disciplinary developments in anthropology and geography have also fostered new approaches in international studies linked with the expanding fields of cultural studies and postcolonial studies (Groennings 22–30; Cornwall and Stoddard 10).

Even with the growing convergence of international and interdisciplinary interests, interdisciplinarity remains relatively invisible in directories of study abroad. And vice versa: Directories of interdisciplinary programs and courses do not identify study abroad programs as a group. Furthermore, even when a program claims to be "interdisciplinary" in promotional materials and course syllabi, it is not necessarily clear whether or how it achieves this goal. To compensate for this void in official description, I asked members of SECUSS-L to identify programs that are in some way interdisciplinary. SECUSS-L is the e-mail discussion list for study abroad personnel, sponsored by the Section on United States Students Abroad of NAFSA: Association of International Educators. List members include study abroad advisors, administrators, program providers, and recruiters. The definition of interdisciplinary I provided them was "an attempt to integrate two or more academic disciplines in a manner that crosses traditional boundaries and stimulates integrative thinking." I then correlated the responses with pertinent insights from the literatures on international education and on interdisciplinary studies, plus further research on program Websites to create a fuller picture of the landscape of interdisciplinary study abroad education.[2] My goal was to ascertain patterns of interdisciplinarity in study abroad, not to create a complete directory of interdisciplinary study abroad programs.

What follows is an analysis and discussion of the interdisciplinary patterns of study abroad programs that emerged in this study. Because area studies emerged as the most prominent framework, I will begin there.

Study Abroad as Area Studies

By and large, study abroad is site-specific. Programs are usually located at one site or they limit student travel within a single country or region. This arrangement has organizational and logistical advantages, though some U.S.-sponsored programs tend to become American enclaves, reducing engagement and immersion in another culture. In both the United States and abroad, the study of a world area tends to be "multidisciplinary." In a review of the field, Richard Lambert reported that area studies is not predominantly or inherently "interdisciplinary." Area specialists come from many disciplines, giving the field breadth of scope. Some blurring of boundaries occurs around topics of common interest, especially in conferences and research projects. However, specialists do not tend to collaborate across disciplines. They work within particular disciplinary and subdisciplinary frameworks (Lambert 189–93). This pattern of multidisciplinarity recurs in the study abroad curriculum. For instance, students traveling to India and China on the University of Calgary's Term Abroad Programs take an assortment of disciplinary courses in fine arts (Indian art, studio art with painting and calligraphy), humanities (Hindi/Chinese language, religious studies, literature), social sciences (political science, history), general studies (comparative perspectives on Canada and China), and kinesiology (an introduction to Chinese martial arts) (Burh).

Within the multidisciplinary array of courses offered in area studies programs, one discipline appears more often than others in study abroad: language. The Institute for Social and International Studies Program in Barcelona, Spain, combines instruction in Spanish with study of social science disciplines. The State University of New York at Albany in Valencia, Spain, combines one course in the Spanish language with three English language courses that cover Spanish culture, literature, art, finance, and economics in the context of the European Union. In conjunction with the University of Buffalo, the Albany campus also administers a program in Madrid at the Instituto Internacional. The courses in Madrid are taught in Spanish, so intermediate or advanced level skills are required. In addition to language study, courses explore Spain's cultural heritage and recent modernization in courses on literature, art, history, and social sciences.

Political transformations in Europe have created new opportunities that are structured as either multidisciplinary combinations or interdisciplinary study of important themes or problems. Klein and Newell's basic definition of interdisciplinary studies is "a process of answering a question, solving a problem, or addressing a topic that is too broad or complex to be dealt with adequately by a single discipline or profession" (39). The Institute for the International Education of Students European Union Program in Freiburg illustrates the first multidisciplinary format. The program examines the European Union from separate perspectives of business, economics, and political science. In addition to field study, students do a Model European Union simulation. By contrast, Antioch College's Europe in Transition: The Challenges of Post-Industrial Society takes more proactive steps toward integration. Four courses focus on cross-cutting themes and problems in recent transformations. The topics include: employment and social policy; ethnicity, gender, and social change; civil rights and immigration; and European political and economic integration. In addition, students do field research and individual research projects. Manfred McDowell, Director of European Programs for Antioch Abroad, emphasizes the intersection of comparative and interdisciplinary approaches. Students come from a variety of institutions plus social, cultural, and national backgrounds. The program has also cultivated a large network of European scholars and contacts in government, business, and social organizations and hosts for family stays.

As these examples suggest, humanities and social sciences are more prominent than the sciences.

Cultural History

The prominence of humanities and social sciences is not surprising. Cultural immersion is a major goal of study abroad (Cornwall and Stoddard 4). As a result, cultural history is a common feature of both multidisciplinary combinations of disciplinary courses and interdisciplinary courses. This tendency appears across world areas. The Ghana Project of the College of William and Mary is a summer program at the Institute of African Studies at the University of Ghana in Legon. A course on "The Ghanaian Culture and Society" acquaints students with the history, culture, and customs of Ghana. Given that the United Kingdom is a major destination for American students, in large part because they do not need to study another language, examples from this region abound. Of the 129,770 U.S. students who studied abroad in 1998–99, the largest percentage—21.4%—went to the United Kingdom (*Open Doors*).

It is not unusual to find combinations of disciplinary and interdisciplinary courses. The University of Kansas Humanities in Great Britain is a summer program in literature, history, and art history. The semester-long variant in Humanities and Western Civilization in Florence and Paris offers six hours of Western Civilization plus two upper-level courses, a special topics course in "European History," and "Art and Architecture of Florence and Paris." The Irish College for the Humanities features courses in history, art, literature, philosophy, music, film, and the Gaelic language, as well as "Irish Culture and Society," "Technology and the Humanities," and "Emotion and Devotion" (combining religion and art). A common general course combines history and literature, and many other courses join art and architecture with political and social history and music within the context of Irish cultural history (Kissane).

Historical periods are also the focus of study abroad. Cambridge University's International Summer Schools that have this focus have been in operation since the end of the nineteenth century. Students can choose a single subject, a variety of subjects, or a coordinated program of complementary courses. Summer school terms are offered in four- and two-week blocks. Individual subjects include art history, history, Shakespeare, science, and English literature. A more conscious integration of period studies occurs in the Medieval Studies block. The University of Tennessee's Normandy Scholars Program concentrates on World War II and its antecedents and results. During the spring semester prior to a three-week study abroad component, students take nine interdisciplinary credits together. Taught by faculty from history and Romance languages, the program also spends some time on twentieth-century French culture. The three-hour course in Caen, France, is scheduled Monday through Thursday, so students have long weekends for independent travel. In addition to the core course, students are required to take a three-hour elective related to World War II and encouraged to enroll in a language course. Upon return home, students complete a research project in conjunction with the foreign study component.

Within the broad framework of area studies, other interdisciplinary fields also appear.

Other Interdisciplinary Fields

A variety of fields may be studied abroad. Closer to home, Trent University in Ontario, Canada, offers students in year-abroad programs courses in Canadian Studies, Native Studies, Comparative Development, and Women's Studies. Trent regards interdisciplinarity as one of its strengths. Students are encouraged to go beyond traditional boundaries to gain a broad understanding of issues relevant to their field of specialization (Awe). Leiden University in the Netherlands has Women's Studies, European Politics and Administration, and Dutch Culture and Government. Antioch College offers Comparative Women's Studies in Europe, Buddhist Studies in India and Japan, Brazilian Ecosystems, and Europe in Transition. The Antioch women's studies program features comparative study. Field research in Germany, Poland, and the Netherlands is followed by independent research in London. In addition to "Political and Social Systems of Women's Lives," the program includes a "Practicum in Feminist Group Process" and a course entitled "The Individual Research Project." Taking concepts and theories out of the classroom is prioritized. Students become participants, observers, researchers, and chroniclers in academic and nonacademic segments of feminist movements.

Not surprisingly, development is a major focus, especially in third-world countries. The Higher Education Consortium for Urban Affairs (HECUA) offers programs in Europe, Latin America, and Asia with a concentration on international development. HECUA students traveling to Ghana have opportunities throughout the region in a variety of fields, including environmental studies, development, African American Studies, and African Studies. In Kenya, they can enroll in "Experimental and Interdisciplinary Studies," which focuses on cultural immersion and global understanding as well as the environment and gender.[3]

Even with the prominence of humanities and social sciences in study abroad, there are opportunities to study science. The primary focus is environmental studies. Similar to the study of cultural history, disciplinary and interdisciplinary courses are often combined. The Union College of Schenectady Program in Marine Studies brings together marine biology with sociology and some engineering and literature. Faculty from biology and sociology teach in the program, which takes place in Bermuda; Woods Hole, Massachusetts; and Newfoundland. Kalamazoo College's Sustainable Development in Thailand couples traditional classroom-based study and seminars with experiential "field-based" learning opportunities in nongovernmental organizations. The School for Field Studies has environmental studies programs in Australia, British Columbia, British West Indies, Costa Rica, Baja, Mexico, and Kenya. In each location, a particular interdisciplinary subfield is the focus: for example, Sustainable Development Studies in Costa Rica and Wildlife Management Studies in Kenya.

There are also other opportunities to study science. Cambridge University's Science Program combines disciplinary and interdisciplinary courses in zoology, plant sciences, environmental studies, and the history and philosophy of science. Programs centered on health care place medical science in the context of the national system. National Health Systems, sponsored by Union College of Schenectady, is a summer program that compares health delivery systems in England, the Netherlands, and Hungary. Students explore how national systems are affected by society, culture, and history. The dominant focus is determined by the faculty member in charge for a particular semester. In the past, a medical ethicist, chemist, and someone from the Graduate Management Institute have participated in the program (Thomas).

The richness of these examples is striking, but the question of integration resurfaces.

CREATING INTERDISCIPLINARITY ABROAD

The question of whether integration actually occurs begs another question: What is integration? In multidisciplinary structures, discipline-based courses are juxtaposed, but there exists no mechanism for the explicit comparison and contrast of the underlying assumptions of differing disciplinary and professional perspectives. The rubric of cultural history that is common in study abroad illustrates the problem. Students explore the history of a region, political structure, economy, literature, arts, and so forth. However, they do not necessarily learn how different disciplinary perspectives inform the study of themes, problems, or questions within that area. Klein and Newell cited a wide range of formats in which integration can occur:

- Course and course segments clarifying the concept of interdisciplinarity.
- Capstone seminars.
- Capstone theses, essays, and projects.
- Coordinated alignment of parallel disciplinary courses.
- Clustering of disciplinary courses around a common integrative seminar or discussion groups.
- Organizational structure based on a topic, theme, issue, problem, or question.
- Specific integrative approaches, theories, or concepts (such as systems theory, feminism, Marxism, textualism).
- Course learning portfolios and academic career portfolios.
- A specific learning model.
- Common living arrangements, shared facilities, and equipment.
- Fieldwork, work experience, travel-study. (Klein and Newell 405)

All these formats appear in study abroad. However, none of them guarantees that integration will occur. It must be actively practiced. Traveling and living abroad can be an interdisciplinary experience in and of itself, in the encounter of different foods, customs, and social structures. Yet students need help integrating their experiences both outside and inside the classroom. Furthermore, as challenging as it can be to venture beyond disciplinary boxes at home, the task can be even more daunting abroad. Faculty who are discipline-oriented do not suddenly become interdisciplinary by boarding an international flight. It takes more than a passport.

Integrating Study Abroad

The gap between the ideal and the real widens in study abroad because of foreign locations. Ideally, faculty teaching in a study abroad program should meet together in advance to familiarize themselves with the nature of interdisciplinary education and the dynamics of team teaching. Collaborative course design remains one of the most powerful ways of creating a shared commitment to interdisciplinary goals. In reality, the plurality of models defies generalization. Faculty may come from different institutions and may not even be teaching common courses. The only given commonality is that they are teaching in the same place at the same time. In this instance, it is all the more important that pre-departure and on-site orientation includes some attention to the nature of interdisciplinary study. The interdisciplinary studies literature is a vital tool, but it must be contextualized by models of integration that have been tested on the study abroad "road."

Theme- and problem-based studies are prominent in these models. Billed as a one-semester interdisciplinary program that develops global perspective, Central European Studies at Masaryk University, Czech Republic-SUNY Oswego offers classes on regional issues, especially recent social, political, economic, and cultural changes in Central Europe. Faculty members draw from economics, social sciences, and the arts. A course on "Re-Modernizing Civic and Political Culture After 1989" illustrates how connections are fostered. The themes include changing inter-ethnic relations, globalization, and interrelations among politics, society, and culture in problems of adaptation. Students also have internship opportunities with Czech and international nongovernmental organizations, businesses, and public institutions. Steve Saum, coordinator of international programs at Masaryk, expects more interdisciplinary possibilities in the future as the national boundaries of European universities are crossed with wider implementation of the European Credit Transfer System, which should make access easier for international students as well.

Some programs adopt an explicit integrative philosophy. The Arava Institute for Environmental Studies in Israel is rooted in a "holistic" approach to regional environmental issues. Program directors attribute this kind of educational experience to the site. Current regional issues include wildlife habitat and coral reef preservation, water conservation, desertification, wastewater treatment and reuse in agriculture, environmental education, and activism and advocacy. In addition to clustered courses in environmental policy, management, and science, the program has social and cultural studies courses that include the history of human presence in the region, the Bible, and the environment. Taught in English, the courses promote technical literacy as well as familiarity with public policy and comprehension of philosophical and ethical concepts necessary to participation in environmental matters, regardless of students' ultimate careers.

As we saw in the earlier discussion of interdisciplinary fields, several integrative elements may be combined. Lexia International is a private organization offering programs in Europe, South America, Africa, Asia, and the Caribbean. Based at major universities or institutes in host cities, the programs provide a multidisciplinary overview of the language, history, politics, economics, and culture of host countries. In addition, students are encouraged to look at historical and contemporary issues in a comparative framework. Lexia programs in Shanghai, China, and in Cape Town, South Africa, share a generic structure. A four-semester "Civilization Seminar" centers on topics and issues that prepare students for a final research project. Teaching is structured in thematic blocks, and lectures prepare students for discussing related themes in and out of the classroom. A two-semester "Research Methods Seminar" introduces a variety of qualitative and quantitative methodologies for the project, with attention to the challenges of research in a foreign culture and language. The four-semester "Field Research Project" is a form of independent study overseen by an advisor. A week at the end of each term is devoted to synthesis, followed by presentation and discussion of results in a group setting. Students have the option of an internship in the host city, and each program has a language requirement.

Experiential learning is also on the list of integrative formats. Study abroad takes advantage of the fact that some geographical areas are living laboratories for particular subjects, such as art in Florence, tropical ecology in Costa Rica, or Buddhism in Nepal (Cornwall and Stoddard 4). Study abroad also shares an important characteristic with other forms of experiential learning, such as internships, service, and living-learning communities. Much of the learning that occurs happens outside the classroom. The "law of unexpected returns" in study abroad recognizes that tremendous gains in personal and intellectual growth derive from living in another culture. However, unless it is contextualized, the experience of living and studying abroad does not necessarily produce integrative understanding or intercultural skills. All study abroad programs should take advantage of experiences outside the classroom by examining connections with and across the enclaves of academic study. The incidental connections that occur are capable of giving any program a more integrative value by broadening, intensifying, and enriching study in a foreign setting.

Internships are powerful means of bridging theory and practice at home and abroad. Westminster College's Oxford Service-Learning is affiliated with the UK Centers for Experiential Learning. In addition to disciplinary core courses in "English Literature," "Contemporary Britain in Historical Perspective," and "British Institutions in Society," students take a fourth course centered on placement in a human service agency. They interact with: children, adults, and seniors; the homeless; victims of emotional and physical abuse; and individuals who are learning and physically challenged or drug- and alcohol-dependent. The first three courses provide insight into the culture, history, and sociology of British society in a combination of classroom instruction and the British model of tutorials. The fourth course, "Profiles of an Agency," is called a "Reflection Exercise." Following orientation and the actual placement, students return to campus for three study days with personal tutorials. A "critical reflection" exercise focuses on understanding a complex social problem. Called a "unifying mechanism," the exercise fosters integrative reflection on the self while confronting a broad base of issues related to the agency, clients, society, and the role of the agency in society.

Institutional partnerships can also be powerful vehicles for integration. The Maastricht Center for Transatlantic Studies is a cooperative effort of about a dozen universities across Europe and North America. Each of two semester-long programs is divided into four teaching blocks of typically three weeks duration. In each block, several faculty offer intensive courses in a variety of disciplines plus environmental science and the professions of business and education. Students can choose up to four courses per semester. Within the teaching blocks, faculty members integrate their courses whenever possible, maximizing students' exposure to different perspectives and teaching strategies. Described as "multidisciplinary, and often interdisciplinary," this approach promotes thematic study of transatlantic issues. The program is also moving toward having faculty work together at the end of their teaching blocks to provide an interdisciplinary approach to a global issue. They might also address a theme common to their particular interests, such as an analysis of Kosovo by people from different countries (Rodenberg).

Individualized studies are also possible abroad. Denmark's International Study Programs (DIS) in public health/pre-medicine draw students from sciences and social sciences. They take core courses in the program and classes in their fields. A similar approach is taken in Environmental Studies and Engineering and Technology. In the Marine Biology and Ecology (MBE) program, students are required to take either "Marine Biology of European Coastal Waters" or "Ecology and Human Impact in the North and Baltic Seas." In actuality, they are encouraged to take both. Joint fieldwork occurs, and the courses complement each other. Jim Gehlar, Director of the University of Tennessee at Knoxville's Center for International Education, observed that the majority of students involved in their exchanges end up pursuing "their own mix of interdisciplinary studies." They tend to take whatever is available for which they have the prerequisites. The same caveat applies to individualized studies in both the United States and abroad. Opportunities for integration should be explicit. They may come in the form of formal units and courses, orientation and exit activities, or learning portfolios that extend across the entire experience.

Although this overview illustrates the varied ways of integrating study abroad, it does not provide detailed knowledge of how to plan and implement a program. One model does.

A CASE STUDY

Eastern Michigan University's Cultural History Tours

Eastern Michigan University (EMU) is a comprehensive regional state university. Its Cultural History Tours (CHT) are unique opportunities to travel throughout Europe or Asia while earning college credit. The program is not limited to EMU students. The majority come from other colleges and universities throughout the United States, and sometimes beyond. The original version, the European Cultural History Tour (ECHT), was created in 1974. It was initially a summer program traveling through Western Europe and the Mediterranean, with courses in European history and art. In the fall of 1987, a full-semester program was added, and the curriculum expanded to include literature and political science. In the winter of 1994, a full-semester Asian variant (ACHT) was created, with courses in Asian history, art, political science, and comparative religion. Adjustment of the European model to include comparative religion in the Asian program acknowledged the importance of religious study to understanding the cultural history of Asia.

Although most study abroad programs are located in one place with occasional limited travel, ECHT and ACHT feature an unprecedented amount of travel: fifty or more cities in up to eighteen countries on semester-long versions. Furthermore, the CHT model maximizes the possibilities for interdisciplinarity by having faculty from up to four disciplines travel and live with students. In effect, it is a mobile residential college and learning community. The model is best understood by "experiencing" what goes into creating and implementing the oldest and largest of the variants, ECHT.

The ECHT Model

ECHT is a survey of the cultural history and current political and cultural environments of the countries that are visited. Courses are offered officially as separate subjects, the dominant model in study abroad. In the semester-long version, students are required to take at least nine semester hours in three different disciplines. However, relationships among subject areas are deliberately emphasized. Put another way, course content tends to look and be disciplinary, but curriculum delivery is interdisciplinary.

Given the diversity of faculty and geographical scope of the program, administration is a complex task. Considerable planning and collaboration are necessary just to move from one country to another, let alone make interdisciplinary connections. Decisions about a host of logistical, curricular, and pedagogical matters are constantly needed. What sites can we visit? In what order? Which days? When and where will we hold separate sessions by discipline? What about sessions for the entire group? Upon arriving in a new city, faculty have an intensive meeting, supplemented by daily conferrals. A separate logistical director takes care of all travel, meals, and lodging, while a faculty member often doubles as on-site academic coordinator. Back home, a full-time director and support staff administer the overall program.

Almost every aspect of the model differs from those same aspects in conventional campus settings. In addition to facing a new culture and environment, faculty are teaching in a highly unusual location. A course back home usually takes place in a fixed location. In contrast, a typical day on ECHT consists of visits to museums, monuments, historic sites, and governmental centers. A typical "classroom" may be an adjacent park, the museum steps, a train station, a hotel lobby, or an actual historic site such as the Roman Forum. Students are guided by the faculty member with the most expertise at a particular site. Other faculty members also contribute their perspectives. For example, the art professor will lead the group through art museums, but the history professor is expected to make connections to historical matters or indicate how a historian's interest in a particular painting or era may be different from an art historian's. The same kind of dialogue can include professors of literature and political science.

Extensive preparation and collaboration are mandatory. Meetings begin a year in advance, centered on discussions of syllabi, core readings, and the dynamics of working together abroad. Even so, the first week or two can be difficult for new faculty. Despite advance preparation and discussions with veteran faculty, the first reality of the program on the move can be daunting. Yet nearly everyone adapts to the pace and style, finding great satisfaction in collaborating with new colleagues, and interacting with students in ways that cannot be matched in a standard classroom environment.

The quality of collaboration is crucial for reducing the sense of overload that new members of the team may experience. In addition to creating a syllabus with disciplinary content that corresponds meaningfully to the itinerary, all faculty must become aware of how their disciplines intersect. Core readings, which represent the various disciplines and perspectives, are at the heart of this process. The issues in these readings will be addressed in both separate class sessions and activities involving the entire group. As with the daily site visits, core readings are mandatory for all students, regardless of which classes they are taking. Hence, they must be carefully and jointly chosen to resonate with disciplinary interests and interdisciplinary connections. Another distinguishing characteristic of ECHT is a lessened sense of turf. Faculty members are experts, but they are co-learners as well. Four-way team teaching requires flexibility. Instructors must be able and willing to think on their feet, improvise, and explore beyond the limits of their own expertise.

As for students, the majority are not aware of the nature of interdisciplinary education before they enroll in the program. They apply for other reasons, including the extent of travel and the ability to transfer courses to their home institutions. For that reason, pre-travel orientation material emphasizes the interdisciplinary aspect of the program. It is also a topic in the formal orientation at the program's first destination. Even with this orientation, students still tend to think in disciplinary ways at the beginning, asking, for example, why they have to go to art museums if they aren't enrolled in an art course or why they have to read a history article if they are not taking history. Nonetheless, changes in perception begin soon after the program is under way.

The informality of traveling and living together is an important catalyst for integration. The flow of ideas and opinions in informal settings and alternative structures facilitates "travel" from one discipline to another. For instance, the visit to Florence allows everyone on the trip to understand and experience the city as a Renaissance Florentine. The history of the Medicis and their dealings with the popes, their relationships to artists such as Michelangelo, the political lessons of Machiavelli, the stories of

Boccaccio, and the dramatic monologues of Robert Browning—all of these come together to provide context and coherence for experiencing the site visits or even just walking around this remarkable city. Students and faculty alike transcend traditional separations of history, politics, art, and literature to move to an interdisciplinary construct, the concept of life in Renaissance Florence. The distance between faculty and students also disappears quickly as everyone lugs backpacks and trudges on and off trains.

Just as learning in study abroad education cannot be contained within a conventional classroom, it is not confined to a fixed period of time either. Ideas and information stimulated by a site visit resurface in subsequent class discussions and in casual conversations among groups of faculty and students while strolling to the next site, waiting for a train, or hanging out at a cafe. Before long, the stuff of ordinary conversation has more to do with the curriculum and the itinerary than the usual small talk of sports and campus high jinks. Faculty members are contributors to the conversations, but not as distant experts behind a podium. Students are likely to engage faculty in these situations because they see them as participants in the program—older and more experienced, but partners in discovery and learning.

After completing a program, most instructors are eager to go again, though commitments at home may prevent a return. Whether or not they return, faculty members indicate in interviews and long-term contact that their teaching styles, professional interests, and even their scholarly work are affected by this experience. Professors returning to their home campuses often show a rededication to the teaching–learning process. Now recognizing the benefits of this stimulating interaction, veterans of interdisciplinary teaching are likely to reenergize those around them. Even in conventional disciplinary contexts, veterans of ECHT and ACHT are likely to engage students in more active modes of learning and make connections to related ideas and examples outside their disciplines. They also encourage and respond to collaboration with other faculty and team teaching.

Anecdotal evidence suggests that student alumni of these programs often show comparable levels of impact. Some who were strongly affected by their first experience abroad engage in further study abroad, international internships, the Peace Corps, independent travel, or living abroad. Many report a heightened and sustained interest in international affairs and intercultural issues. Back on their home campuses, after a sometimes difficult reentry into "normal" life, most students are better able to see relationships and connections in their academic work and discern patterns in other contexts. It is not uncommon for study abroad alumni to exhibit greater poise, self-confidence, and judgment. And they usually maintain close contact with those who shared their study abroad experience, no matter how far apart they may live.

CONCLUSION

If study abroad is to achieve its full interdisciplinary potential, several additional areas need attention. The first is advising. Even in standard on-campus environments, advising is often a weak link in the chain of interdisciplinary studies. Advisors and program coordinators should be aware of the interdisciplinary potential of study abroad. When they are helping students find programs, interdisciplinary possibilities should be an important consideration, not an afterthought or oversight. Unfortunately, many study abroad advisors and members of general advising staffs are not attuned to such programs, especially if sponsored by another institution. They have plenty to do to get their students into programs that are appropriate, available, and affordable. They must also deal with financial aid, housing, visa requirements, transcripts, health and safety issues, orientations, and other pressing issues.

The second area of need is integrating study abroad with the rest of a student's academic career. Most study abroad programs are credit-bearing; often they are the most vital and vividly remembered learning experiences of a student's time in college. However, study abroad usually remains separate from the "regular" curriculum. It winds up carrying a double cost—not only the added expense of foreign travel but the perception that it is time away from the "real work" of students' majors (Cornwall and Stoddard 4; Johnston and Spalding 420). Whether study abroad is a required or an optional component of a degree program, campuses should create formal opportunities for long-term reflection. Reentry is a crucial phase. Yet, again, the plurality of program types means that generalizations about how reentry is handled are difficult. The general lack of connection between study abroad to the rest of academic life makes the role of preliminary advising even more important to the study abroad experience. It also suggests that teaching and learning abroad should be a synthesis of what is happening inside and outside the immediate classroom with long-term implications for general education, majors, careers, and personal lives.

A third area of need arises from the second. For the most part, efforts to internationalize the curriculum have occurred apart from efforts to teach multiculturalism. They also occur within isolated disciplinary and geographical spheres. The concept of "interculturalism" should infuse all forms of international education. According to Cornwall and Stoddard, interculturalism works at the intersections of disciplines and cultures to dismantle the boundary between domestic and international diversity. Interculturalism also fosters an understanding of global processes that goes beyond most visions of interdisciplinarity (28–30). No matter what their content is, study abroad courses fall short if they do not include opportunities to reflect on civic responsibilities in a world in which globalization has dismantled the boundaries of "home" and "abroad."

Students go abroad for many reasons. They want to travel, learn about other cultures, and prepare for careers. Likewise, the internationalization of the disciplines is occurring for many reasons. The most powerful cause, though, is global economic transformation (Groennings 27–29). In a globalized marketplace, study abroad must service more than economic and technological objectives alone. The interdisciplinary skills of cultural understanding and negotiating different ways of knowing make study abroad in any form one of the most powerful forms of liberal education.

The fourth and final area of need is criteria of good practice. The earlier models and lessons, coupled with insights from the literature on interdisciplinary studies in U.S.-based programs, suggest a basic checklist for study abroad programs.

Checklist of Questions for Interdisciplinary Study Abroad

- Is the interdisciplinary nature of a program or course explained in promotional print and Internet sources, course syllabi, and other course materials?
- Is interdisciplinarity merely implicit, or is there an explicit, clarified focus on integration in all phases, from orientation to course delivery?
- Does the program go beyond multidisciplinary combinations of different subjects to offering explicit opportunities for reflecting on differences of disciplinary perspectives and their interconnections around particular topics, issues, and problems?
- Is integration a random interest or an ongoing process?
- Are the integrative skills gained from interdisciplinary study clarified?
- Are time and resources invested in faculty development, preparing individuals for collaborative teaching and acquainting them with the nature of interdisciplinary education?
- Do faculty work together in teaching, designing the program and course, and creating course materials, including assessment activities?
- Are the interdisciplinary dimensions of participating disciplines and pertinent interdisciplinary subfields and fields recognized?

Sonnie Carpenter of the *Marymount College Study Abroad* program provides a last word from my survey of the SECUSS-L discussion list. Marymount was the first women's college to offer study abroad. It sponsors programs in the United Kingdom, Ireland, and Australia that allow students to cross disciplines. "Many of the universities abroad," she responded, "are figuring out that they have to allow for crossing disciplines in order to keep the study abroad students enrolling." This chapter takes the first step toward helping them figure out how to make it happen, and this book will lead them to the fuller range of knowledge and resources in the literature on interdisciplinarity. As Groennings observed, to the extent that international studies are "inherently interdisciplinary," they are conducive to integrating the disciplines. They catalyze creativity at the junction of disciplines and their relationship to external change, potentially accelerating the fuzzing of discipline boundaries (29). Study abroad is and will remain one of the most dynamic forces of change.

NOTES

1. I thank Julie Thompson Klein for her invaluable advice, countless insights, and wealth of knowledge during the research and writing of this chapter.

2. It is important to note that the results of my findings are limited to the number of replies received.

3. For information on Ghana and Kenya, see http://isp.edu/ncsa.

WORKS CITED

Awe, Cynthia Bennett. E-mail to the author. 10 May 1999.

Burh, Joanne. E-mail to the author. 5 May 1999.

Carpenter, Sonnie. E-mail to the author. 5 May 1999.

Cornwall, Grant H. and Eve W. Stoddard. *Globalizing Knowledge: Connecting International and Intercultural Studies*. The Academy in Transition Series. No. 4. Washington, DC: Association of American Colleges and Universities, 1999.

Gehlar, Jim. E-mail to the author. 5 May 1999.

Groennings, Sven. "Higher Education, International Education, and the Academic Disciplines." *Group Portraits: Internationalizing the Disciplines*. Eds. Sven Groennings and David S. Wiley. New York: American Forum, 1990. 11–31.

Johnston, Joseph S., and Jane R. Spalding. "Internationalizing the Curriculum." *Handbook of the Undergraduate Curriculum: A Comprehensive Guide to Purposes, Structures, Practices, and Change*. Eds. Jerry G. Gaff and James L. Ratcliff. San Francisco: Jossey-Bass, 1997. 416–35.

Kissane, Michael. E-mail to the author. 6 May 1999.

Klein, Julie Thompson, and William H. Newell. "Advancing Interdisciplinary Studies." *Interdisciplinarity: Essays from the Literature*. Ed. William H. Newell. New York: The College Board, 1998. 393–415.

Lambert, Richard. "Blurring the Disciplinary Boundaries: Area Studies in the United States." *Divided Knowledge: Across Disciplines, Across Cultures.* Eds. David Easton and Corinne Schelling. Newbury Park, CA: Sage, 1991. 171–94.

McDowell, Manfred. E-mail to the author. 13 May 1999.

Open Doors on the Web. Institute of International Education. 10 May 1999. http://opendoorsweb.org.

Rodenberg, Terry. E-mail to the author. 10 May 1999.

Saum, Steven. E-mail to the author. 5 May 1999.

Thomas, William. E-mail to the author. 14 May 1999.

For listings of study abroad programs, see the following annual directories:

Academic Year Programs

Peterson's Study Abroad. Princeton, NJ: Peterson's, 2001.

Academic Year Abroad. New York: Institute of International Education, 2001.

Summer Programs

Peterson's Learning Adventures Around the World. Princeton, NJ: Peterson's, 2001.

Vacation Study Abroad. New York: Institute of International Education.

Online Sources

www.petersons.com
www.studyabroad.com
www.allabroad.com

Internet Addresses for Program Models

Arava Institute for Environmental Studies. http://arava.org.

Brazilian Ecosystems—Antioch College. http://www.antioch-college.edu/aea/.

Central European Studies at Masaryk University, Czech Republic—SUNY Oswego. http://www.rect.muni.cz/cesp.

Denmark's International Study Programs (DIS). http://www.disp.dk.

European Union Program in Freiburg—The Institute for the International Education of Students. http://www.iesabroad.org.

College of William and Mary Programs Abroad. http://www.wm.edu/academics/reves/programs_abroad/.

Higher Education Consortium for Urban Affairs (HECUA). http://www.hecua.org.

Humanities in Great Britain and Humanities and Western Civilization in Florence and Paris, University of Kansas. http://www.ukans.edu/~osa.

Institute for Social and International Studies Program in Barcelona, Spain. http://isis.pdx.edu

Irish College for the Humanities. http://www.iol.ie/~ichkerry.

Lexia International. http://www.lexiaintl.org.

Maastricht Center for Transatlantic Studies. http://www.tuh.nl/mcts/.

Marine Studies—Union College, Schenectady, NY. Contact William Thomas. thomasw@union.edu.

Medieval Studies, Cambridge University. http://www.cam.ac.uk/CambUniv/ContEd/IntSummer.

Minnesota Studies in International Development. http://www.umabroad.umn.edu/MSID/msid_GENERAL.html.

National Health Systems—Union College, Schenectady, NY. Contact William Thomas. thomasw@union.edu.

Normandy Scholars Program—University of Tennessee. Contact Jim Gehlhar. gehlhar@utk.edu.

School for Field Studies. http://www.fieldstudies.org.

Science Program at Cambridge University. http://www.cam.ac.uk/CambUniv/ContEd/IntSummer.

Sustainable Development in Thailand, Kalamazoo College. http://www.kzoo.edu/cip.

Trent University, Ontario, Canada. Contact Cynthia Bennett Awe. cawe@trentu.ca.

University of Calgary Term Abroad Programs in India and in China. http://www.ucalgary.ca/UofC/students/ISC/Exchange/termabr.html.

Valencia, Spain—SUNY Albany. Contact Joan N. Savitt, jsavitt@csc.albany.edu.

Westminster College, Oxford Service-Learning. http://www.btinternet.com/~ukcentres.

CHAPTER 11

Interdisciplinarity and the Adult/Lifelong Learning Connection

Lessons from the Classroom

Roslyn Abt Schindler

My undergraduate degree in Interdisciplinary Studies prepared me well for my professional work and my continuing education at the graduate level.

> Rev. Lottie Jones-Hood, Ph.D., ISP Alumnus and Pastor
> of the First Congregational Church, Detroit, Michigan

Interdisciplinary education gave me a solid foundation upon which to build future career choices and objectives.

> Arnold Wicker, ISP Alumnus and Commander,
> Detroit Police Department

I feel not only better prepared for career advancement, but more importantly, better prepared for life, period.

> Tom Peters, ISP Alumnus and Electrical Planner,
> Great Lakes Steel

Experience is supposed to be a good teacher, and this chapter is about just that. How has experience teaching adult learners in an interdisciplinary way—or, as they are now often called, lifelong learners—created a whole new pedagogy, a new "merger" of teaching and learning methods and ideas? How does the experience that adult learners bring to the interdisciplinary classroom enhance both their own and their teachers' learning experiences and their teachers' instruction? In this chapter, I will respond to these questions using my professional experiences as well as those of other teacher-scholars in the fields of interdisciplinary studies and adult/lifelong learning. My hope is that this chapter will be helpful for faculty who are new to teaching adult learners in an interdisciplinary way. For those experienced in this field, it will serve as a reinforcement of effective ideas and methods and as an inspiration to explore new ones. Above all, the chapter will reveal concrete methods based on sound theories that will make teachers feel more comfortable teaching these special students.

Just as adult learners have some initial fears and anxieties about returning to or beginning college, some faculty might have some fears about teaching students who are older and who might have more life experiences than they do. Thus, the process of teaching lifelong, interdisciplinary learners entails a joint journey in which professor and student help and support each other in an exciting and mutually beneficial relationship. What makes this journey even more exciting is the fact that interdisciplinary studies and adult/lifelong learning enjoy a natural affinity. Julie Thompson Klein, author or editor of numerous pioneering works in interdisciplinary studies, uses a wonderfully appropriate quotation by Theodor Fontane, a well-known, late-nineteenth-century German novelist, as an epigraph in her 1990 book, *Interdisciplinarity: History, Theory, Practice*: "*das ist ein zu weites Feld*" ("that is too broad a field") (40). The context here is all the more relevant as interdisciplinary studies and adult/lifelong learning are, indeed, two "*weite Felder*" ("broad fields"). And these two broad fields connect most effectively within a pedagogical context. Indeed, as I will demonstrate in this chapter, they form a marriage made in heaven.

I am a long-time faculty member in the Interdisciplinary Studies Program (ISP) at Wayne State University in Detroit, Michigan. This program fosters a pedagogy that represents an intersection of two important deep fields, lifelong learning and interdisciplinarity. Our program's hope is to produce students who are able to assess, in sum, the why, what, and how of interdisciplinary and lifelong learning as well as the values that each field has brought to bear on their lives. From electrical planner, advertising executive, cable television executive, and church pastor, to stationary engineer, consultant in graphic design production, university registrar, manager of a volunteer department, and registered nurse, adult interdisciplinary students gain core skills and capabilities "to use disciplinary, professional, and interdisciplinary knowledge in order to solve problems and explore complex issues" (Interdisciplinary Studies Program, *Why ISP?*). I believe that due to the different life experiences and cognitive levels of adult learners, interdisciplinary teaching for them should feature the following:

1. Confidence-building,
2. Attention to context,
3. Practical, problem-solving, even job-related, skills,
4. A more individualized approach to learning than might otherwise be followed,
5. Collaborative learning opportunities.

In this chapter, I will focus on how to cultivate each of these five components.

BUILDING CONFIDENCE

> One reason I was so appreciative of the College of Lifelong Learning (CLL) is that there were other adult learners like myself, so I didn't feel so out of place. I really appreciated being respected as an adult learner and having my years of wisdom respected. I appreciated being able to integrate the best of what I had with the best of what the school offered, in order to complete my education and to continue along my professional path. (Benjamin Jones, ISP alumnus)

> ISP helps to make university education more accessible to adults with family, work, and other responsibilities. I was hesitant about competing with younger students in a traditional classroom, but ISP focuses on the needs of students like me. If it wasn't for CLL, I would never have gotten a degree. (Al Briscoe, Jr., ISP alumnus)

For adults to engage in interdisciplinary study, there must be pedagogical and programmatic emphasis on confidence-building for these special students, the first point of this chapter's thesis. Adult students begin or return to college with significant anxieties, fears, insecurities, self-doubts, and disequilibrium that naturally come from returning to school after a long absence. Noted adult educator-scholar Malcolm S. Knowles offers extensive insight into the characteristics of adult learners. According to him, adults "need to know why they need to learn something before undertaking to learn it" (83). Moreover, they have a self-concept that includes a strong sense of responsibility and self-direction as well as a life-centered (or task- or problem-centered) orientation to learning. In contrast to more traditionally aged students, they tend to be more responsive to intrinsic motivators (self-esteem, quality of life, job satisfaction, etc.) and to reflect a wider range of individual differences in terms of background, learning style, motivation, needs, interests, and goals (Knowles 83–85).

Added to this listing, a consideration by another noted scholar, David Halliburton, is especially relevant. Halliburton considers adult students to be "'at risk' in the face of life challenges. They will experience heightened anxiety and disequilibrium in the course of their studies" (465). They must discover or rediscover their own voices. Their ideas and belief systems are challenged, requiring a very important form of validation and affirmation of their self-worth. Or, to say it differently, a kind of transformation is required—of the adult student, the instructor, and the curriculum—to enhance and empower the student participant, the major goal of any adult-oriented interdisciplinary curriculum (Gerbic and McConchie 2–3).

Yet these students' very uncertainty can be a strength because it prompts them to be open to the kind of exploratory inquiry that does not necessarily culminate in a definitive answer or set of conclusions. In her 1995 essay, "Interdisciplinarity and Adult Learners," Klein makes a similar point. Beyond noting that "the core elements of interdisciplinary learning . . . correlate with core elements of adult learning," she affirms that adult learners' "disequilibrium and doubt" tend to make it easier for them to allow for the necessarily "shifting landscape of interdisciplinary inquiry" (119, 123). These students' interdisciplinary inquiries result most frequently in continuing broad and deep inquiry, creative exploration, unconventional examination, and original problem-solving: in sum, multifaceted, proactive analysis and effective synthesis, the fundamental guideposts for interdisciplinary studies.

To build confidence, introductory interdisciplinary seminars for adult students would do well to include concrete and varied ways to help them return to the world of academic reading, writing, and critical thinking. Courses that include short reading texts and short paper assignments (which may be revised for a higher grade) are best in this context as students are able to complete them easily and quickly, helping them build confidence. There are many other confidence builders, which are also critical for adults. Frequent teacher–student conferences with regular feedback concerning progress are very important: they offer students the opportunity to express concerns and fears and to seek and benefit from one-to-one assistance. Teacher accessibility may be enhanced further through e-mail and telephone dialogue between class sessions.

Incorporation of adult students' rich experiences and expertise into class discussions and assignments makes students gain confidence not only in their own abilities but also in what they contribute to the whole. This incorporation links quite naturally to promoting active student participation in curriculum development and a student-centered curriculum, one that addresses students' concerns and needs—especially their need for new challenges and for recognition of their abilities and other strengths. Above all, there must be constant positive reinforcement of the students' decision to engage in an academic program at a time that some may consider to be approaching the sunset of their lives.

EMPHASIZING CONTEXT

> By the time I had completed my remaining year and one-half [of ISP's undergraduate degree program], I couldn't understand why everyone didn't opt for this approach to education. To me, it was nearly everything . . . that a college education should be. (From Carole Keller's master's thesis, *Why MISP?: A Non-Traditional Graduate Program for Non-Traditional Students*)

> The ISP . . . appealed to me since it offered a well-rounded curriculum, touching on many areas of relevance to a working adult, and the favorable trait of being 'interdisciplinary' appeared often in trade journals, promising a bright future. (Mitch Scheidel, ISP alumnus)

Although engaging in interdisciplinary inquiry can be difficult, adult students—because of their maturity and experience—are generally able to meet the challenge. Unlike most traditionally aged students who enter college with an absolutist frame of mind (where all questions have a right or wrong answer and truth is absolute and knowable), adult learners often come into college capable of more complex thought processes. They are able to see that truth depends on context. David Halliburton focuses on the positive correlation between adult learner's thinking capabilities and the demands of interdisciplinary studies. He argues that "problem-finding and task definition are higher order capacities." In this context, he views adult learners as problem-solvers who are at a higher cognitive level, confirming that adults adapt well to "task-oriented team work and call upon the necessary interpersonal skills for problem solving" (465–67).

Contextual learning, the second point of this chapter's thesis, is, therefore, another crucial aspect of successful adult/lifelong learning pedagogy, as it is within interdisciplinary studies as well. The focus on context translates as students' ability to examine a specific issue, problem, or topic from multiple perspectives, to integrate and synthesize different approaches, and to engage in creative inquiry. In other words, adults want to know not only the "what" (content), but also the "why" and the "how" (context), of knowledge (Farrand 24–25). They are involved with epistemological questions without necessarily knowing what that word means at the start of their inquiry. As Klein notes, adults "exhibit a greater degree of integration than normally achieved by undergraduates. Adult learners will already have made some connections between various disciplines" ("Interdisciplinarity and Adult Learners" 122).

Based on their state as mature individuals, adults are deep into linkages. Karen McDevitt reflects on her interdisciplinary degree: "Having completed the Bachelor of Interdisciplinary Studies, I was convinced that the continuation of my education would be difficult at best in any narrowly disciplined program. My interests (gender studies and media culture) not only cross several disciplines, but require an integration—a synthesis—of information" (Interdisciplinary Studies Program, *MISP Brochure*). Karen is referring to the content and process, structure and substance of her learning—the connectedness or integration of her learning, a hallmark of interdisciplinary studies. According to Klein, "the heart of interdisciplinarity is the *interplay* of perspectives that occurs in balancing depth, breadth, and synthesis. Depth insures the necessary disciplinary, professional, and interdisciplinary knowledge and information for the task at hand. Breadth insures a multidisciplinary variety of perspectives. Synthesis insures integrative process and construction of a holistic perspective that is greater than the simple sum of its parts" (*Mapping* 11–12).

This interplay is increasingly valued within the broad spectrum of reforms in general and liberal education. In a 1998 essay on the importance of a liberal education, William Cronon argues that one of the most important goals of education should be to

> follow E.M. Forster's injunction from *Howard's End*: "Only connect." More than anything else, being an educated person means being able to see connections that allow one to make sense of the world and act within it in creative ways. Every one of the qualities I described here—listening, reading, talking, writing, puzzle solving, truth seeking, self-criticism, working in a community, nurturing and empowering people—is finally about connecting. A liberal education is about gaining the power and the wisdom, the generosity, and the freedom to connect. (4)

Clearly, interdisciplinary studies with its emphasis on making connections when undertaken by lifelong learners who tend to make these connections more easily than other students can promote a unique and powerful form of liberal education.

The narrative summary of a 1992 senior project by an Interdisciplinary Studies Program alumnus provides excellent continuing evidence for the beneficial interaction between adult/lifelong learning and interdisciplinary studies. In his project, *The Adult Undergraduate Experience: Critical Reflections About Being in College While Being in Life*, Bill McDermott surveyed forty-seven adult learners (thirty-six graduating seniors and eleven alumni) to develop a model of cognitive attitude in adult undergraduates in an interdisciplinary studies program. Students' attitudes changed in terms of their capacity for reassessment through critical thinking, active problem-solving, openness to other perspectives, reflective skepticism, and liberating tendencies. According to the author's summary, "[t]here is a maturity that understands the shortsightedness of fragmentation. . . . Nothing exists in isolation" (n.p.). Bill McDermott's fellow ISP graduate, Craig M. Farrand, whose outstanding senior essay (1993) is entitled, *Interdisciplinarity: The Adult Student, the University and Life*, certainly agrees, drawing on the authority of leading scholars (David Halliburton and Jean Piaget, among others) as well as the experience and expertise of ISP faculty and adult student survey responses. Moreover, Bill's, Craig's, and other students' capstone work, incorporating both primary and secondary research, demonstrates a successful contextual pedagogical strategy for adult learners in an interdisciplinary studies program: a senior essay or project that synthesizes both the structure and content of their learning and is, therefore, a direct concrete outcome of the interdisciplinary studies and adult/lifelong learning connection.

In their essay, "Advancing Interdisciplinary Studies," Julie Klein and William Newell offer an excellent listing of additional ways to foster students' contextual or integrative thinking. Among the suggestions are: "coordinated alignments of parallel disciplinary courses; clustering of disciplinary courses around a common integrative seminar or discussion groups; specific integrative approaches, theories, or concepts (such as systems theory, feminism, Marxism, textualism); course learning portfolios; field work experience, travel-study" (13).

SOLVING PROBLEMS

I was asked to adapt a local cable-access television station into a media center, and sought a graduate program that would help. I needed training that addressed telecommunication networks, curriculum design, video production, media management, and cultural change. To obtain the program that I wanted, I would have had to borrow from several disciplines. The MISP Individualized Studies Track provided exactly what I needed for this emerging industry. (John Kotarski, MISP alumnus)

The reason I came to the MISP was because it allowed me to follow the course of study that I envisioned. I am able to pursue my interest in public policy and administration but from a wider, yet more integrated, perspective than the more defined master's program in that field would have allowed. (Truman Hudson, Jr., MISP alumnus)

I came to the MISP to bring about a career change through the amalgamation and careful supplementation of my education and work experience. Included in my goal is the ability to creatively solve problems from an interdisciplinary perspective. (Valerie Allen-Hardesty, MISP alumna)

Because of their ability to think contextually, adult students easily recognize that a single discipline is insufficient to address most issues or problems. For them, the seemingly simplest everyday problem or the most complex world issue requires multiple insights that are integrated into "a more comprehensive perspective" (Klein and Newell 3). For example, a computer or a refrigerator salesperson who needs to convince a buyer must discuss components of the purchase that draw from economics, mathematics, engineering, aesthetics, history, marketing, advertising, and so on. In the sales pitch, the salesperson touches on these disciplines quite unconsciously, and the buyer considers these disciplines individually and together equally unconsciously in decision making until both parties arrive in an interdisciplinary classroom, only to discover that they are, indeed, interdisciplinary thinkers and "doers." Another example, this one from the world stage and affecting us all, is the problem of global warming. This monumental and problematic phenomenon requires comprehensive and integrated insights into history, the sciences, politics, economics, geography, engineering, mathematics, and more.

The emphasis on practical, problem-solving, and job-related skills in an interdisciplinary studies classroom is not only relevant to adult learners but also a critical aspect of their ability to bridge the gap between their world of work and the world of academics, specifically the world of interdisciplinary studies. An interdisciplinary approach to learning, which involves solving problems and addressing issues, appeals to adults because they are highly pragmatic learners. Because they must solve problems on a daily basis in their home, at work, and in their community, they have a strong need to transfer or apply what they learn and to be competent in that application. Deborah Vess writes, "Proponents of interdisciplinary studies have long argued that interdisciplinary work fosters the growth of critical thought, greater empathy for problems addressed, and the ability to apply knowledge to many different contexts" (1). Adult learners are also holistic thinkers: They perceive the world as a whole, in an integrated fashion, not as a combination of separate parts. They strive to combine or integrate component parts to make sense of the learning experience or the problem at hand. In other words, an interdisciplinary approach to learning—interdisciplinary pedagogy—appeals to adult learners in terms of their own needs and priorities as well as the experience and knowledge they bring to the classroom.

Teachers can most successfully support students' learning and problem-solving skills by emphasizing that problem-solving is a systemic, methodical process that includes several steps as well as conceptual and practical ideas. First, a teacher must pose a concrete problem or case study, including a hypothesis in some cases. Next, he or she should provide students with guiding questions and a collaborative structure in which to work (e.g., small groups of three or four). The teacher should also help students seek appropriate sources for research. Then, the teacher should emphasize the following characteristics of successful problem-solving: careful observation; listening and reading; objectivity; openness and receptivity to various points of view; broad and deep, active and accurate research; analysis and synthesis to achieve results. It is also important to stress the necessity for students to seek appropriate advice outside the peer group. Finally, students must realize that their hypothesis or anticipated solution may not, in the end, work out; rather, the problem-solving process may direct or redirect them to "square one" or to an entirely different hypothesis or set of hypotheses.

INDIVIDUALIZING LEARNING

I was initially attracted to the ISP because of the hours and its mature students whose life experiences added new dimensions to the classroom. (Edna Jackson, MISP alumna)

[Classes] are scheduled at times and in places more convenient to working adults, making things easier for nontraditional students. . . . I think they . . . actually push the student to do more than a traditional program, because there's a carry-through from term to term. . . . I really think the professors . . . are much more hands-on than [would be in] a more traditional educational program. There's more of a one-on-one relationship between students and faculty. (Timothy McGee, ISP alumnus)

In addition to bolstering problem-solving skills, adult/lifelong learning pedagogy should ideally meet students' needs pertaining to location, day, time, and delivery mode—in effect, a more individualized approach to learning than might otherwise be followed. This aspect is the fourth point of this chapter's thesis. Adult or lifelong learning, says K. Patricia Cross, an internationally known and respected scholar in that field, covers "formal, nonformal, and informal patterns of education . . . and is also characterized by flexibility in time, place, content, and technique of learning" (261–62). Cross argues further: "Lifelong learning is not a privilege or a right; it is simply a necessity for anyone, young or old, who must live with the escalating pace of change—in the family, on the job, in the community, and in the worldwide society" (ix). Written in 1981, Cross's statements could not be more relevant and, hence, valid today. And one might easily replace the words "lifelong learning" with "interdisciplinary study" in her second statement. Indeed, all the alumni quoted in this chapter agree that interdisciplinary study is a necessity in much the same way that Cross argues and for the same reasons. Thus, the interactive journey continues.

The more individualized approach called for by adult/lifelong learning and appropriate to interdisciplinary study includes flexible assignment choices and deadlines as well as a flexible delivery system. The latter has historically meant location, day, and time, and, to some extent, diverse modes of delivering instruction: for example, television courses and distance learning in more "primitive" forms. In more recent years, the term "delivery system" has taken on more technologically advanced meaning, including online courses and degree programs, interactive television instruction beamed out to the far reaches of any region of any land, and so on—distance learning in its most sophisticated and varied implementation. Busy adults with home, work, and community responsibilities are attracted to modes of flexible learning that make their ability to (re)enter education convenient and viable in terms of their varied lifestyles and learning styles.

In order to appeal to adult learners' varied learning styles, faculty should offer a diverse range of assignments or methods of learning within the context of both a flexible delivery system and adults' experience with familiar environments—family (particularly children-oriented), work, and community. Adults enjoy game- and role-playing, case studies, group research projects, field study, experiential and service learning, and discovery-based learning. These kinds of assignments or projects encourage interactive group work that builds confidence and promotes contextual or integrative learning and outcomes. These methods of learning also often bridge the known and the unknown. Bridging the known and the unknown is especially helpful for adult learners as they come or return to college with both general and specific anxieties (the first point of this chapter's thesis). Within the context of familiar experiences, adults also benefit greatly from developing a portfolio, whether for professional, educational, creative, and/or research purposes; the portfolio facilitates integration of learning in a most productive, active, and long-lasting way. These pedagogical strategies are in keeping not only with adult students' focus on the practical, problem-solving, job-related skills discussed earlier, but are the same effective tools and methods typically heralded by interdisciplinarians.

COLLABORATING

Both the ISP and MISP can be ideal for adult students who are self-motivated and self-disciplined. . . . The opportunity exists to concentrate on areas of study that are of particular interest to any one individual, while at the same time benefit from exposure to the interests that are held by others in a class. Adult students have the distinct advantage of coming to class with not only widely varied professional experiences, but also a deep set of personal, life experiences. Sharing these, while getting to know the other students, is what made the ISP and MISP enriching adventures for me. (Karen McDevitt, ISP and MISP alumna)

The fifth point of this chapter's thesis is that interdisciplinary teaching for adults should feature collaborative learning opportunities. Although it is a distinct feature meriting individual emphasis, this fifth point also incorporates the previous four elements of teaching mentioned in this chapter. Collaborative learning opportunities help establish and sustain a feeling of community, mirror what happens in the workplace (i.e., are practical and even job-related), reflect flexibility in teaching technique, emphasize context, and build confidence. Collaboration constitutes the essential strategy of interdisciplinary work, and it is a way for adult learners to exercise their natural tendencies as social, interactive beings and their preference for and long standing experience with oral communication in all aspects of their lives: work, play, family, and community (Farrand 21–22). As Klein notes, collaborative learning is especially suited to the adult learning context because older students and instructors can better participate in a collaborative manner as co-learners and co-teachers in "task-oriented teamwork" ("Interdisciplinarity and Adult Learners" 123). In short, peer interactive learning is an excellent teaching strategy that benefits both students and instructors.

The instructor in an adult/lifelong learning classroom should most often be a "guide on the side" rather than a "sage on the stage." He or she guides students to collaborate in reading groups, peer editing groups, or interdisciplinary problem-solving exercises, for example. Moreover, it is important to emphasize that these groups meet in class rather than outside of class: adults rarely have time, given their family, work, and community responsibilities and commitments, to meet outside of class. This lack of time, a major characteristic of their lifestyle, is translated into their learning style, which the instructor should incorporate into his or her teaching style. This process continues the theme of flexibility that is so necessary for adults and so appropriate for interdisciplinarity. Small group work with specific instructions as to process and goals, coupled with plenary group discussion either before or after the completion of the project, tends to maximize effective interaction among students and with the instructor. Even if students initially feel a bit awkward in small group settings, they soon overcome those inhibitions and begin to feel very comfortable interacting with their peers, especially if the group has a stable, rather than variable, membership to maximize reciprocal, ongoing support. The groups move toward mutually beneficial goals of improvement: in reading strategies, writing achievements, critical thinking skills, interpersonal skills, and interdisciplinary problem-solving skills. Group work, like all forms of active learning, promotes "long term retention of concepts" (DeZure 11). As mentioned earlier, this collaborative mode is often familiar to students from the workplace.

The instructor benefits from this teaching strategy by being able to orchestrate a truly "open" classroom, where students work, exchanging ideas and insights, at their own pace within a designated framework and timetable. The instructor is a coach and a team leader, building trust and cheering students on to victory. The instructor exhibits the very passion for learning that he or she hopes to inspire in students (Farrand 78). He or she remains the "content expert," but not in the traditional sense of lecturing for long periods of time, a time-honored method of academics. Rather, the instructor provides creative stimuli for learning—short lectures, films, specific discussion questions or issues to consider, and so on—and encourages students to contribute their own rich experiences to the learning panorama. They immerse themselves as a learning community in a true interactive teacher–student, teaching–learning experience. Problem-solving in an interdisciplinary context becomes a collaborative, enjoyable adventure in which all students engage with enthusiasm and their best efforts. Whatever the course topic, students get fully involved. And collaboration need not (always) be face to face, of course. In this advanced age of computers with the endless possibilities through the Internet and beyond, students can experience the technological permutations and combinations available to collaborate effectively with peers and instructors.

In the superb concluding chapter, "Professionalizing Interdisciplinarity," of his 1998 edited book, *Interdisciplinarity: Essays from the Literature*, William H. Newell includes key reasons that students are so successful with interdisciplinary studies. Among these reasons, which correlate so clearly with adult learner motivation and success, are: cognitive skills acquired, affective outcomes, long-term career impacts, enhanced general knowledge, employer satisfaction, and close peer support (538–39). Newell's inclusion of close peer support is of paramount importance, not only to the learning outcomes, but also to the enjoyment students derive while participating in the educational process. It is clear that their learning is both broad and deep as well as long-lasting because of the collaboration among students and between students and instructor as mutually supportive partners in a productive, ongoing relationship.

CONCLUSION

There is no single best interdisciplinary pedagogy, interdisciplinarians agree. We learn from scholars in adult/lifelong learning that there is no single best pedagogy in this area either. Rather, in each field, numerous possibilities exist. However, there is a unique connection between the two fields that gives rise to an enhancement of both fields and their pedagogies by virtue of the compatible elements that emanate from and are active in them. All this adds significance and weight to an important point made by Klein: "Understanding the nature of adult learning, interdisciplinary learning, and the relationship between the two will be increasingly important in the preparation of teachers and the continuing education of current faculty" ("Interdisciplinarity and Adult Learners" 125). Indeed, the connection between these two fields offers the possibilities for and the promise of pedagogical exploration that will enhance each and both together. It is an ongoing journey, and it is a privilege and a pleasure to be a traveler alongside colleagues and students alike.

It is appropriate, in light of the emphasis in this chapter on student testimony, to give Craig M. Farrand the last word. His senior essay has already served to inform this chapter's discussion. In that essay, Farrand concludes that there is a relationship of "mutual trust and respect between instructors and adult students" in an interdisciplinary studies program, "with gains being felt on both sides of the process" (79). From Craig Farrand and many others, we learn that the gains encompass the realization of the learning and teaching goals and expectations for each group. All evidence indicates that an interdisciplinary studies classroom that has taken into account the needs and attributes of adult learners is an ideal environment for these special students. To recall the five points of this chapter's thesis: these students gain practical, problem-solving, even job-related skills; enjoy a more individualized approach to learning than might otherwise be followed; are immersed in a contextual exploration—the how and the why—far behind the absolutist stage of thinking; build confidence that endures in their personal and professional lives as well as in any further academic pursuits; and, finally, participate in collaborative learning opportunities that create a meaningful and long-lasting bond among them as peers and with their instructors. It is, to be sure, a marriage made in heaven.

WORKS CITED

Cronon, William. "'Only Connect': The Goals of a Liberal Education." *The Key Reporter* 64, no. 1 (Winter 1998–99): 2–4.

Cross, K. Patricia. *Adults as Learners: Increasing Participation and Facilitating Learning*. San Francisco: Jossey-Bass, 1981.

DeZure, Deborah. "Why Some Groups Fail." *Whys and Ways of Teaching* 7, no. 1 (September 1996): 11–12.

Farrand, Craig M. *Interdisciplinarity: The Adult Student, the University and Life*. A senior essay submitted to the Interdisciplinary Studies Program of the College of Lifelong Learning at Wayne State University in partial fulfillment of the requirements for the degree of Bachelor of Interdisciplinary Studies. April 1993.

Gerbic, Philippa, and Andrew McConchie. "Collaborative 'Real World' Projects That Foster Integrative Understanding." National Conference of the Association for Integrative Studies. Naperville, IL. 1 October 1999.

Halliburton, David. "Interdisciplinary Studies." *The Modern American College.* Ed. Arthur Chickering. San Francisco: Jossey-Bass, 1981. 453–71.

Interdisciplinary Studies Program. *MISP Brochure*. Detroit: Interdisciplinary Studies Program, n.d.

———. *Our Students Say . . . College Degree Options for Adults*. Detroit: Interdisciplinary Studies Program, n.d.

———. *Why ISP?* Detroit: Interdisciplinary Studies Program, n.d.

Klein, Julie Thompson. "Interdisciplinarity and Adult Learners." *The Journal of Graduate Liberal Studies* 1, no. 1 (Fall 1995): 113–26.

———. *Interdisciplinarity: History, Theory, Practice*. Detroit: Wayne State University Press, 1990.

———. *Mapping Interdisciplinary Studies*. The Academy in Transition Series 2. Ed. Jerry G. Gaff. Washington, DC: The Association of American Colleges and Universities, 1999.

Klein, Julie Thompson, and William H. Newell. "Advancing Interdisciplinary Studies." Newell, *Interdisciplinarity* 3–22.

Knowles, Malcolm S. *The Making of an Adult Educator: An Autobiographical Journey*. San Francisco: Jossey-Bass, 1989.

McDermott, Bill. *The Adult Undergraduate Experience: Critical Reflections on Being in College While Being in Life*. A senior project submitted to the Interdisciplinary Studies Program of the College of Lifelong Learning at Wayne State University in partial fulfillment of the requirements for the degree of Bachelor of Interdisciplinary Studies. December 1992.

Newell, William H., ed. *Interdisciplinarity: Essays from the Literature*. New York: The College Entrance Examination Board, 1998.

———. "Professionalizing Interdisciplinarity: Literature Review and Research Agenda." Newell, *Interdisciplinarity* 529–63.

Vess, Deborah. "Implementing an Interdisciplinary Core Curriculum: The Experience of a Small Public Liberal Arts University in Georgia." *Association for Integrative Studies Newsletter* 21, no. 1 (March 1999): 1–6.

PART V

Support for Interdisciplinary Teaching

CHAPTER 12

Academic Advising in Interdisciplinary Studies

Virginia N. Gordon

The college years, for most students, are a time to grow intellectually, socially, and personally. How this growth transpires, of course, is unique to the individual student's own background and experience. Many colleges and universities are truly committed to providing an environment in which this growth is fostered. The advent of learning communities, service-learning experiences, internships, and other integrative study formats are witness to this commitment to holistic learning. Many campus services and activities also are dedicated to helping students develop and grow in beneficial ways. Academic advising is one of the most important services for helping students become aware of their intellectual and emotional growth, in particular, and for helping them monitor the progress in their development. This ongoing contact is never more critical than in advising students who are involved in the many forms of interdisciplinary studies.

A common, if misleading, perception of academic advising is that its main (and sometimes only) function is to help college students schedule classes. Over the past several decades, this narrow definition has been replaced by a more developmental and all-encompassing one (Frost; Gordon; Winston et al). One definition views advising as "a decision-making process during which students realize their maximum educational potential through communication and information exchanges with an advisor" (Grites 7). Crockett suggests that advisors serve as coordinators of students' educational experiences.

The developmental approach has received great acceptance as an ideal model for advising since it is student-centered and draws on the theoretical notion that individual students are unique in the personal attributes they bring to the educational experience. These personal characteristics include a student's academic, career, and personal interests and goals, past achievements, level of motivation, and cognitive maturity, to name a few. Developmental advisors are sensitive to the unique characteristics inherent in each student and tailor their advising approaches accordingly. Implicit in developmental advising philosophy is that students have an ongoing relationship with an advisor who, over time, learns their academic strengths and limitations.

A developmental advisor, therefore, is student-centered and purposefully involves students in their own learning. The relationship between advisor and student is one of mutual responsibility for the student's intellectual growth. Developmental advising for interdisciplinary students is a perfect vehicle for creating this shared learning environment. It supports individuals' intellectual growth by enticing them to explore their interdisciplinary interests. An interdisciplinary advisor encourages students to become involved in reality-testing these interests through the many options that interdisciplinary study offers. While developmental advising incorporates knowledge and use of students' interests and capabilities, in some cases, this personal involvement may lead to a mentoring relationship that constitutes an even higher level of advising interaction. Mentoring signifies an ongoing advising involvement at the personal level on the part of both advisor and student and is an ideal way to support a student's academic, vocational, and personal development.

The academic advising process is such a critical component of any type of interdisciplinary studies program that advisors need to be included as part of the team that is responsible for its creation and structure. Although faculty advisors are often directly involved in the formation of integrative study programs, professional advisors can also serve as important contributors. Professional advisors are often free from the confines of specific disciplines and are knowledgeable about how information and teaching methods may connect one department's offerings with another's. (In some interdisciplinary settings such as learning communities, freshman seminars, or student success courses, advisors may also be involved as teachers.) Both faculty and professional advisors can emphasize the importance of building regular advising contacts into any interdisciplinary structure.

A developmental advising approach is especially relevant to interdisciplinary studies since many students, especially first-year students, often have no experience or knowledge of what is involved in interdisciplinary opportunities. They may need assistance in identifying the many interdisciplinary opportunities on campus, especially since many of these may be hidden. As Klein notes, "A significant amount of [interdisciplinary] activity takes place under other names and in other guises" (*Crossing* 20) such as in internships, practicums, travel-study, and first-year seminars. Beyond locating interdisciplinary curricular opportunities, students may also need help in recognizing the many academic and career-related skills that many interdisciplinary experiences provide such as problem-posing and problem-solving capacities, communication to diverse audiences, and multilogical thinking.

Students can be involved in interdisciplinary studies in many ways. Interdisciplinary courses or majors are considered more traditional structures, yet organizational structures such as learning communities, educational centers, or consortia are becoming more common (Klein and Newell). Newell insists that "the curricular strategy of interdisciplinary study and the pedagogical strategies of learning communities, collaborative learning, living-learning, experiential learning such as service learning and study abroad, and multicultural learning can all be productively thought of as forms of '*integrative study*'" ("Powerful" 1). Advising in these different integrative study formats may require slightly different approaches or structures, but the advising tasks of helping students select an interdisciplinary format, monitoring their learning experience, and assessing the value of their experience remain the common goals.

This chapter will outline some of the basic elements in developmental interdisciplinary advising including communication skills, the progression of the advising process itself, and the importance of advisor training and development in the specific areas of expertise desirable in interdisciplinary advisors.

COMMUNICATION SKILLS

In any phase of interdisciplinary advising, the use of effective communication skills is obvious but sometimes taken for granted. The outcomes desired as a result of using optimal communication techniques are: (1) to provide a personal, caring, and supportive advising environment; and (2) to individualize advising around the student's needs, abilities, and interests. Communication skills that can enhance interdisciplinary advising include: establishing rapport, giving information, and challenging and confronting.

Understanding students' personal characteristics and needs is important in helping them select an interdisciplinary program. To do this, the advisor must establish a level of trust. Listening to and observing what students say and how they say it can offer insights into how they view themselves, their own learning process, and the world around them. Listening to students can provide insights into their perceptions of what interdisciplinary studies involves and their level of commitment to the endeavor. Students who enjoy being challenged intellectually, who are flexible, and who are able to entertain new thoughts and beliefs are often good candidates for different interdisciplinary experiences (Stember 343; Armstrong 175). On the other hand, students who are more comfortable with highly structured settings where new ideas are presented in traditional ways may not find certain types of interdisciplinary experiences as rewarding.

Asking open-ended questions and paraphrasing or restating students' answers are techniques that signal the advisor's interest and concern. Since about two-thirds of communication is nonverbal, advisors should be sensitive to students' nonverbal cues as well as nonverbal messages they may be sending.

It is sometimes difficult to provide a great deal of information in a brief advising session. Too much information presented too quickly can confuse or overwhelm a student, especially one who is trying to make a decision about an interdisciplinary option for the first time. Advisors need to offer information verbally in a clear and concise manner, while reinforcing or expanding it with printed information, which the student can study later. Information students can retrieve on the Internet may require additional explanation.

Areas of information in which interdisciplinary advisors need expertise include basic curricular knowledge such as the institution's general education requirements, course requirements for departmental majors and minors, and elective courses. They also need information about the interdisciplinary opportunities on their campus, such as interdisciplinary courses, majors, minors and concentrations, capstone seminars, tutorials, cluster colleges, interdisciplinary centers, independent study, or study abroad. Other possible options might include learning communities, research possibilities, or off-campus integrative opportunities that might interest their advisees, such as inter-institutional programs and internships.

Interdisciplinary advisors also need expertise about various disciplines since explaining how different disciplinary views may be integrated requires an understanding of how the parts fit into the whole. As Klein and

Newell indicate, "Disciplines are distinguished from one another by the questions they ask about the world, by their perspective or world view, by the set of assumptions they employ, and by the methods which they use to build up a body of knowledge (facts, concepts, theories) around a certain subject matter" (25). Advisors can discuss with students what the different disciplines are, how courses in various disciplines might differ, and how the implicit interest areas and the competencies acquired in certain disciplinary courses might relate to different career fields.

In some cases, a referral to another office or person may be needed to obtain more specific information. Advisors should make sure students know who to contact, what information they are seeking (what questions to ask), and what to do with the information once they have acquired it.

Sometimes it is appropriate to challenge students by asking questions that force them to think in new ways. Occasionally, advisors may need to push students to explain or defend positions or actions that seem irrational or counterproductive. For what reasons are students selecting interdisciplinary experiences? To enhance their own learning experiences, for example, or because an interdisciplinary course is taught at an hour that fits their schedule? Or perhaps they are avoiding an interdisciplinary experience because of an irrational fear or misunderstanding of what is involved?

Advisors can also help students clarify their values as those values pertain to choices and actions. After a degree of mutual trust has been established, in rare situations, the advisor may feel confrontation is appropriate. If advisors sense students are avoiding certain ideas or actions, confrontation may advance them to new levels of thinking or to an examination of attitudes or habits that are counterproductive.

THE INTERDISCIPLINARY ADVISING PROGRESSION

Not only is academic advising critical in helping students select a type of interdisciplinary offering such as a major, course, or learning community, but it can also play an equally important role in helping students monitor their cognitive and affective progress while engaged in an interdisciplinary experience. Advising can also be used as a "feedback" vehicle for helping students and faculty assess the value and relevance of a particular integrative strategy. The interdisciplinary advising process, therefore, can be viewed as a continuum of progressive phases. These include: (1) selecting an interdisciplinary experience, (2) monitoring the experience, and (3) assessing the value of the experience. The progression of these advising tasks is detailed next.

Advisors can play a pivotal role in helping students select the type of interdisciplinary experience that can yield optimum benefits given the student's academic interests and abilities. Students who select an interdisciplinary option for the first time not only need to understand how this experience might be different from a traditional approach, but also need to be apprised of what is expected of them in assignments, in- and out-of-class participation, and evaluation where applicable. An effective advisor will discuss the benefits and challenges of different curricular options and will be supportive as students weigh alternatives. Two areas of knowledge that are especially useful for advising in this phase are knowledge of the curriculum and a familiarity with how students mature and develop, especially in personal and cognitive areas.

Most students' knowledge of curricula is based on what they learn from the catalog (when they read it), their peers, and academic advisors. When selecting courses over a four-year period, most students experience only 5 percent of what is offered by the institution. When required courses are subtracted from the hours needed to graduate, some students may only be able to choose from only 1 to 2 percent of what is in the catalog (Grites and Colijn).

A generalist's knowledge of curriculum is essential in interdisciplinary advising since it cuts across many disciplines' diverse concepts and ideas. This means an interdisciplinary advisor must have a critical awareness of how disciplines differ and what each offers students in regard to their interests and goals. In advising about the general education curriculum, for example, first-year students may want to know how an interdisciplinary course might be different or more interesting to them than a course in a specific department that also meets the general requirement. A junior may want to know what is involved in an interdisciplinary major. An effective advisor will be able to describe the differences and similarities across interdisciplinary options, such as a cluster of courses, an interdisciplinary major, or an independent study, and how each of these might involve and challenge students' intellectual development. For example, when a student is considering whether to enroll in a learning community, the advisor can inform the student to expect it to provide greater academic skill acquisition, integration of content material across disciplines, less fragmented sources of information, and personal and social support (Strommer).

Laff views the advisor as the "research director" for the student. In this role, the advisor helps students understand how departmental courses can "combine with cognate work in peripheral disciplines, independent study, and other resources on campus to create coherent fields of study" (30). According to Laff, students need to be "guided" to a greater understanding of

how disciplines relate to their own personal interests and abilities. A generalist's knowledge of the pros and cons of each discipline is essential if this
curricular match is to be conveyed to and understood by the student.

In their role as research director, advisors also need to help students explore ways that their coursework may be integrative. Klein and Newell describe four levels of integration and synthesis available in most college
curricula. These levels are: (1) students take a selection of courses from different departments; (2) the institution offers students an opportunity for
integration through insights gleaned from a disciplinary course, sometimes
taught as a seminar; (3) faculty join students in the process of synthesis
through courses focused on interdisciplinary topics; and (4) material from
different fields of knowledge are integrated into a "new, single, intellectually coherent entity" (13).

When describing these levels of integration in curricula, advisors must
also consider the capability for knowledge integration of their advisees as
they recommend different interdisciplinary programs. Although level one
courses offer the least effective opportunity for helping students integrate
knowledge, they are the most common. Students who take courses or are
involved in programs at level two must often assume responsibility for
achieving integration. Although some level three offerings provide the degree of interaction and instruction that integration requires, others may
not. Level four offerings operate at the highest level since there is a "conscious effort to integrate material from various fields of knowledge" (13).

Not only can integration of knowledge be provided through courses and
seminars, but it can also be encouraged through other vehicles such as
fieldwork, study abroad programs, and living-learning centers. Advisors
can play an important role in helping students consider integrative opportunities outside the classroom by referring them to the organization or campus office where pertinent information may be obtained.

In addition to critically understanding the integrative opportunities on
campus, effective interdisciplinary advisors need to understand how students develop cognitively during the college years. Knowledge of student
development theory can provide a framework for understanding not only
how students learn, but how ready an individual student might be for an interdisciplinary experience. This knowledge includes an understanding of
students' competencies to handle the academic content and their intellectual abilities to analyze and integrate diverse and possibly conflicting bits of
information. General knowledge of how students progress in their personal
and cognitive growth provides insights that can be targeted at individual
students.

Two developmental theorists, Arthur Chickering and William Perry, offer theoretical frameworks for this approach. Chickering points out that college students grow and develop in an orderly way, accomplishing certain developmental tasks as they move through the college years. He describes seven developmental tasks or vectors that need to be completed if students are to move smoothly into adulthood. These seven include: developing competence, managing emotions, moving through autonomy toward interdependence, developing mature interpersonal relationships, establishing identity, developing purpose, and developing integrity.

These developmental tasks are continually being mastered throughout life, and Chickering describes a differentiation and integration process within each task in which students move through cycles of ever-increasing levels of complexity. Although it may appear that these tasks have been resolved, circumstances may require a need to revisit them later. Each student thus follows a unique path and timeline in personally accomplishing these tasks.

Three of Chickering's seven developmental tasks are especially relevant when advising for interdisciplinary programs. The first vector, that of *developing competence*, includes developing intellectual, physical, and interpersonal competencies. Chickering and Reisser define intellectual competence as a "skill in using one's mind. It involves mastering content, gaining intellectual and aesthetic sophistication, and most important, building a repertoire of skills to comprehend, analyze, and synthesize" (45). This understanding of how students develop intellectual competence is central to the teaching and advising functions. Advisors are in contact with students who are at many different levels of intellectual development. Students who are less capable of critical thinking skills can benefit from interdisciplinary courses, for example, because they will be challenged to stretch their abilities to comprehend, analyze, and synthesize course content. On the other hand, advisors may sense that some (often upper-class students) have the capacity to develop higher levels of competence by challenging them with "new frames of reference that integrate more points of view" (45).

Encouraging a higher order of critical thinking is integral to interdisciplinary study. Many elements of course content, for example, may need to be synthesized so that the depth and breadth of information and knowledge are "grounded in commonalties but are still responsive to differences in disciplines" (Klein and Newell 15). Because multiple perspectives need to be synthesized, many thinking skills, such as comparing, contrasting, and differentiating, are developed. Eventually successful interdisciplinary students may move to a "*sense of competence*" where they are confident in their ability to master virtually any intellectual challenge placed before them.

Another vector relevant for advising interdisciplinary courses or programs is that of *developing purpose*. Chickering and Reisser describe developing purpose as "increasing (one's) ability to be intentional, to assess interests and options, to clarify goals, to make plans, and to persist despite obstacles" (50). Helping students select interdisciplinary courses or programs involves an examination of the student's interests and goals. Goal setting is also critical in forming interdisciplinary majors since there is rarely a prescribed plan of study. In some cases, these students may need to design their major to fulfill a specific purpose. This calls for a close advisor–advisee relationship because interdisciplinary students often need more guidance and monitoring than those in traditional majors.

A critical aspect of advising is helping a student create an educational plan that not only includes long- and short-term goal setting, but an action plan to accomplish those goals. Electing to be part of a learning community, for example, might accomplish a first-year student's goal of wanting a smooth transition into college. Figuring a way to combine a student's seemingly disparate interests in dance and accountancy might be a longer-term goal.

The third vector important in advising is *developing integrity* since it involves a student's core values. As Chickering and Reisser state, "Students bring to college an array of assumptions about what is right and wrong, true and false, good and bad, important and unimportant" (51). When students hear new and sometimes disturbing ideas in or out of the classroom, their values and beliefs may be challenged. Some advisors have experienced the student who insists on dropping a course because exposure to certain ideas is too uncomfortable or upsetting. Many interdisciplinary courses typically revolve around contemporary social problems (Klein, *Crossing* 1). As Newell points out, many interdisciplinary courses feature critical thinking where students "are encouraged to recognize and formulate a critique of their own irrationally held beliefs and biases" (Newell, "Academic" 223). This type of topic can create cognitive decentering for some students and might be upsetting. An advisor may need to help them reflect on what they are learning and assist them in identifying their own position and how and why it might differ from that of others. Helping students acknowledge the existence of new and different values or beliefs may require an understanding of individual students' experiences and background. As students continually clarify their values and beliefs, they eventually personalize them and develop consistency between their values and their behavior.

Whereas Chickering identifies the critical developmental tasks that students confront during the college years, William Perry offers a useful theory of cognitive development, one that is especially relevant to interdisciplinary advising. Perry describes how students move from a closed view of what they learn to a more broad and open way to assimilate knowledge. As students become capable of more complex reasoning, they are able to challenge and be challenged by new ideas and new ways of thinking. Interdisciplinary advisors and teachers can help students make this transition by helping them understand the difference between information and knowledge. Students with a more closed view may see knowledge as a collection of information and view learning as a simple information exchange. In other words, it is the responsibility of others to convey this knowledge to them; they are passive recipients. Intellectual development requires a large degree of personal interaction with the educational environment, and advisors are in a perfect position to encourage and foster this development. Knowledge of Perry's concepts can provide interdisciplinary advisors with a cognitive stage framework focusing on intellectual and ethical development.

The Perry model comprises nine positions or stages, each presenting a qualitatively different mode of thinking about the nature of knowledge. Perry likens these modes to the lenses through which students view the world. The stages tend to reflect the student's perceptions of the teacher's or advisor's role and the student's role as learner.

The nine positions may be grouped into four more abstract categories of dualism, multiplicity, relativism, and commitment. Dualistic students think in terms of right versus wrong or black versus white and view learning as information exchange between an expert (i.e., a teacher or advisor) and themselves. Dualistic learners have difficulty with reflection, comparison, and analysis. They believe right answers exist somewhere for every problem, and since advisors and teachers are authorities, they have the answers. Dualists expect advisors to "tell them what course to take" or "what major is best" for them. An advisor might help students identify several alternatives and weigh the pros and cons of each, while making it clear the choice is theirs. In this way, the advisor is responding to students' present levels of thinking and helping them move into a more multiplistic way of thinking by suggesting options.

Some dualists have trouble with the critical thinking skills that are often required in interdisciplinary experiences. If students are having difficulty in an interdisciplinary course, for example, advisors might want to help them assess their skills in these areas. Interdisciplinary advisors can reinforce the notion that there are multiple perspectives or alternatives to the ideas raised in class and that thinking in absolutes does not allow for openness to new ideas. Advisors also need to be aware that dualists assume a simplistic connection between major and career. This might be a real concern to students who are looking for the one career that is "right" for them. In addition to initiating a discussion about alternatives, advisors may want to refer the student to the instructor in the course in which they are having difficulty or to the career resources on campus if the concern is vocationally oriented. Advisors may also want to challenge students to think creatively about how to combine differing research and career interests.

The multiplistic student considers the idea that there are multiple alternatives to every problem, but still thinks there is one best solution. To such a student, diversity is acceptable, and knowledge is viewed in quantitative terms. "People have a right to their own opinions," so no opinion is wrong. However, multiplistic students believe that if they work long and hard, eventually the authority will give them the "right" answers. Until this point, they may not have been aware of so much new information or considered the ideas and values of others. Advisors may detect a sense of confusion on the part of multiplistic students. Advising strategies may include helping them acknowledge this confusion and devise strategies for coping with their uncertainty. Comparing alternatives can be accomplished through a line of reasoning that is consistent, understandable, and predictable.

Interdisciplinary advisors need to help multiplistic students establish evaluative criteria that are consistent, given that making choices of courses, majors, or other interdisciplinary opportunities may seem overwhelming at first. Competent interdisciplinary advisors can influence students' decisions about disciplinary and interdisciplinary options that most closely match and yet may challenge their capacity for thinking and learning.

Perry indicates that there is a qualitative shift when students begin to engage in *relativistic* thinking. Analysis and synthesis are possible. Relativistic students are comfortable with different perspectives and are able to make judgments about the relative merits of an idea or alternative. Relativistic students are on the way to becoming self-directed learners. Like Chickering's individual working on the vector of developing integrity, relativistic students examine their personal values. This knowledge about students gives advisors an especially important insight into advising upper-level undergraduates. Such a relativistic pattern of thought is important in interdisciplinary courses or formats that require a deeper level of analysis and synthesis.

Interdisciplinary advisors can help relativistic thinkers to become more "critically self-reflective" (Klein and Newell 223). Advisors may want to challenge any beliefs or biases that appear to be irrational in their advisees' thinking and promote fair thinking about ideas and opinions different from their own.

According to Perry's model, students who have reached *commitment* are willing to take full responsibility for their learning and recognize that new learning will require continual seeking and processing. Given the complex level of thinking involved in this developmental level, advisors will probably not often see a traditionally aged, first-year student who has reached this level of commitment. Yet, because interdisciplinary study often encourages higher-level thinking, advisors may see some upper-class students who have reached the commitment stage because of their continuing interdisciplinary exposure. The advisor's role when working with students in commitment can be that of sounding board and supporter.

MONITORING THE INTERDISCIPLINARY EXPERIENCE

Knowledge of how students develop is just as important in the monitoring phase of interdisciplinary advising as it is in the selection process, since individual students' experiences will be colored by their ability to integrate what they are learning. Perhaps one of the most important contributions advisors can bring to the interdisciplinary advising process is helping students make meaning of their experience as it is happening. Integration of knowledge involves moving from depth to breadth along with questioning the value of what they are learning (Klein, *Crossing* 212). As Boyer points out, when disciplinary boundaries are crossed, a more integrated view of knowledge can be realized.

This was brought home to me one day in advising two different students. One undergraduate complained about his "boring" schedule because the courses he was taking were "redundant." Upon questioning he disgustedly indicated the material covered in his three courses was too much alike. Later, an older adult student who was taking a similar schedule of courses excitedly described how he was gaining new insights and ideas from his courses. He was impressed at how the content of one course dovetailed with another. Through his ability to integrate the courses' material, he was making exciting connections between disciplines. As an advisor, I was fascinated with the contrast in the two students' reactions to essentially the same experience. Obviously, the older student was cognitively able to integrate the content of courses in three separate disciplines into a holistic understanding of how fragments of knowledge can relate to each other.

The first-year student did not have the cognitive maturity to integrate the possible connections in the coursework in which he was involved. Using Perry's ideas, the advisor would be sensitive to the younger student's inability to perceive the relationships that the more mature, older student was able to recognize. A developmental advisor would point out to the first-year student the beauty of coursework that integrated important ideas and concepts, emphasizing the fact that we artificially divide knowledge into disciplines for our own purposes. Using the student's description of how the coursework overlapped, an interdisciplinary advisor could help the student understand how ideas from different disciplines might interact under a common theme or complement each other.

While helping students monitor their progress in interdisciplinary programs, advisors may find some advisees with value conflicts. Sometimes the topics in interdisciplinary courses are more value-laden than discipline-oriented courses. As mentioned earlier, some students may not want to remain in a course or program where content conflicts with their own values or beliefs. By discussing with an advisor their impressions, reactions, and satisfaction with the experience, students may become more aware of possibilities for new ways of thinking and learning. Practical applications for what is being learned (or unlearned) can be reviewed and clarified. Advisors must also be aware of how their own value systems influence the way they approach a certain problem or student.

ASSESSING THE VALUE OF THE INTERDISCIPLINARY EXPERIENCE

What are the advantages of taking part in an interdisciplinary experience and how can desired outcomes be measured? Astin found that interdisciplinarity had a positive and broad effect on the cognitive and academic development of students who participated. He also found that interdisciplinary studies had a positive effect on self-reported growth measures (424–25). Pascarella and Terenzini found that curricular experiences that included thematic courses that required integrated learning encouraged critical thinking (619).

During earlier advising contacts when students select an interdisciplinary option, it is the responsibility of the student and advisor to discuss not only the goals or outcomes students hope for, but what they can realistically expect from the experience. During the monitoring phase of the advising relationship, a student's progress in meeting goals can be reviewed and perhaps redirected if the student's needs change or become clearer.

The department, office, or organization sponsoring a particular interdisciplinary program will most likely undertake an evaluation. These summative evaluation efforts are geared toward evaluating the interdisciplinary course or program itself. Evaluation of interdisciplinary programs is much needed, but little has been done in this area (Klein and Newell 17). Preliminary efforts to assess learning in interdisciplinary programs indicate that some positive changes occur in students, such as growth in critical thinking, academic development, and increased intellectual self-concept (Astin; Field, Lee, and Field; Pascarella and Terenzini). Although evaluative efforts are critical to the potential development and improvement of interdisciplinary offerings, it should be emphasized that these official evaluations may be very different from the students' evaluations of the interdisciplinary experience. Students who participate in these programs need to take responsibility for assessing how they personally benefited or did not profit from the experience. Advising sessions are a natural place for this to occur.

Two kinds of goals or outcomes can be discussed in advising sessions. In the "information-giving" phase, students should clearly understand the goals and structure of the interdisciplinary program before enrolling in it. The second goal is to help students discuss how *they* want to benefit from the experience, personally, academically, and even vocationally. After identifying goals that are realistic and attainable, the advisor and student might want to formalize them in writing. For example, after being a member of a learning community for a year, a student should be able to answer this question: What academic and personal changes have transpired? Are they the same ones the student anticipated when she began her freshman year? How will the interdisciplinary experience enhance the possibility of a senior's being accepted into a graduate program? How can he articulate his experiences in a graduate school application? What marketable skills (e.g., solving complex problems, thinking conceptually, communicating verbally and in writing) has the student acquired that can be discussed with a prospective employer?

When advising is viewed as a progression of events, the process will reflect continuity and personalization. Students will know that one person on campus understands their academic strengths and limitations, and they will feel the support and acceptance that comes from a personal advising relationship. The advising tasks of helping students select, monitor, and assess an interdisciplinary experience can bring a sense of continuity and purpose to the advising exchange.

ADVISOR DEVELOPMENT

Armstrong emphasizes the importance of faculty development for teaching in interdisciplinary programs since many faculty are not prepared "to do the sort of interdisciplinary work the institution requires of [them]" (175).

The model for faculty development he proposes suggests that "faculty participants seek to effect the same intellectual synthesis they expect from their students" (177). He also proposes that the institution reward interdisciplinary efforts if "such efforts are to be successful" (180). The same may be said of the preparation required for academic advising for interdisciplinary programs.

When developing a program for training academic advisors to assist interdisciplinary students, some of the issues involved in regular advisor development efforts remain the same. As previously indicated, curricular knowledge, knowledge of student development (especially cognitive development), and communication skills are basic to effective advising. The focus, however, must be on the specific needs of interdisciplinary advisors, whether they are professional staff or faculty assigned as advisors to the students they are teaching.

Other possible content areas that often lead to productive discussions include:

- Developmental advising philosophy and how it can be applied in various interdisciplinary offerings.
- Student learning styles and how this knowledge can be applied to interdisciplinary advising and teaching.
- A review of student development theory and how students at different levels of cognitive maturity might react to different modes of interdisciplinary teaching and learning.
- A review of how students make educational decisions (i.e., how they understand the decision-making process and what strategies might be employed in the advising exchange).
- Career development theory and how students can apply their interdisciplinary experiences to the career decision-making and job-search processes.
- How interdisciplinary experiences can help students identify and clarify their values.
- Understanding the needs of special populations enrolled in interdisciplinary programs (e.g., older adult students, students of color).
- Direct applications for advising in specific interdisciplinary programs (e.g., professional staff advisors who are advising departmental interdisciplinary majors or faculty advisors who are advising the same students they are teaching in a learning community).

Other local needs can be addressed in advisor development programs. Because interdisciplinary advising requires special knowledge and skills, the importance of regular advisor development programs cannot be overstated.

SUMMARY

Developmental advising is an ideal model for academic advising in any type of interdisciplinary program, given that student decisions about such opportunities require an understanding of how their personal qualities might predict satisfaction and success in such endeavors. Interdisciplinary advisors must be able to relay accurate curricular information to students while they are weighing the options available at their institution. When discussing what students want to accomplish during the interdisciplinary experience, advisors can help them determine whether the outcomes they desire are realistic. As students progress through an interdisciplinary option, their advisor can encourage reflection on what the student is learning and experiencing. The advisor can also help students evaluate the value of the experience when it is completed by reviewing what was learned and determining whether the student's expectations were met. Suggestions for topics in an interdisciplinary advisor development program were offered.

Perhaps one of the greatest benefits of advising students in interdisciplinary programs is the potential growth in knowledge and skills of advisors themselves. If the advising process is perceived as a learning environment, both student and advisor play the roles of teacher as well as learner. Klein and Newell state that one goal of interdisciplinary studies is to provide "a more comprehensive perspective . . . of the question, problem, or issue" (12). The goal of advising can also be viewed as offering a more comprehensive understanding of the student, the interdisciplinary format, and the full potential of the advisor–student relationship that can evolve. When regular contact has been established, the advising setting involves questioning, reflecting, and assessing what has transpired. When these elements are present, both the student and advisor benefit.

WORKS CITED

Armstrong, Forrest H. "Faculty Development through Interdisciplinarity." Newell, *Interdisciplinarity* 171–80.

Astin, Alexander W. *What Matters in College? Four Critical Years Revisited.* San Francisco: Jossey-Bass, 1992.

Boyer, Ernest L. *College: The Undergraduate Experience in America.* New York: Harper & Row, 1987.

Chickering, Arthur W. and L. Reisser. *Education and Identity.* 2nd ed. San Francisco: Jossey-Bass, 1993.

Crockett, D., ed. *Academic Advising: A Resource Document.* Iowa City: American College Testing Program, 1979.

Field, M., R. Lee, and M. L. Field. "Assessing Interdisciplinary Learning." *Interdisciplinary Studies Today*. Eds. J. T. Klein and W. Doty. New Directions for Teaching and Learning. No. 58. San Francisco: Jossey-Bass, 1994.

Frost, S. H. *Academic Advising for Student Success: A System of Shared Responsibility*. Washington, DC: ASHE-ERIC Higher Education Report No. 3, 1991.

Gordon, V. N. *Handbook for Academic Advising*. Westport, CT: Greenwood Publishing, 1992.

Grites, T. J. *Academic Advising: Getting Us through the Eighties*. Washington, DC: ASHE-ERIC Higher Education Research Report No. 7, 1979.

Grites, T. J., and Colijn, G. J. "Coherent Curricular Choices." *NACADA Journal* 9, no. 2 (1989): 11–15.

Hursh, B., Haas, P., and Moore, M. "An Interdisciplinary Model to Implement General Education." Newell, *Interdisciplinarity* 35–50.

Klein, J. T., and Newell, W. H. "Advancing Interdisciplinary Studies." Newell, *Interdisciplinarity* 3–22.

Laff, N. P. "Developmental Advising for Undecided Students: Rethinking the Relationships." *Issues in Advising the Undecided Student*. Ed. V. N. Gordon. Columbia, SC: National Resource Center for the Freshman Year Experience, 1994.

Newell, W. H. "Academic Disciplines and Undergraduate Interdisciplinary Education: Lessons from the School of Interdisciplinary Studies at Miami University, Ohio." Newell, *Interdisciplinarity* 213–224.

Newell, William H., ed. *Interdisciplinarity: Essays from the Literature*. New York: College Entrance Examination Board, 1998.

Newell, W. H. "Powerful Pedagogies." *Reinventing Ourselves: Interdisciplinary Education, Collaborative Learning and Experimentation in Higher Education*. Eds. B. L. Smith and J. McCann. Bolton: Anker Press, 2000.

Pascarella, E. T. and P. T. Terenzini. *How College Affects Students: Findings and Insights from Twenty Years of Research*. San Francisco: Jossey-Bass, 1991.

Perry, W. G. *Intellectual and Ethical Development in the College Years*. New York: Holt, Rinehart, & Winston, 1970.

Stember, M. "Advancing the Social Sciences Through the Interdisciplinary Enterprise." Newell, *Interdisciplinarity* 337–52.

Strommer, D. W. "Teaching and Learning in a Learning Community." *Learning Communities: New Structures, New Partnerships for Learning*. Ed. J. H. Levine. Columbia, SC: National Resource Center for the First-Year Experience and Students in Transition, 1999.

Winston, R., S. Ender, T. Miller, and T. Grites. *Developmental Academic Advising*. San Francisco: Jossey-Bass, 1984.

CHAPTER 13

Transforming Interdisciplinary Teaching and Learning Through Assessment

Michael Field and Don Stowe

Do not go where the path may lead, go instead where there is no path and leave a trail.

Ralph Waldo Emerson

INTRODUCTION TO THE ASSESSMENT MOVEMENT

O ver the past twenty years, interest in the assessment of student outcomes has grown dramatically. State legislatures, governors, and various governing entities, faced with accountability concerns, have given some political urgency to assessment's agenda.[1] In an era of diminishing resources and multiple demands for funds, handing out money to higher education on its assumed merits has been frowned on. As a result, at least in part, of political pressures, trustees, benefactors and legislators demand an economic analysis, seeking some indication of the "bang" factor for their bucks. Such demands were underscored when, in 1988, Secretary of Education William Bennett issued a directive requiring all federally approved accreditation organizations to include evidence of institutional outcomes in their criteria for accreditation (Palomba and Banta 2).

Driven both by the desire of faculty to understand the teaching and learning process and by external pressures for accountability, universities and colleges have adopted a variety of initiatives and mechanisms in-tended to measure and document student learning. Resources devoted to the careful and systematic documentation of student achievement have multiplied rapidly in the last decade. By 1995, according to *Campus Trends*, 94 percent of institutions were engaged in assessment, and 90 percent had increased their involvement in assessment as compared to five years earlier (Palomba and Banta, 3). Many institutions have appointed full-time direc-tors or coordinators of assessment, and, at the departmental level, faculty are often assigned released time for assessment tasks.[2]

At the same time that pressures for accountability from legislators were building, higher education professionals experienced a series of challenges to the status quo, embodied in such widely publicized works as *Involvement in Learning* in 1984 and *Integrity in the College Curriculum* in 1985. These re-ports, and others that followed, crystallized elements of a critique of stu-dents' experiences as fragmented, distorted by premature specialization and lacking in intellectual coherence. Calls for reform in general educa-tion and for the introduction of a set of intellectual experiences common to all undergraduates intensified. Reinforcing such criticisms, a growing ten-dency toward a psychology of consumerism now reveals a public eager to ask the same hard questions of higher education that they are asking every-where else: What am I getting or will I get for my investment of time and money? Assessment has often been characterized as the ideal response to this panoply of demands and as the engine to revitalize higher education. At times, it has even been presented as a panacea (Erwin 2–5).

Educators' early enthusiasm for assessment was understandable, as the assessment movement seemed to answer the concerns of the public and legislators and to offer exciting alternatives to the traditional ways of mea-suring student learning and programmatic or institutional quality, such as student grades, the number of books in a university's library, the size of an institution's endowment, or the number of Nobel Prize winners on a fac-ulty. Advocates of this early assessment movement argued for direct mea-sures of student learning, carried out systematically. The question at issue was not how well prepared a program is to deliver an education, but what students actually learn.

Emphasis in these early years of the 1980s was often placed on standard-ized tests administered at the beginning and end of an educational program in order to document "value added," that is, actual growth in student un-derstanding and/or skills that could be attributed to the educational pro-gram. More recently, although the notion of value added survives, the focus of assessment has shifted somewhat to accommodate more subtle tech-niques for gathering data and the related ideas of continuous improvement and defined competencies (Ewell, "National Trends" 107; Farmer and Napieralski 476–92). Although many assessment advocates now tend to emphasize qualitative approaches, most experts, however, agree that there are significant advantages and disadvantages to both standardized, objective measurement instruments and qualitative processes such as the analysis of student portfolios or the use of focus groups to provide valuable sources of assessment information. Along with this move toward more qualitative measures of assessment, there has recently been a shift from teaching-based to learning-based models of assessment (Barr and Tagg; Cross). Whereas teaching-based assessment focuses on increasing and improving instruction, learning-based assessment emphasizes the enhancement of student learning.

Finally, the realities of conducting assessment in a time-limited environment have encouraged the embedding of assessment activities into the traditional activities of the classroom. Some faculty members have been understandably resistant to giving up class time to conduct assessment activities. Many other faculty, however, have concluded that assessment can be an essential element of their own scholarship. Thus, they have adopted the practice of incorporating assessment (through the one-minute paper, goal ranking and matching, focused listing, etc.) within the framework of their class since it supports honest, reflective, scholarly practice (Angelo and Cross; Eder, personal interview).

In this chapter, we first consider some of the pitfalls of the current mainstream assessment movement and then explore the interesting nexus of interdisciplinarity and assessment: To what extent are the fundamental questions and assumptions of assessment affected by their application to an interdisciplinary endeavor? How can interdisciplinarians side step some of the pitfalls of the mainstream movement? After examining the diverse goals of interdisciplinary studies and the unique challenges of interdisciplinary assessment, we provide a summary of evolving assessment practices appropriate to interdisciplinary settings. The chapter concludes with some suggested principles to apply in developing interdisciplinary assessment practices that are both challenging and fruitful.

A MODEST CRITIQUE

Despite the potential of assessment to reframe the way teaching and learning are understood in the academic world, there is relatively little evidence to date that its considerable promise has been or ever will be fully realized. Perhaps in reaction to the rapid and widespread adoption of its goals, or the occasional exaggerations of its most fervent advocates, there are signs of some self-doubt. Indeed, the title of the 2000 AAHE Assessment Conference was *Rising Expectations for the Assessment Movement: Can We Deliver?* Nevertheless, efforts at assessment seem nearly ubiquitous. The number of institutions involved and the resources available to promote and engage in assessment are not, however, convincing evidence of the movement's effectiveness, any more than the volumes available in a university's library or the number of its faculty holding doctorates can demonstrate that students are actually learning anything. Because of the way assessment has been defined and practiced, its rapid adoption, and the absence, in many cases, of systematically collected data, it is questionable whether the assessment movement will soon demonstrate that the expenditures of time and money dedicated to it had anything like the impact claimed for it.

As a result of the growing prominence of the assessment movement, discussions of educational effectiveness in regional accrediting agencies, boards of trustees, and higher education coordinating boards tend to focus less on the level of educational resources and far more than ever before on assessment that can demonstrate real learning. Unfortunately, however, the published literature to date presents many more narratives and anecdotal reports about how to assess than evidence of the real value of assessment on a massive scale. And the scale has been massive, if the amount of money and the number of institutions and programs diligently working at assessment are fair measures.

Mainstream assessment suffers from several other sorts of problems. A fundamental problem lies in the dualistic nature of assessment: it is both a means of political accountability and a principled means of educational reform. In many cases, the best way to assess for educational improvement is quite different from the best way to assess in order to respond to external pressures for accountability. Assessment professionals are thus often torn between competing demands. In part because of the external mandates for assessment and the political forces that underlie those mandates, faculty members are often suspicious and resistant to assessment. Although it is possible to overstate faculty resistance, a significant aversion to assessment among faculty is a continuing problem (Schilling and Schilling ix).

Additional problems include the lack of consensus on the purposes of assessment, disputes about the uses of assessment data, and inappropriate or incomplete methodology. These problems have many roots. First, learning outcomes are sometimes expressed so idealistically as to defy measurement. Occasionally, this is caused by an uncritical combination of learning outcomes and programmatic goals. For example, the program goal of good citizenship is more elusive than a learning outcome that requires application of a principle such as freedom of speech. Second, goals are occasionally combined in a manner that makes the analytic processes of conventional assessment difficult to implement. Outcomes may be expressed in an awkward combination of program, departmental, and course goals or simply in unmanageable combinations such as the display of oral, scientific, and computer literacy all in the same breath. Third, some programs display serious inconsistencies between the desired learning outcomes and their choice of measurement instruments. For example, although a program may have a clear set of learning outcomes, it may adopt, perhaps out of desperation, a standardized test that does not report on learning outcomes deemed important by the program. Finally, goals established for assessment plans are often written exclusively in terms of departmental or programmatic processes instead of learner behavior. For example, it is common to see goals such as increasing student enrollment or adding faculty lines in assessment plans. Assessment at the program level is useful and appropriate, but it is no substitute for assessing student learning.

Beyond these difficulties looms one additional obstacle, obvious but often unnoticed. In the academic world, where annual reports, grant applications, and institutional prose abound, claims about ambitious assessment goals and initiatives often mask the absence of actual activity. In other words, we sometimes find a fundamental failure to get started.

Despite these problems, assessment is far from dead. The assessment movement has not complied with the early, cynical predictions that it would be gone by the end of the century. At the beginning of a new century, assessment is firmly entrenched in the ethic of institutional effectiveness assumed by regional and national accrediting bodies as well as state governing agencies. Assessment has become a contemporary rallying cry in every sector of higher education. Thus, one finds assessment efforts throughout the academy, ranging from individual courses to departments, programs, and entire institutions. Outside the degree-granting arena, assessment is also nearly ubiquitous in continuing education programs, housing, and student activities.

In addition to these areas, most interdisciplinary programs are beginning to formulate and implement assessment plans, either as an effort to improve teaching and learning, or in response to an external mandate, or perhaps from both motives. Regardless of motive, assessment has been used effectively to improve the credibility of interdisciplinary programs (Schilling, personal interview). As interdisciplinary programs continue their quest for mainstream credibility, it is not surprising to find these programs confronting the challenges of assessment.

INTERDISCIPLINARITY AND ASSESSMENT

With some notable exceptions (Field, Lee, and Field; Klein; Newell) most discussions of assessment to date have focused on the traditional academic disciplines. The idea of interdisciplinarity has become a considerable force in higher education, however, at least at the level of public rhetoric. Any new dean or college president, it is coyly observed, must include three ideas in all talks: strategic planning, fund-raising, and interdisciplinary efforts. Although the interdisciplinary community welcomes even such nominal recognition, added attention as a high-stakes player is accompanied by the obligation to bring diverse interdisciplinary efforts into the mainstream and document the outcomes of such efforts.

Like those expressed about assessment, attitudes toward inter-disciplinarity range between two extremes. It is seen either as a good way to achieve desired educational outcomes and perhaps even an educational panacea, or it is viewed as an ephemeral idea or a less effective or at best merely as effective approach as conventional disciplinary approaches in producing desired outcomes. In the context of this book, we prefer the posi-tion that interdisciplinarity is the most authentic way to achieve desired educational outcomes. Interdisciplinary approaches to knowledge may re-sult in conventional outcomes such as writing competency, oral communi-cations proficiency, and computer literacy. However, because we believe interdisciplinarity more authentically represents the domains of knowl-edge and the intricate if not ineffable connections among them, we offer as a hypothesis that interdisciplinarity provides a superior way to achieve de-sired cognitive outcomes in the areas of critical thinking as well as a variety of affective and developmental outcomes. We further contend that there may be many serendipitous and positive outcomes of interdisciplinary edu-cation that have not been completely identified or placed in the canon of desired outcomes.

Thus, assessment gives us a platform not only to assess the achievement of designated outcomes of interdisciplinary studies but also to identify and categorize other kinds of learning. There is indeed some evidence to sup-port the claims of positive interdisciplinary outcomes, but it is still primar-ily anecdotal or inferential rather than quantitative or experimental. Consequently, an important challenge facing the interdisciplinary com-munity is to design systematic ways of evaluating such claims. The appro-priate test for alternative conceptions of interdisciplinarity is what outcomes they produce when they are put into practice (Newell 537–40). Although assessment may ultimately validate the authenticity of interdisciplinarity, there are many obstacles to overcome.

ASSESSMENT CHALLENGES SPECIFICALLY RELATED TO INTERDISCIPLINARY STUDIES

The roots of interdisciplinarity, especially the idea of the unity of knowledge, are classical in origin, but the interdisciplinary revival of the classical ideal must prove its worth in a culture of evidence. With an academy organized around the idea of the disciplines, interdisciplinarity has been accorded verbal support while often being relegated to what Karl Schilling has called an "across-the-street" status. As interdisciplinary programs gain legitimacy on their campuses, their move from the margin to the mainstream has been accompanied by growing pains.

In late fall of 1998, the Board of the Association for Integrative Studies (AIS) appointed an assessment study committee to advise the interdisciplinary community on issues related to assessment. The committee launched a national survey of interdisciplinary programs to determine the status and impact of the assessment movement among diverse interdisciplinary programs. It sent a request for assessment-specific information and assistance to over 1,000 members of AIS, as well as over 500 other requests to graduates of the Institute of Integrative Studies, Interdisciplinary Program Directors, and participants in the Evergreen Project, a study of model learning communities. By late spring of 1999, the committee had received only eighty-nine responses, over half of which were asking for guidance and assistance with interdisciplinary assessment.

The information received and the low response rate suggest that assessment practices among the majority of interdisciplinary programs are still in their infancy. Although a few programs have been involved in assessment for some time and have matured somewhat, many programs began assessment quite recently, often as a response to administrative or political pressure. Although external pressures for accountability are looming, few interdisciplinary programs can report much significant activity, as indicated by such comments as the following:

> Although we have many interdisciplinary projects under way, we do not have good assessment plans in place.

> The interdisciplinary major is less than ten years old, and we have done less formal assessment of it.

> No assessment tools available but would like to keep apprised of your work and would like to use these assessment tools.

> We are just starting interdisciplinary programs at our University. No assessment methods yet, but I look forward to hearing about what others are doing.

Our assessment . . . is still in its infancy.

As is the case with many institutions, we are currently looking at ways to achieve meaningful assessment of all our programs, and I would be most interested in receiving information on practices at other schools.

The first report of the committee in the fall of 1999, aided by response data and our own professional involvement in the assessment arena, offers a conventional snapshot of the status of interdisciplinarity and assessment. Given the rational-linear context that assumes that assessment begins with well-defined learning outcomes, we arrive at several conclusions. First, there is no single, widely accepted definition of interdisciplinarity, no accepted theory of interdisciplinarity, and no single model of an interdisciplinary program. Consequently, a broad range of programs and enterprises, with very different methodologies and goals, may all be properly considered interdisciplinary. Thus, it is difficult to arrive at any interdisciplinary assessment guidelines, given the heterogeneous nature of interdisciplinary programs and courses. To further complicate matters, the conventional conception of assessment has focused on specific skills and abilities. It is reasonable to argue that interdisciplinary programs embracing complexity and ambiguity may not be well served by single measures or reductionist strategies (Klein 26).

Second, there is still no widespread consensus on the expected learning outcomes of interdisciplinary studies, despite the conventional notion that agreed on outcomes should precede assessment. As the assessment movement shifted its emphasis from process to outcomes, interdisciplinary programs were challenged by the magnitude and complexity of their predicted outcomes. Cognitive and affective developmental outcomes, for example, are more difficult to assess than the ability to write a complete sentence or use a specific formula.

Third, assessing the ability of students to do synthesis or integration, which many interdisciplinary scholars cite as the hallmark of interdisciplinarity, offers unique challenges, given the rather broad nature of the construct. Consensus on the meaning of synthesis or integration does not exist. Perhaps solid, honest, nuanced scholarship will lead interdisciplinarians to a better understanding of what synthesis really is and how it can be measured.

As our study of interdisciplinary assessment has continued, it has become clearer that the conventional, linear logic of assessment works well, up to a point, in assessing interdisciplinary outcomes. In other words, following a conventional model of assessment can yield interesting information that satisfies the demands of external accrediting agencies. In fact, our survey suggests that many interdisciplinary programs seem to be making progress in their choice of conventional measurement techniques. Where assessment is being conducted, multiple strategies are often defined and implemented. Occasionally, there is a lack of congruence between goals and techniques adopted to measure those goals. Some assessment strategies appear to be adopted rather uncritically or purely as a matter of convenience. Nevertheless, based on this recent survey, those already involved in assessment in the interdisciplinary community are employing an impressive and diverse array of assessment techniques.

What our preliminary findings also indicate is that the fluid nature and complexity of interdisciplinarity are not well served by quick, unquestioning obedience to conventional processes. Currently, we see five crucial challenges to assessing interdisciplinary learning:

1. Finding a fit in the typically linear assessment arena for creative, interdisciplinary programs seeking complex cognitive, developmental, and serendipitous outcomes.
2. Describing expected outcomes in non-utopian language while leaving room for discovery of unanticipated outcomes.
3. Defining the core interdisciplinary construct of synthesis or integration in a measurable manner.
4. Identifying both conventional and creative assessment techniques for gathering data on interdisciplinary learning.
5. Keeping the focus of assessment on improving cognitive, affective, and developmental outcomes, thus improving interdisciplinary curricula and pedagogy.

In the following section, we address some of these challenges by exploring some possible assessment practices for interdisciplinary studies.

EVOLVING INTERDISCIPLINARY ASSESSMENT PRACTICES

A cornerstone of conventional assessment is progress toward clear and operationally defined learning outcomes. However, the depth and diversity of anticipated interdisciplinary outcomes, the richness of interdisciplinary programs, and the possibility of unanticipated outcomes provide the exhilaration of exploration and discovery. Therefore, as interdisicplinarians develop assessment plans according to conventional assessment wisdom, they should remain vigilant for evidence of unanticipated as well as anticipated outcomes. With this caution, evolving assessment wisdom provides two portals through which one may view outcomes: indirect and direct.

Indirect assessment methods include surveys, interviews, and focus groups. Students or other observers reflect on the quality and quantity of student learning outcomes; learner outcomes are not directly observed. Direct methods assess whether or not students have achieved desired learning outcomes. Although they most often come in the form of examinations (multiple-choice, true–false, standardized, or locally developed), other direct methods come in the form of performances that require students to create their own unique responses rather than choose from a set of predetermined responses (Palomba and Banta 116).

Indirect Techniques of Assessment

The application of indirect assessment techniques, especially in class and among alumni, dominated early assessment practices among interdisciplinary programs. Surveying is a common example of an indirect assessment technique. The practice of surveying is commendable; it is an excellent way to get an assessment program started and to make students and faculty alike conscious of their common learning aspirations. As noted earlier, indirect methods of assessment ask learners to reflect on what they have experienced and achieved rather than demonstrating directly what they have learned.

Written questionnaires, telephone surveys, focus groups, and interviews may be used to assess levels of student satisfaction and employment (Palomba and Banta 87). Surveys may prove especially useful in the initial stages of developing an interdisciplinary assessment plan for a reason that is not immediately obvious. Doug Eder (personal interview) suggests that what is measured is that which is valued by students and faculty. Consequently, the inclusion of an item on a survey asking about synthesis or empowerment may motivate students and faculty alike to seek the valued outcome. However, as we continue to approach a consensus on the meaning and outcomes of interdisciplinarity, we believe that effective assessment will require both indirect and direct measures of learning, with an increasing emphasis on direct techniques.

Direct Techniques of Assessment

Given the shift in the focus of assessment, from judging the worth of programs to providing feedback for ongoing improvement of teaching and learning, we encourage interdisciplinary programs to incorporate more direct assessment techniques into their assessment plans. Although the issue is not settled, direct assessment techniques such as standardized and locally developed tests have not completely enabled interdisciplinary programs to "close the loop"—that is, to have a data-based discussion about teaching and learning. Performance-based or authentic assessment techniques offer some new avenues for the assessment of interdisciplinary programs.

In a performance environment, students actively demonstrate their learning rather than simply select a response on a standardized test (Palomba and Banta 95). The theory is that the quality of the curriculum, teaching, and student learning is revealed authentically through student performances on real tasks (Eder, personal interview). In performance assessment, it is important to distinguish between the assessment environment and the measurement technique. Performance assessment environments include simulations, juried presentations, projects, internships and fieldwork, and carefully developed portfolios (Palomba and Banta 95–96). These authentic environments are not assessment techniques; they are, however, circumstances conducive to the application of some measurement activity. Performance environments offer attractive assessment opportunities for interdisciplinary programs.

There are many interdisciplinary environments conducive to authentic assessment. Senior seminars, internships, field placements, simulations, juried presentations, written projects, case studies, oral presentations in the classroom, and longitudinal portfolios of a student's work all provide fertile grounds for authentic assessment. Authentic assessment strategies embedded in a rigorous senior seminar, field experience, or portfolio process offer great promise both for improving teaching and learning and validating the interdisciplinary approach to education.

Douglas Eder, a distinguished voice in the assessment movement and director of assessment at Southern Illinois University at Edwardsville, is a proponent of the senior assignment. The senior assignment is a scholarly process that occurs by contract between a senior and a dedicated faculty member and results in a tangible product. The product provides evidence of the curriculum and teaching that preceded it and can be assessed. Faculty may also approach the senior project descriptively, asking more general questions such as "what is" as opposed to "how well." Conversations among faculty regarding intended and unanticipated outcomes form a rich and productive environment for improving teaching and learning.

After choosing a performance environment, faculty need a technique to measure performance. The use of rubrics and protocols that respond to intended outcomes may provide the needed link between assessment environment and outcomes.

Rubrics

Observational protocols and scoring rubrics offer exciting options for directly assessing interdisciplinary learning outcomes within performance environments. The application of rubrics is on the rise, since some form of a scoring rubric can be applied in all authentic assessment environments (Fulkert 78). A rubric, scoring guide, or rating scale provides "the rules" for expected outcomes. Rubrics describe a vital link between teaching and learning. This link requires the faculty member to define, before the fact, expected learner outcomes along a continuum. The rubric is designed to describe the characteristics and level of expected performance. Effective rubrics and well-collected data provide opportunities for interdisciplinary students and faculty to reflect upon what has been learned and what may be improved to enhance learning (Bush and Timms 104).

There are two types of scoring rubrics: analytic and holistic. An analytic rubric divides an authentic performance into parts and provides a rating for each part. If faculty want to create a rubric for assessing an oral presentation, they might decide that three indicators are very important: (1) knowledge of subject, (2) organization, and (3) vocal delivery. A three- or four-point scale could be developed for each important indicator. For example, the levels on a three-point scale rating knowledge of subject could be defined as "not acceptable," "acceptable," and "more than acceptable." A doctoral student at Ohio University is currently taking the general idea of rubrics and applying the thoughtful work of Barbara Walvoord and others called Primary Trait Analysis (PTA) to develop rubrics that may help assess the interdisciplinary construct of synthesis (Carol Canavan, personal interview). PTA is an analytic scoring method that identifies the factors or "traits" that will be included in the scoring and then builds a scale for scoring student performance on each trait. It will be useful if an analytic scoring rubric can be developed for each of the anticipated outcomes of interdisciplinary study, especially the outcome of synthesis.

By contrast, a holistic rubric focuses on a performance, presentation, paper, field-experience, and so on, as a single entity. The score represents an overall assessment of the product (Bush and Timms 109). Holistic rubrics may not provide all the nuanced information we would like to have, but some of the potential outcomes of interdisciplinarity are not easy to separate into primary traits. For example, within the AIS Assessment Committee, there is an ongoing debate about the nature of synthesis. Perhaps synthesis can be understood as a combination of distinguishable skills that may be measured and weighted individually. On the other hand, perhaps such an analytic understanding of synthesis proves elusive. Gordon Vars (personal interview) offers an alternative view of synthesis and assessment. He suggests that the idea of synthesis may be so complex that its essence may only be assessed in the context of a holistic act that he describes as "connoisseurship." If so, faculty members who are familiar with the subtleties of synthesis would be obliged to act as competent but critical judges of students' abilities to synthesize and to render a holistic, informed opinion.

The combination of scoring rubrics, whether analytic or holistic, and authentic performance environments has opened the door to exciting possibilities in interdisciplinary assessment. Rubrics or observational protocols, when applied to student performances in presentations, simulations, projects, and portfolios, may enable interdisciplinary programs to begin having data-based discussions that will empower the programs to improve teaching and learning. In the rapidly evolving culture of evidence, performances embedded in the context of a senior assignment or carefully developed portfolios of student work offer attractive assessment environments to interdisciplinarians.

Examinations of student portfolios and senior assignments assembled over time are in some ways like an archaeological dig, and can yield both indirect and direct evidence of learning. Faculty can uncover evidence of critical, creative, or integrative thinking; examine the curriculum and pedagogy in which the evidence was born; and provide quantitative as well as narrative evidence of how students have grown (Palomba and Banta 97).

The value of portfolio assessment for interdisciplinary outcomes lies in the longitudinal nature of the process. Not only does the portfolio provide an authentic snapshot of the beginning and ending of the academic experience, it also offers a look at what happened along the way. Portfolio examination can provide rich and expressive evidence of experiences and development while furnishing compelling evidence of developing knowledge and skills (Schilling 6–7). This information can be used effectively to validate the interdisciplinary process and to communicate the process to internal and external audiences.

Other Promising Interdisciplinary Authentic Assessment Techniques

In addition to assessing intended outcomes, those conducting portfolio or other performance-based assessment may uncover evidence of unanticipated outcomes of interdisciplinary study. Given that the claims by practitioners of interdisciplinarity are numerous and diverse, but the preponderance of the evidence regarding outcomes is often anecdotal (Newell 537), we suggest that interdisciplinarians conduct their assessment activities not only from an outcomes-centered model but also from a "goal-free" model that generates data built inductively around questions of importance (Schilling and Schilling 30). Interdisciplinary learning outcomes may then be developed and revised as a consequence of a thoughtful analysis of what students have learned. Interdisciplinarians who are not comfortable with a linear approach to outcomes assessment may begin with a nonlinear process, asking important questions such as "What did our students learn this year?" Ongoing discussions of this type will ultimately yield a set of intended outcomes that may be assessed more directly while still leaving room for faculty to explore portfolio data in a qualitative, archaeological manner.

Karl Schilling's thoughtful essay, "Making the Case for Quality in Programs Across the Street: Interdisciplinary Assessment for Interdisciplinary Programs," offers an intriguing narrative about the experiences of the Western College Program faculty at Miami University and gives an excellent example of a qualitative, descriptive approach to assessment. Schilling relates how the faculty attitudes were transformed through a progression of assessment experiences. After struggling to make interdisciplinary program assessment work with conventional methodology, the faculty broke free from a singular model and shifted to a model in which they were gathering materials from students that allowed them to tell a story of growth, change, and unexpected outcomes. While shifting from a model that told "how well" to a model that described "what is," the Western College Program faculty discovered the power of descriptive assessment to elicit change. Schilling and his colleagues used a variety of assessment techniques including portfolios, structured interviews, ethnographic observations, alumni surveys as well as the Cooperative Institutional Research Profile (CIRP) and the College Student Experiences Questionnaire (CSEQ). Schilling describes how the information gathered in the assessment process not only got the faculty involved and energized but also helped the interdisciplinary studies program survive during a time of financial exigency.

RECOMMENDATIONS

Given the fluid nature of both assessment and interdisciplinarity, it does not serve the profession to be unduly prescriptive. The fundamental question is how seriously do we take the assessment challenge of transforming teaching and learning through interdisciplinary curricula and pedagogy. It may be easy enough to develop assessment plans employing conventional linear wisdom and emphasizing indirect techniques, but this is not sufficient. While explicitly acknowledging the need for the disciplines, we see authentic interdisciplinarity as a powerful means for achieving complex levels of cognitive and affective development (Klein 30–31). Even though it is relatively easy to articulate this goal, it is quite challenging to define components of cognitive and affective development in measurable ways and equally challenging to measure the constructs. Our suggestions are not intended to be prescriptive but rather heuristic, starting from a platform of reason and experience and encouraging others to proceed well beyond our initial boundaries.

At the moment, there appear to be several hallmarks of promising interdisciplinary assessment programs. First, the program should be steeped in the understanding that, fundamentally, assessment is used to improve teaching and learning. All activities and outcomes should be measured against the achievement of these two related purposes. Although some well-meaning accrediting or oversight organizations may seek to impose a singular assessment plan on multiple programs, this practice is not entirely successful. In fact, some well-founded assessment efforts to improve teaching and learning are actually proving instructive to the accountability side of the house. Doug Eder refers to this as the process of the tail wagging the dog.

Second, the assessment program should be locally developed to reflect the faculty's unique and evolving understanding of interdisciplinarity. Third, faculty need to be intimately involved in the assessment process, however difficult that involvement may be to achieve. The notion of embedding assessment within a course, especially a senior seminar, has proven helpful here. Fourth, a good interdisciplinary assessment program is in a state of constant flux. In an information-rich environment, or what T. Dary Erwin calls a "culture of evidence," everything is constantly on the table—from outcomes to curriculum to pedagogy to underlying philosophies. Peter Ewell notes that assessment is just as useful for formulating and enhancing our understanding of learning outcomes as it is for determining outcomes ("Assessment Update"). Within this environment of managed chaos, the following principles seem appropriate to the development of an interdisciplinary assessment process (Hatfield 2–5; Eder, personal interview):

A. Acknowledge that no assessment plan will ever be perfect.

B. Define the mission of the interdisciplinary program. At a minimum, the mission should define whom the program will serve, in what manner the student will be served, and the anticipated outcomes. The mission of the program should be linked conceptually to the mission of the home institution. An understanding of institutional goals and values is critical to the development of a program mission.

C. Identify the scope of the interdisciplinary assessment plan. Will the plan measure outcomes only? The learning outcomes approach to assessment is widely accepted in higher education and represents only the minimum standard of effective assessment. The AIS Assessment Study Committee is currently considering a recommendation that the scope of interdisciplinary assessment include at least four elements: (1) intended and serendipitous learner outcomes in the cognitive, affective, and developmental domains; (2) interdisciplinary curriculum design and implementation; (3) interdisciplinary pedagogy; and (4) program context. Peter Ewell recently asked three questions to counter the outcomes-only environment of assessment: What did you do? What happened, and What mattered? ("Assessment Update"). Ewell regards assessment as a complex and dynamic process that carries with it the obligation of thoughtful analysis and judgment.

D. Define expected outcomes in measurable terms, but also expect unexpected or serendipitous outcomes. Be prepared to report and reflect on these matters as much as on the anticipated outcomes. If synthesis is a primary goal of interdisciplinarity (and indeed it should be), specify that as an intended outcome. Integrative thinking is an elusive thing, not readily captured. The essence of Peter Ewell's wisdom is that assessment monitors *indicators* of learning—external traits usually associated with the desired learning.

E. Define curriculum and instruction strategies intended to achieve intended outcomes.

F. Install assessment methods that match the goals of the program. Define multiple assessment methods. Include quantitative as well as qualitative measures. Include a mix of direct and indirect measures of learning. Before a program begins collecting data, it is wise to determine the types of data that are already being collected. Often, a program can work in conjunction with an ongoing project of Institutional Research, since the data needed are being collected for some other purpose. Identify available resources before generating new data. While looking for the intended outcomes, remain aware that data on unanticipated outcomes may be as instructive as data on the intended outcomes.

G. Develop a systematic plan for gathering data: prioritize goals, set timelines, and identify clear lines of responsibility.

H. Implement the plan on a continuous basis.

I. Use the data! Evaluate the data periodically. Adopt a philosophy of continuous improvement. Continuous improvement occurs when data are collected and evaluated on a regular basis, allowing for minor adjustments in inputs and processes.

J. Communicate the results to stakeholders.

K. Act, if action is indicated.

L. Engage in sincere reflective practice. Periodically review the process of assessment.

M. Report the documented outcomes of interdisciplinary education in appropriate scholarly contexts.

CONCLUSION

The range of interdisciplinary programs, their diverse populations, and intended as well as serendipitous outcomes form the rich landscape of interdisciplinary studies today. Although adopting conventional, linear assessment wisdom is seductive, it would be premature and unduly prescriptive to establish a single set of norms for assessment among interdisciplinary programs. After all, interdisciplinary studies teaches us not merely to exist among the tensions, paradoxes, and ambiguities of our lives, but to revel in and thrive among those intellectual forces. Each interdisciplinary program faces a similar challenge: develop a compelling story of the program, supported by an array of information and data, that will help faculty continue to improve the quality of the educational experience for students (Schilling 11).

NOTES

1. This work represents a conscientious albeit imperfect synthesis of the thoughts of many. The authors owe a special debt to our other colleagues on the AIS Assessment Committee: Doug Eder, Karl Schilling, and Gordon Vars. Our committee would not exist except for the vision and action of the AIS Board of Directors and its Executive Director, William H. Newell.

2. Although a full examination of assessment's surprising growth is beyond the scope of this chapter, it is worth noting that the emergence of the assessment movement is, in itself, a phenomenon worthy of interdisciplinary study, for it has roots in the perspectives of several disciplines.

WORKS CITED

Angelo, Thomas A., and K. Patricia Cross. *Classroom Assessment Techniques: A Handbook for College Teachers.* 2nd ed. San Francisco: Jossey-Bass, 1993.

Association of American Colleges. *Integrity in the College Curriculum: A Report to the Academic Community: The Findings and Recommendations of the Project on Redefining the Meaning and Purpose of Baccalaureate Degrees.* Washington, DC: Association of American Colleges, 1985.

Barr, R. B., and J. Tagg. "From Teaching to Learning: A New Paradigm for Undergraduate Education." *Change* (November–December 1995): 13–25.

Bush, Marcia and Michael Timms. "Rubric and Portfolio-Based Assessment: Focusing on Student Progress." *Assessment in Business Education.* Eds. Jim Rucker and Ramona Schoenrock. Reston, VA: National Business Education Association, 2000. 103–120.

Canavan, Carol. Personal interview. June 15, 2000.

Cross, K. P. "New Lenses on Learning." *About Campus* (March/April 1996): 4–9.

Eder, Douglas. Personal interview. June 15, 2000.

———. *"Senior Assignments."* http://www.siue.edu/~deder/assess/sra.html.

———. "Authentic Assessment: Elements for use In Interdisciplinary Studies." Presentation at the Association for Integrative Studies Conference, Portland, OR, October 2000.

Erwin, T. Dary. *Assessing Student Learning and Development: A Guide to the Principles, Goals, and Methods of Determining College Outcomes.* San Francisco: Jossey-Bass, 1991.

Ewell, Peter. T. "National Trends in Assessing Student Learning." *Journal of Engineering Education* (April 1998):107–13.

———. "Assessment Update." Presentation at the Assessment Forum of the Freshman Year Experience Conference, Columbia, SC. February 2000.

Farmer, D. W., and Napieralski, E. A." Assessing Learning in Programs." In J. G. Gaff, J. L. Ratcliff, and Associates, *Handbook of the Undergraduate Curriculum: A Comprehensive Guide to Purposes, Structures, Practices, and Change.* Eds. J. G. Gaff, J. L. Ratcliff, and Associates. San Francisco: Jossey-Bass Publishers, 1997. 476–92.

Field, Michael, Lee, Russell, and Field, Mary Lee." Assessing Interdisciplinary Learning." *Interdisciplinary Studies Today.* Eds. J. T. Klein and W. G. Doty. San Francisco: Jossey-Bass Publishers, 1994. 69–84.

Fulkert, Ronald F. "Authentic Assessment." *Assessment in Business Education.* Eds. J. Rucker and R. J. Schoenrock. Reston, VA: National Business Education Association, 2000. 71–90.

Hatfield, Susan R. "Department Level Assessment: Promoting Continuous Improvement." Idea Paper #35, IDEA Center, Kansas State University, May 1999.

Klein, Julie Thompson. *Assessing Interdisciplinary Learning K-16: Listening to the Sounds of Integration.* Unpublished manuscript submitted for publication, 1999.

National Institute of Education. *Involvement in Learning: Realizing the Potential of American Higher Education: Final Report of the Study Group on the Conditions of Excellence in American Higher Education.* Washington, DC: GPO, 1984.

Newell, William H. "Professionalizing Interdisciplinarity: Literature Review and Research Agenda." *Interdisciplinarity: Essays from the Literature.* Ed. William H. Newell. New York: College Entrance Examination Board, 1998. 529–63.

Palomba, Catherine A., and Trudy W. Banta. *Assessment Essentials: Planning, Implementing, and Improving Assessment in Higher Education.* San Francisco: Jossey-Bass, 1999.

Schilling, Karl L. "Making the Case for Quality in Programs Across the Street: Interdisciplinary Assessment for Interdisciplinary Programs." Manuscript submitted for publication, 1999.

————. Personal interview. June 15, 2000.

Schilling, Karl L., and Karen Maitland Schilling. *Proclaiming and Sustaining Excellence: Assessment as a Faculty Role*. ASHE-ERIC Higher Education Report Volume 26, No. 3. Washington, DC: George Washington University, 1998.

Vars, Gordon. Personal interview. September 30, 1999.

Walvoord, Barbara E., and Lucille P. McCarthy. *Thinking and Writing in College: A Naturalistic Study of Students in Four Disciplines*. Urbana, IL: National Council of Teachers of English, 1991.

CONCLUSION

Achieving Interdisciplinary Innovation

Leading and Learning in Community

Faith Gabelnick

Real learning gets to the heart of what it means to be human. Through learning we recreate ourselves. Through learning we become able to do something we never were able to do. Through learning we reperceive the world and our relationship to it. Through learning we extend our capacity to create, to be part of the generative process of life.

Senge, *The Fifth Discipline*

When faculty and administrators confront the challenges of interdisciplinary learning, they often look for "solutions" through curricular and pedagogical innovation. Many of the topics of the preceding chapters—team teaching, writing across the curriculum, and communities of learning—are frequently touted as "silver bullets" because they seem to offer a complex approach that can stimulate or promote a variety of integrative transformations in class or on a campus. People often resist and then vigorously attach to one or another of these innovations in the hope that, at last, one or another curricular strategy will solve or at least address a particular course, departmental, or institutional challenge, such as retention, morale, faculty development, or student motivation for learning. And, as the authors of this volume suggest, these strategies can and do successfully improve student learning, enhance the connections between faculty and students, and reinvigorate creative faculty. Yet, in thinking about innovative interdisciplinary pedagogy, one must be as exploratory as possible, taking into account not only the particular pedagogical approach but also the framework in which that approach will occur. This framework not only entails the time, place, and curricular context, but even more important, it consists of the psychosocial predilections of those who are attempting something different.

Who takes the lead in establishing and sustaining interdisciplinary pedagogical innovations is an important question because it raises issues about the nature of teaching and learning and the interrelationship of any pedagogical innovation to the curriculum, the students, the faculty member, and ultimately to the larger organization in which the change is occurring. Too often, interdisciplinary changes are tied to certain individuals on campus, and when these people retire or shift their focus, innovations can disappear or at least fail to become sustained by entering the fabric of the curriculum (For specific examples, see Trow 188; Hershberg 198).

Thus, in considering interdisciplinary pedagogical innovation, we must place those curricular moves in a larger context of learning and leading transformational change. In this concluding chapter, we shall examine factors that influence the change process and those qualities of learning that contribute to interdisciplinary transformations on our campuses. Learning is a social process, and adaptive strategies to enhance the learning are often called innovations. Yet, too often these "innovations" are what Wátzlawick calls "first order change," which is a type of change that simply moves the furniture around. Second order change shifts a paradigm of understanding and allows a space for new constructive thought and action. One might expect that any innovator worth her salt would wholeheartedly embrace substantive change; however, the reality is often more modest than the dream.

Innovation, change, and transformation are all associated with loss as well as gain. And it is often the case that interdisciplinary innovations become so complicated or expensive that they cannot be sustained. When the grant support runs out or the dynamic faculty member goes on sabbatical, the innovation subsides, and people quietly nod and say, "I knew it couldn't/wouldn't last." Because we live in a dynamic world of change, our ambivalence toward this world can serve as an impediment to the very programs or agenda we claim we want to accomplish. Thus, our understanding of the change process can be very helpful in comprehending our role in initiating, sustaining, and then continuing to participate in interdisciplinary pedagogical innovation.

CREATING AND SUSTAINING INTERDISCIPLINARY
CHANGE: THE CHALLENGE FOR LEADERS

Joseph Jaworski, in his book, *Synchronicity*, explores the many themes, patterns, and synchronistic events that led him to leave his profession as a trial lawyer and pursue a path as a creator and enabler of change. Founder of the American Leadership Forum, Jaworski and others designed a program that brought together a group of young and/or emerging leaders and built them into a community of learners. Using experiential learning, didactic content, professional development seminars, and collaborative projects, Jaworski and his associates purposefully structured a learning experience and environment that fostered an enduring learning community. Those who have completed the ALF program stay in contact with each other, and the "reunions" are opportunities for these lifelong learners to continue to share and learn from each other and keep track of how they are making a difference in the world.

Jaworski does not write specifically about innovative interdisciplinary pedagogy or curricula, but he does write about three important elements for creating change in organizations that are directly applicable to creating and sustaining interdisciplinary innovations in academic organizations. These elements refer to our psychological stance or perspective as we contemplate change. At first glance, they appear to be deceptively simple, but we submit that contemplating the shifts in perspective is necessary to become a leader of innovation and is vital for enduring innovative work.

Jaworski notes that three important shifts need to occur in order for us and our organization to change. These shifts are: (1) *how we see the world*, (2) *how we understand relationships*, and (3) *how we make commitments*. Each of these shifts involves a phenomenological change, and each is contingent on one another. Any innovation that helps people to learn in a more complex way will implicitly provide strategies for people to accomplish these three shifts. Paradoxically, these shifts may occur within a student well beyond the actual experience in class, yet the innovation was able to generate, even prospectively, a different way of seeing and being in the world. It is this shift, not the innovative strategy itself, that stimulates transformational learning.

How We See the World

We have been taught to look for predictability in our world. We like to label or name the elements of our world, and we like certainty. At the same time, campuses are filled with conversations about future possibilities: how and where we will teach; who will comprise the faculty; what the university or college of the future will look like—structurally and physically; where it will be located; and how our students will become engaged in a broader society. In listening or observing these dialogues we conclude that colleges and universities at one level are all about change and development and at another level are conservators of century-old practices and attitudes about the nature and content of knowledge.

On the one hand, the traditional academic organizational and governance structures, such as majors or other disciplinary programs, tenure, or even the architecture of universities carry a sense of authority and permanence akin to religious belief. Attempting to tamper with these structural "certainties" is sometimes akin to heresy and carries with it the same types of "deadly" consequences for the leader who introduces change. Yet, on the other hand, academics create new interdisciplinary programs and invent extraordinary ways of teaching and learning in them; they will vigorously pride themselves on their creativity in the classroom, in the research labs, in the administrative halls—so long as the perceived basic philosophy and core values of the institution remain intact. Therefore, whenever an innovation is introduced to a campus, the "buzz" is usually about how much of a change is likely to be introduced. Ironically, one of the most common ways to accomplish change is to claim that the innovation is not an innovation, that it is being accomplished at other institutions, and that this innovation will have little or no impact on university resources.

Underneath the discussions about change or the processes that resist change is a deeply held common belief that the educational system as we know it is fundamentally Valuable and Good and that those who work at these institutions serve a Higher Purpose whose general task is to make the World a Better Place. As noted in the previous chapter by Michael Field and Don Stowe, discussions of outcomes assessment often perturb academic constituencies because they appear to challenge this bedrock set of beliefs in the fundamental validity of the academic enterprise, in other words, *how we see the world.* How can you demonstrate that what you are doing is producing the results or outcomes you claim, asks the educated public? This question unsettles academics because responding to it leads us to examine open-mindedly why we do what do. The fear is that we may discover that some of what we do has little educational impact and ought to be stopped and that some of what we do does not make a great change in the lives of students but perhaps ought to continue in a different way. Although we want to believe that most of what we do has high correlates for producing the type of educated citizen we claim we want to graduate, the reality is that we are not often prepared organizationally or psychologically to validate that belief. Can there be interdisciplinary transformational change without challenging some of these dearly held basic assumptions of academica? Probably not. Can there be interdisciplinary change without some type of "cost" to the institution? Probably not. Can leaders inaugurate change without also transforming the culture in which the change is to occur? Probably not.

Change at institutions is often driven by external factors. Students are changing and coming to our institutions with different life and cultural experiences. Moreover, when they graduate, students must confront an increasingly diverse and globalized society. As a result, we adapt by instituting study abroad programs and multicultural courses (see Chapter 10 in this volume). As students arrive at college with superior technology skills and needs, we must move toward using technology effectively in our learning environments (see Chapter 5). As students come with different attributes, especially age, we need to change the times and types of class offerings to accommodate adult learners (see Chapter 11). As the market place has become the most competitive for higher education institutions, we have learned business strategies and fund-raising skills. Even as we have tried to hold on to our traditional beliefs and ways of learning, the world has become more plastic, less predictable, more open-ended. And so, as we move into a more contingent, mediated yet unpredictable century, the world of learning and leading is changing.

Questions and questioning, learning about learning, become a way of being. One inquiry opens up a set of new questions to think about, and possibility becomes a partner to creativity. On many, many campuses, change—and especially change that fosters interdisciplinarity—is occurring, and resistance to change is occurring. Many predictions about the end of education as we know it abound in journals and newspapers as if once we make that first step to change, we leave everything else behind. Making this first shift in how we see the world is experienced by many as akin to walking off the edge of a cliff. It is the most extraordinary first step in any type of transformation, because the perceived world truly changes and, once that happens, many possibilities appear that were never before considered.

Not surprisingly, people defend against looking at the world in different ways because they fear that they will lose a series of comforting and long-lived assumptions about how they are to live and thrive in that world. For example, if one questions the nature of the academic discipline, the catastrophic fear is that "someone" might eliminate the concept of the disciplinary major. After eliminating the major, we would wonder about what would become of the thousands of disciplinary faculty who "practice" in these majors and the hundreds of graduate programs that prepare them for this practice. A vista of unemployed academics would loom. Even framing hypothetical questions publicly can flood a campus with fear and uncertainty. And so, although there are endless discussions on campus about revisions of majors, the invention of cross-disciplinary or self-designed majors, or even the elimination of some majors that are not drawing students, there is very little discussion on most campuses about whether or not we should be organized around majors. Similarly, although faculty spend years working to achieve tenure and then serving on tenure review committees, for the next group of aspirants, there is relatively little open discussion about the contemporary purpose of tenure and how the professorate will and must change. Discussions about change are framed in the least disruptive ways, and when faculty votes occur, most times, tradition roars back into the room. This is the way that the academic industry preserves the status quo.

Suppose we envision a world that is more open, dynamic, interconnected, and interdisciplinary. Suppose we see our universities, not as a series of small countries or territories but as a landscape of interdisciplinary learning communities, interacting and leveraging resources, and sharing a set of common values about learning, civic engagement, and professional development. We might have a different budgeting process, a different way to understand faculty achievement, a different way to learn with and from our students, a different way to structure our campuses. Might we not frame this shift in terms of possibilities for enrichment and not as scenarios for loss and desperation?

Ultimately, how we see the world in the twenty-first century will have a major impact on how we teach and lead in our interdisciplinary communities of learning. The continuing tension in higher education and American society between individuality and community lies at the heart of the matter. Future educational paradigms will be based fundamentally on openness and the ability to learn and to use that learning in a variety of work and living environments. If we hold on to a particular way of seeing the world, we keep ourselves locked inside our fears of change and miss the tremendous opportunities for generativity that lie ahead.

How We Understand Relationships

Margaret Wheatley's book, *A Simpler Way*, portrays a world that is interconnected in every way possible. Her photos show the repeated patterns in nature, and her text reveals a natural world that is a dynamic, interconnected system. When one reads this book, one wonders how it could be any other way. The connections, at all levels of our consciousness, abound, and we are suffused with a sense of wholeness and well-being. Why then do we spend so much of our lives breaking down these connections and setting up barriers to communication?

In academia, we chop up our knowledge base into schools, colleges, divisions, departments, and disciplines; we provide hierarchical titles and roles for faculty and staff; we distribute funds on seniority bases, or criteria of sufficiency. We give awards and endlessly find ways to separate people into "the Good, the Not-So-Good, and the Stars." Classes that actually foster the connection among disciplines and between the learning and living are few. Students sit in classes as anonymous participants. Faculty often do not know each other outside their departments or divisions. Everywhere there is separation, not connection. Curricular innovations, such as team teaching and learning communities, purposefully attempt to connect different disciplinary knowledge bases through collaboration among faculty or the thematic liking of traditional courses. As Valerie Bystrom has described in Chapter 4, learning communities often break down the barriers of fifty-minute classes to engage students and faculty across a broader time span. According to Jay Wentworth and Jim Davis in Chapter 2, team teaching dismantles the traditional authority of the teacher and blends disciplinary forms of knowledge. Both team teaching and learning communities challenge the academic structure by encouraging learning to span several disciplines; and they can build a different way of learning together that values collaboration not competition to accomplish assignments. Leading and learning in community mirrors the natural world that Meg Wheatley describes because the world is perceived as both chaotic and orderly, variously patterned, and endlessly changing, alive to possibilities and honoring connections.

Martin Buber's classic text, *I and Thou*, speaks to the importance of developing mutuality as a way of enhancing our humanity. If we experience the world as fundamentally connected, then our views about relationships reflect this unity and connection. Our understanding of relationships then moves away from power and competition toward collaboration and vulnerability. As learners, we begin to understand that we do not/cannot learn alone. Collaborative learning strategies as well as feminist pedagogy and service learning are constructed on this principle of relatedness. As Nancy Grace points out in Chapter 8, this principle of relatedness can inspire those of us who are in the role of teacher to work with our students in ways other than as an authority figure. We begin to act like a mentor and coach; we facilitate our students' learning; we begin to speak to our own areas of ignorance and then we begin to see ourselves as learners, too. If we are in the role of students, we begin to understand that knowledge is not finite, that information can be found in many places, and that learning with other students and other faculty does not have to produce a grade. Relationship be-comes the basis for learning, and we understand that unless we establish strong relationships, our learning will be compromised.

An important part of this shift in the nature of relationship involves a capacity to experience, tolerate, and speak to disappointment and loss. The end of an academic term can be experienced as the possible end of a special set of relationships, not simply the end of a class where a grade is given. If we do not provide a space for reflection and grieving, we thereby try to protect ourselves from acknowledging loss in order to maitain a more distanced, utilitarian view of our education. Grieving and reflecting on one's experiences thus become an important element of growing and changing and therefore need to be a part of an innovative learning culture. It is our flight from death, our wish not to grieve that fundamentally blocks learning and change resulting from that learning. Change must involve loss. We ask our students to change their learning environments every se-mester, every class. We ask them to learn in different ways, regardless of their preferred learning style, yet subtly, pervasively, we try to keep our world predictable and orderly. When we are truly being innovative, we re-member the human need for connection and the inevitable grief that oc-curs when that connection is broken.

Truly confronting how we develop and sustain relationships is very diffi-cult because of the natural tendency to avoid pain and the pain of loss, and this is one of the fundamental reasons why institutional change is so diffi-cult. Human beings are changing every moment; their lives grow and con-tract, and possibilities at twenty years old may be past accomplishments or missed opportunities at age fifty. We submit that students are the main driv-ers of change and they are also the main impediments to change: they come to an educational institution to learn new skills and academic information. It is often their interest in learning beyond the classroom and impels the development of internships, study abroad programs, or other types of expe-riential learning. Yet, within the classroom, students can be quite conser-vative and will question innovations as a form of game playing. They may not see the connection between some of the activities being designed and the information that is expected to be learned. However, if students trust their teacher—in other words, have a sense of relatedness and connection to the teacher—they will engage in the class and will be more open to par-ticipating in innovative pedagogy.

Looking at interdisciplinary curricular and pedagogical innovation from the faculty and administrative perspective also yields paradoxical insights: Faculty, especially tenured faculty, make a long-term, even lifetime com-mitment to an institution and, as part of the tenure process, establish a set of relationships that define their academic community. Administrators, especially senior administrators, make a commitment to a series of tasks and accomplishments not, necessarily, to a series of relationships and not surprisingly are often viewed as transients by the faculty. Nationally, we know that administrators are more mobile than faculty—and probably students, who, by and large, tend to attend schools within a 500-mile radius of their homes. Change implies mobility, and when the most mobile group tries to implement change, the campus can react to these initiatives as an administrative fad and dismiss them. As Stanley Bailis argues in Chapter 1, even though most curricular and pedagogical innovations are started by faculty, the administrative commitment can be a compelling force. When the supportive administrator leaves, a particular innovation such as the development of a certain interdisciplinary program or a cross-disciplinary diversity initiative may find itself at risk.

Depending on how and who initiates change on a campus will impact any innovation unless the mechanisms for institutionalization are great. A campus community comprised of changing human beings embraces any change very carefully because the university must continue beyond these innovations, and the custodians of the institution—the faculty—feel a deep obligation and responsibility to preserve their idea and ideal of a traditional community of scholars. The inertia in an educational institution pulls us back to familiar strategies even as we try to stretch the boundaries of our imagination.

However, once we make a shift in how we see the world, some of these resistances also shift. Now we see that the world is contingent on the relationships in that world, and if we work differently with our colleagues and students, our expectations of the kinds of relationships that are possible also change. This is clearly the case with successful and enduring interdisciplinary innovations: students and faculty report deeper learning, more complex relationships when the roles, the relationships, shift. Because the learning in interdisciplinary studies courses is contingent and connected, the possibilities for teaching also enlarge; the opportunities to work together expand; the assignments are more imaginative; and the baselines for expectations for teaching and for learning rise (Klein and Newell 18). Those who become members of an interdisciplinary learning community, in the best sense of that idea, are able to establish deeper relationships with one another and approach learning from multiple perspectives. If a shift truly occurs, if faculty and students complexly understand what learning in community means, then they will use that knowledge to institute other changes and they will change themselves.

How We Make Commitments

In these dynamic times, the idea and experience of commitment is a vital but fleeting concept. We can remember a time barely ten years ago when workers or potential workers (e.g., college students) might have had the expectation that their careers would be fairly stable and that the employer would continue to have an investment in the stability of its workforce. In the twenty-first century, this assumption of continuance is disappearing. Neither the employer nor the employee brings to work an expectation of loyalty or commitment to an organization. Rather, the commitment has been transferred to the individual and the particular knowledge base and set of skills any individual can bring to a particular problem at a particular moment. This condition is gradually impacting higher education as students and employers value less and less a degree from any one institution. In a buyer's market, colleges and universities become one of many sources of education and training. And in a buyer's market, what is being sold are knowledge and skills. The knowledge is being packaged in a variety of forms, and this market segmentation is exploding. Technology makes it possible for students all over the world to construct their own educational plans and to use a variety of educational providers to fulfill those plans. Institutions of higher education are simply one resource to use in building one's knowledge base. Even the concept and need for a college degree are challenged.

One could ask why we even think about educational innovation or learning in community when "community" as we have experienced it is already being transformed. What does commitment look like in a transformational environment, and what can endure when the assumptions about how we are leading our lives are shifting so dramatically?

As has been noted, pedagogical innovations are often seen as ways to address certain institutional concerns such as retention, morale, faculty development, and institutional distinction. Yet too often innovation occurs at the edge of the curriculum and is not embedded into the heart of the academic enterprise. Think about past interdisciplinary programmatic innovations such as Ethnic Studies, Environmental Studies, or Women's Studies, interdisciplinary efforts such as learning communities and team teaching, or cross-disciplinary initiatives such as Writing Across the Curriculum. When the institutional commitment is conditional and local and/or connected to a particular group of faculty or administrators, the program is weakened or struggles for years and years to attain some kind of "legitimacy" on campus.

Thinking about a shift in how we make commitments means that we must be purposeful in thinking about why we want to create and sustain "new" approaches to teaching and learning. And our answer must reside in a whole systems view of an institution and a holistic plan for what the innovation can represent. For example, establishing an interdisciplinary general education course that includes service assignments in the community and a good dose of case-based inquiry does not often mean that the university as an institution is committed to interdisciplinary, inquiry-based learning (although it ought to mean just that). It means, at minimum, that the university is providing a space for some interdisciplinary education to occur for some students and faculty. Similarly, placing interdisciplinary learning communities among special populations or confining their existence to special programs does not necessarily signify that the institution is changing its other programs in relation to these populations. Because true institutional change is not embedded in the creation of interdisciplinary learning communities, learning communities like many other so-called innovations, last for a period of time and then yield to the next iteration of campus change.

If an interdisciplinary innovation such as a learning community or a study abroad experience is to endure, then the entire system must also reflect on how to embrace the changes. For example, areas of campus such as the registrar's office, the admissions office, and the alumni office would have to think about their roles in a different way: Admissions would have to revise its publication materials to invite students who might enjoy interdisciplinary studies; the registrar's office would have to shape its procedures to allow for more complex cross-listing; and the alumni office might want to feature stories about alumni who had expanded their own careers in an interdisciplinary way. As Virginia Gordon emphasizes in Chapter 12, the training and approach of advisors would also have to be altered. Curriculum committees, tenure and promotion committees, and hiring committees would have to rethink their requests for documentation of scholarship when active, interdisciplinary learning strategies would produce more field-based, cross-disciplinary, teaching-oriented, collaborative, and even student-centered research. Any interdisciplinary innovation, however small, located in a single class, has the potential to explode thought and connection. It is not to be tried as a quick fix. Enduring change is not cosmetic; it is systemic; and leading such change requires patience and a view of an institution as a complex, interrelated entity.

When interdisciplinary innovations are created out of a shift in how we see the world and how we establish relationships, then institutional commitment is necessary, not conditional. The work also shifts from being a kind of experiment or temporary innovation to being a vigorous engagement with important curricular and value-based assumptions. These innovations are then seen not as vehicles for solving particular problems but as ways of fostering constructivist thinking, collaborative engagement, teamwork, and a habit of connected relatedness. In an interdisciplinary environment of commitment, trust flourishes, and connection to one another and perhaps to the institution deepens. As shown in Chapter 2, 4, and 10, when people rely on one another, they work in community. They can argue and test out new ideas; they can validate evidence, and they can move into uncertain territory. The flow of meaning that can be created through learning in community links to other aspects of the curriculum and to others, on campus and off campus.

Educational innovations that are created out of an institutional commitment to interdisciplinary learning then have meaning for many. Opportunities to reflect on discoveries and experiences are not contained within the walls of a classroom or special program, but find voice and influence among those not formally engaged in that particular effort. Those discoveries become linked to the institutional plans and elaborated in other examples of shifts in how one sees the world, how one establishes and continues relationships, and how one makes and continues commitments. We are then ready to say that the institutional culture has shifted, and in that shift, a space is created for more change. When one resides on a campus where interdisciplinary innovation is held with respect and thoughtfulness, possibilities for transformation appear endless. Students may take courses online (see Chapter 5); they may enroll in learning communities (Chapter 4), study abroad (Chapter 10), engage in self-designed, research-based inquiries (Chapter 8), create interdisciplinary performances (Chapter 6), or volunteer in a community service organization. The bottom line is their learning; the faculty support their efforts, and administrators work to enable more to happen.

The challenge for interdisciplinary leaders, those who enable interdisciplinary innovations to exist and those who teach and learn in interdisciplinary community, is to urge and maintain a dynamic whole-systems perspective on their work. This challenge will demand a rapidly cascading change in how we see the world. Leaders do not always bring this point of view because they do not necessarily see themselves as part of a learning community in a very broad sense. Leaders live in a world that asks for concrete solutions to enormously complex problems, and their focus, understandably, is to drive toward addressing those problems. Shifting that more directed, goal-driven stance to a more open, process-oriented, flexible, and inclusive posture is the most difficult educational innovation, but is exactly the challenge posed by teaching and learning in an interdisciplinary learning community. The kinds of transformational learning that interdisciplinary learning communities can foster replicate in microcosm the macrocosmic learning and leading that also must occur in order to sustain, in a deep way, the innovative, transformational experience.

Learning as a Way of Being

When we consider the dramatic changes in the students who are studying at colleges and universities and the pressure those institutions feel to address the needs of these "customers," the challenge to higher education seems enormous and even depressing. Yet futurists like Peter Schwartz and Peter Leyden, writing in *Wired* magazine, note that the advent of the Information Age can be seen as an enormous positive opportunity for learning and for our society as a whole. They write:

> We are watching the beginnings of a global economic boom on a scale never experienced before. We have entered a period of sustained growth that could eventually double that world's economy every dozen years and bring increasing prosperity for—quite literally—billions of people on the planet. . . . [T]hese two megatrends—fundamental technological change and a new ethos of openness—will transform our world into the beginnings of a global civilization, a new civilization of civilizations, that will blossom through the coming century. ("The Long Boom" 116)

What they and other futurists predict is that a shift in how we see the world, moving from an expectation of predictability and formality to an engagement with possibility and a continuous construction and reconstruction of our world and its opportunities will allow us to dream and play, learn and work, in ways we cannot yet have imagined. This "letting go," however, is subtle and scary, and yet it is precisely what we must try to effect as interdisciplinary educational leaders.

Peter Vaill's recent book, *Learning as a Way of Being*, speaks to this shift in how we must navigate. In this previous work, he noted that leaders and learners are now operating continuously in a world of "permanent white water." What this means is that we cannot expect that once we manage one crisis or one period of turbulence, we can expect peaceful times. In fact, what is expected is that our world will be and is constructed of a series of turbulences and that these turbulences are the norm. Thus, when we, like the authors in this volume, exhort faculty and students to learn about critical thinking and complex decision making and to develop better verbal and written competencies, we are saying that these skills will be needed to work in a more plastic, less predictable environment.

Vaill sees this new world as a wonderful opportunity for transforming the ways we learn. Like others we have noted, he speaks to the fact that learning must be connected to how one understands oneself in one's work role and one's private life. We are not isolated, separate entities, and, in fact, our ways of living are becoming intricately connected with our ways of working. How we understand the world and how we approach learning are inextricably connected to who we are internally. Thus, his latest book, *Learning as a Way of Being*, systematically compares more traditional, academic learning approaches to a more expanded, innovative, experientially based stance. This stance speaks directly to the ways interdisciplinary innovations can be constructed in order for them to endure and contribute to institutional transformation.

Each of the following types of learning actively engages and empowers the interdisciplinary learner. When one engages in these types of learning, one does not rely on the teacher, but rather creates a partnership with a more experienced learner. This shift from a teaching to a learning paradigm means that students and their teachers each have much at stake in the learning enterprise. They must work in the present to explore, connect their minds with their bodies, and assess critically the outcomes of their discourse and their experimentation. When one engages in these types of active learning, the traditional accoutrements of faculty life begin to fall away. If learners are self-directed, then what is the role of grading, we might ask. If we connect explicitly our feelings with learning, then we become more vulnerable and thus more able to admit our mistakes. Learning truly becomes an active noun because it involves exploration, discovery, wrong turns, and stunning mistakes.

Interdisciplinary innovations use many of these types of learning:

1. *Self-directed learning*: Nonprescribed learning—no road maps; invention, integrated with one's values, skills, life experience. This type of learning, for example, is exemplified in inquiry-based, interdisciplinary learning as described by Chris Myers and Carolyn Haynes in Chapter 9.

2. *Creative learning*: Inventive learning—divergent thinking, exploration, discovery. Performance-based teaching as discussed by Jeff Abell in Chapter 7 promotes this form of learning.

3. *Expressive learning*: Learning in the here-and-now—connecting feelings with discovery and expressing it in the external world. Feminist pedagogy and multicultural learning—in particular their focus on coming to voice as described in Chapters 6 and 8—highlight this form of learning.

4. *Feeling learning*: Vulnerable learning—making mistakes, trying out, acknowledging limits of competence. Although this form of learning can be incorporated into any interdisciplinary course, the developmental mentoring

relationship between student and advisor as defined by Virginia Gordon in Chapter 12 offers an ideal opportunity for feeling learning.

5. *Online learning*: Deinstitutionalized learning—on-the-job learning. Strategies for how to accomplish this are articulated by Robert Bender in Chapter 5.

6. *Continual learning*: Lifelong learning—continuation of learning themes; feeling like a beginner again and again, testing oneself and one's knowledge base. Roslyn Abt Schindler offers ideas for how to accomplish this type of learning in Chapter 11.

7. *Reflexive learning*: Learning about learning—paying attention to the learning process; folding back reflections into lifelong learning themes. Many of the writing assignments proposed by Seabury in Chapter 3 prompt this form of learning.

When we link explicitly learning and living, the shifts in perspective become apparent and almost commonplace. The role of the learner is taken up by the student and the faculty, and the internal and external themes of their relationships, their lifelong experiences, develop into what Senge calls a "Purpose Story." How each community of learners unravels and learns its story then becomes a launching point for reintegration into the larger system—the college and the community. Vigorous interdisciplinary learning environments contain many stories, as illustrated in every chapter in this book. In these chapters and in interdisciplinary programs across the globe, students speak to the joy of cross-disciplinary study, to the freedom of dialogue among themselves and their teachers. The faculty tell of being rejuvenated, of working with their colleagues in a new, more meaningful way. Telling these stories becomes an active way of assessing the success of the innovation and, at the same time, discovering new ways of understanding how people are learning. Telling the stories shows that we are a healthy organization; that we are on a journey that is both general and specific, purposeful and theoretical. Stories reveal how we see the world, how we understand relationships, how we make commitments. They form the core of institutional identity; and these stories are transforming from the heroic teacher who is embedded with the wisdom of the ages toward a more democratic, participatory community.

Senge writes, "Real learning gets to the heart of what it means to be human" (14), When faculty and students engage in "real learning," they involve human beings in a deep way in the process of living. Thus, interdisciplinary innovations become alive, dynamic arenas to pursue one's being. When we lead and learn in interdisciplinary community, we discover our roles over time; we purposefully commit to shared values and goals, and we acknowledge a diversity of viewpoints, perspectives, and backgrounds. When people choose to become members of an interdisciplinary community—in all their various roles—they make a commitment to examine and reexamine what membership in that community entails. Living in a world of permanent white water, in a world where the definitions of what it means to learn are changing, those who claim to undertake change must examine how that change effects every aspect of the system in which they work. Far from heading over a cliff, interdisciplinary work brings life to an organization and connects it with the enduring spirit of living and learning in community.

WORKS CITED

Buber, Martin. *I and Thou*. 2nd ed. Trans. R. G. Smith. New York: Scribner, 1958.

Hershberg, Theodore. "The Fragmentation of Knowledge and Practice: University, Private Sector and Public Sector Perspectives." Newell, *Interdisciplinarity* 195–212.

Jaworski, Joseph. *Synchronicity: The Inner Path of Leadership*. San Francisco: Berrett-Koehler Publishers, 1998.

Klein, Julie Thompson, and William H. Newell. "Advancing Interdisciplinary Studies." Newell, *Interdisciplinarity* 3–23.

Newell, William H., ed. *Interdisciplinarity: Essays from the Literature*. New York: College Entrance Examination Board, 1998.

Schwartz, Peter, and Peter Leyden. "The Long Boom: A History of the Future, 1980–2020." *Wired* 5, no. 7 (July 1997): 115–29.

Senge, Peter M. *The Fifth Discipline: The Art and Practice of the Learning Organization*. New York: Doubleday, 1990.

Trow, Martin. "Interdisciplinary Studies as a Counterculture: Problems of Birth, Growth, and Survival." Newell, *Interdisciplinarity* 181–94.

Vaill, Peter. *Learning as a Way of Being: Strategies for Survival in a World of Permanent White Water*. San Francisco: Jossey-Bass, 1996.

Wátzlawick, Paul, John H. Weakland, and Richard Fisch. *Change: Principles of Problem Formation and Problem Resolution*. New York: Norton, 1974.

Wheatley, Margaret, and Myron Kellner-Rogers. *A Simpler Way*. San Francisco: Berrett-Koehler Publishers, 1996.

INDEX

also Journals (electronic) in the classroom; Listservs in the classroom; Peer learning, online; Web-based courses

Tetreault, Mary Kay, 166–67

Transformational change. *See* Organizational change

Vaill, Peter, 287–88

Wagner College, Practical Liberal Arts Program, 131–32

Washington Center for Improving the Quality of Undergraduate Education, 88–89

Wayne State University, Interdisciplinary Studies Program (ISP), 222

Web-based courses, 109–14

WebCt. *See* Course management software

Women's studies: challenges for, 162; international focus of, 163. *See also* Feminist pedagogy

Woolf, Virginia, 164

Writing across the curriculum (WAC): history of, 38–40; problems with, 60 n.4; sustaining commitment to, 44–45

Writing instruction in interdisciplinary courses, 38–64

Writing-intensive courses: assignments, 47–58; definition of, 40; issues and problems with, 40–46, 60 n.3; "writing to learn" versus "writing in the disciplines" approach, 40, 49

Yang, Philip Q., 128